Refiguring the Ordinary

Refiguring the Ordinary

Gail Weiss

Indiana University Press
Bloomington & Indianapolis

This book is a publication of

Indiana University Press
601 North Morton Street
Bloomington, IN 47404-3797 USA

http://iupress.indiana.edu

Telephone orders   800-842-6796
Fax orders   812-855-7931
Orders by e-mail   iuporder@indiana.edu

The paper used in this publication meets
the minimum requirements of American
National Standard for Information
Sciences—Permanence of Paper for Printed
Library Materials, ANSI Z39.48-1984.

Manufactured in the United States of America

Library of Congress Cataloging-in-
Publication Data

Weiss, Gail, date–
    Refiguring the ordinary / Gail Weiss.
    p. cm.
    Includes bibliographical references
(p.   ) and index.
    ISBN-13: 978-0-253-35157-9 (cloth :
alk. paper)
    ISBN-13: 978-0-253-21989-3 (pbk.:
alk. paper) 1. Phenomenology.   I.
Title.
    B829.5.W45 2008
    128'.4—dc22   2007046928

1 2 3 4 5 13 12 11 10 09 08

For my parents,
Irene and Harry (Max) Weiss

Reality is never more than a lead towards an unknown
on the road to which one can never progress very far.

Marcel Proust, "The Captive,"
Remembrance of Things Past, volume 3

Contents

Acknowledgments

It is hard to bring any book to a close because there is always another text one should read that is relevant to one's project, another issue that one wants to introduce or discuss further. When one's topic concerns how both individual and collective understandings of the "ordinary" are constituted and reconstituted in a manner that can be liberating for some people while, at the same time, oppressive for others, there is literally no end to one's inquiry because, as I am suggesting in the pages that follow, the construction of the ordinary is a continuous, open-ended, dialogical process. For this reason, although this is certainly a complete text (and a rather long one at that), the project itself is incapable of being completed, and I hope it will be taken up by others in turn.

Just as it has been difficult to call this book finished, it is also difficult to write these acknowledgments because there have been so many formative influences on this text. Most of them are discussed throughout the chapters themselves; however, I do want to especially thank a few people for their support and feedback during the years I worked on this book. First, of course, is my family. The nonstop hustle and bustle of our daily home life has grounded my own sense of the ordinary and has provided numerous salutary (and not so salutary) distractions as I worked. As this book has matured, so have our children. The publication of this text in 2008 also marks the year our oldest child, Jason, graduates from high school. Thus, *Refiguring the Ordinary*'s publication coincides with the end of a special era in our family of seven that I will miss enormously even as we all move on to new adventures in the years to come! I especially want to thank our caregivers of the last few years, Julia Morales (and her daughter Rebeca, who is my twins' best friend), Courtney Popov, Wendy Lazar, and Cathy Holland. Jason, Robin, Rachel, Simon, Colin, Sam, and I are so grateful to have had you be part of our family. It is truly a special person who voluntarily takes on the task of taking care of five kids when there are plenty of one- and two-kid families who would have been more than happy to have them instead!

Aside from my family, I have always received incredible stimulation and support from my fellow continental feminist philosophers, a group that includes well-established as well as up-and-coming scholars. Over the past few years, as I've given earlier versions of these chapters as presentations at national as well as international conferences, my community of interlocutors has expanded exponentially, enriching this project enormously. It is impossible to list all the people who provided me with invaluable feedback and great companionship at these events; however, I would like to acknowledge some of the organizations that have brought us together as well as special conferences where we have spent hours listening to one another's work and sharing our lives. The Merleau-Ponty Circle was my first philosophical home, and I am always grateful to its members for their astute philosophical insights, friendship, and support. The interdisciplinary faculty, postdoctoral, and graduate students who composed the Mediated Body Group at the University of Maastricht have motivated me to think more carefully about contemporary scientific and medical technologies that have become an integral part of embodied experience, and have offered me new perspectives on bodily interiority. The European-based Feminist Phenomenology and Hermeneutics group, which has met biannually for several years, has made me much more aware of how hard my talented feminist colleagues overseas have had to fight to acquire any sort of stable academic position in the traditional, patriarchal philosophy departments that still dominate Europe, departments in which feminist philosophy is often not considered to be "true" philosophy because it is not seen as offering truths or even as having access to truth in the first place. Both this group and the Maastricht group have made me much more discerning in assessing the relevance of claims I am making outside my own U.S. context, a crucial task for any serious scholar.

The Society for Phenomenology and Existential Philosophy (SPEP) and the International Association for Philosophy and Literature (IAPL) are two central communities in my life, and many new ideas for chapters and arguments, as well as lists of new texts I needed to examine, have been hastily scribbled down in the midst of a stimulating SPEP or IAPL session! My colleagues in the Human Sciences Program at The George Washington University have been the most supportive interdisciplinary community anyone could ever ask for, and I hope our innovative program is allowed to have the future it deserves despite the shortsightedness of corporate-minded administrators at our university who have never really "understood" or sufficiently valued the collaborative work we are doing. The philosophy department at GW is now full of many new junior colleagues, and I especially appreciate the friendly, open spirit that dominates all of our exchanges. I am also grateful to GW for a sabbatical leave during the 2001–2002 academic year, which enabled me to get this project solidly off the ground.

My local continental feminist colleagues and close friends, Ellen Feder and Debra Bergoffen, are always a source of intellectual stimulation, humor, and comfort as we navigate our ways through the trials and tribulations of our respective Washington, D.C., universities. Ellen and I have shared countless cell phone conversations discussing philosophical arguments, professional concerns, relationships, children, and just about everything under the sun, and it is an immeasurable comfort to know she is always "just a phone call away!" Wonderful contemporary scholars who have especially pushed my thinking on the various issues I take up in these pages include Linda Alcoff, Alia Al-Saji, Judith Butler, Ed Casey, the late Mike Dillon, Ros Diprose, Helen Fielding, Liz Grosz, Larry Hass, Sara Heinämaa, Galen Johnson, Eva Kittay, Sonia Kruks, Robert McRuer, Jim Morley, Ann Murphy, Kelly Oliver, Dorothea Olkowski, Gayle Salamon, Hugh Silverman, Peg Simons, Beata Stawarska, Nikki Sullivan, Rosemarie Garland Thomson, Abby Wilkerson, and the late Iris Young.

I am very grateful to Dee Mortensen, senior editor at Indiana University Press, whose support and enthusiasm for this book has been unwavering since the very first time we discussed it together. I especially want to thank the two anonymous reviewers who read the manuscript with such care and offered excellent suggestions to improve it! Laura McLeod, assistant sponsoring editor at IU Press, managing editor Miki Bird, project editor Neil Ragsdale, Carol Kennedy, who did the copyediting of the manuscript, and Valerie Hazel, who generated the index, did the crucial behind-the-scenes work that enabled this book to see the light of day. I am also indebted to my brother-in-law, Peter Brooke, for letting me use another of his beautiful paintings, *Stopgap Exit*, as the cover for this book.

I would like to acknowledge the presses listed below, who published earlier versions of the following chapters: "Context and Perspective," in *Merleau-Ponty: Hermeneutics and Postmodernism*, ed. Thomas Busch and Shaun Gallagher (SUNY Press, 1992), 13–24; "Ambiguity, Absurdity, and Reversibility: Responses to Indeterminacy," *Journal of the British Society for Phenomenology* 26, no. 1 (1995): 43–51; "Reading/Writing between the Lines," *Continental Philosophy Review* 31, Kluwer Academic Publishers (1998): 387–409; "The Body as a Narrative Horizon," in *Thinking the Limits of the Body*, ed. Gail Weiss and Jeffrey Jerome Cohen (SUNY Press, 2003), 25–35; "Can an Old Dog Learn New Tricks? Habitual Horizons in James, Bourdieu, and Merleau-Ponty," *Cultural Matters* 2 (electronic journal) (Spring 2003); "Imagining the Horizon," in *New Critical Theory: Essays on Liberation*, ed. William S. Wilkerson and Jeffrey Paris (Rowman and Littlefield, 2001), 249–262; "City Limits," *City: Analysis of Urban Trends, Culture, Theory, Policy, Action* 9, no. 2 (July 2005): 215–223; "Urban Flesh," *Philosophy Today* 49, no. 5, special SPEP vol. 30, "Directions and Directives: A Snapshot of Current Continental Philosophy" (2005): 116–127, and in *Feminist Interpretations of Merleau-Ponty*, ed. Dorothea Olkowski and Gail Weiss (Penn State University Press, 2006), 147–165; "Death and the Other: Rethinking Authenticity," in *The Voice of Breast Cancer in Medicine and Bioethics*, ed. Mary C. Rawlinson and Shannon Lundeen, *Philosophy and Medicine* 88 (Springer Press, 2006), 103–116, and in *Feministische Phänomenologie und Hermeneutik*, Hrsg. Silvia Stoller, Veronica Vasterling, and Linda Fisher, Orbis Phaenomenologicus (Würzberg: Verlag Königshausen and Neumann, 2005), 256–269; "Challenging Choices: An Ethic of Oppression," in *The Philosophy of Simone de Beauvoir: Critical Essays*, ed. Margaret A. Simons (Indiana University Press, 2006), 241–261; "Mothers/Intellectuals: Alterities of a 'Dual' Identity," in *The Other: Feminist Reflections in Ethics*, ed. Helen Fielding et al. (Palgrave Macmillan, 2007), 138–165.

Last, but not least, I would like to offer special thanks to my long-suffering husband, Sam Brooke, for giving me the time and space I've needed to work on this book and for picking up the slack on the home front whenever I've been faced with pressing paper, grant, course, conference, and book deadlines, which is pretty much all the time!

Refiguring the Ordinary

Introduction

Life changes fast.
Life changes in the instant.
You sit down to dinner and life as you know it ends.
The question of self-pity.
—Joan Didion 2005

As the author Joan Didion emphasizes in the epitaph above that recurs hauntingly throughout her autobiographical memoir, *The Year of Magical Thinking*, no matter how stable it may seem, the "taken-for-granted" quality of ordinary life can be irrevocably disrupted at any point in time. Every person experiences this disruption on occasion, even though what counts as "ordinary" can differ radically from one person to another. While the disruptions themselves tend to dominate one's attention when they occur, when life is running smoothly and predictably most people are usually less inclined to question the status of the familiar. Like Gregor Samsa in Kafka's *The Metamorphosis*, even in the face of extraordinary events, one may still fail to interrogate the grounds that establish the framework for what counts as "ordinary." This raises the question, as the phenomenologist Maurice Natanson might have put it, "How is it with the ordinary?"

Despite the reassuring stability that the very concept of the ordinary often invokes, it is clear, as mentioned above, that the parameters of "ordinariness" vary for each human being. They are dependent not only upon individual likes, dislikes, aptitudes, and deficiencies but also upon familial, community, and cultural conditions and expectations, not to mention environmental factors. What counts as ordinary experience for one individual can be an extraordinary experience for another and vice versa. The ordinariness of any given experience is established not only by the gestures and activities that take place within it but also in and through the familiar horizons of significance against which it unfolds, and it is these latter with which this book is concerned.

Phenomenology, as Edmund Husserl defined it in the early twentieth century, involves a suspension or "epoché" of our ordinary approach to the world of our concern. To describe the familiar after it has been rendered unfamiliar through the bracketing of the presuppositions one usually brings to bear on one's everyday experiences is the unique method the phenomenologist pursues. Rather than viewing the subjective starting point for these descriptions as an inescapable barrier to achieving intersubjective verifiability, Husserl claims that if it was systematically followed, phenomenology itself could become a "rigorous science" that would provide the foundation for all the other sciences (including the natural as well as the human sciences). For, as Husserl points out, even the natural sciences begin with the subjective experience of the scientific observer, with her perceptions, thoughts, and methodological commitments. Accordingly, he argues that the inherently subjective nature of all experience should be understood not as an insuperable obstacle but instead as one's only vehicle for arriving at valid descriptions of the world in which one lives.

Just as quantum mechanics shows us that the scientist's measurements alter the phenomena being measured, when we attempt to describe our ordinary experiences as if they were unfamiliar, the experiences themselves are transformed in the process. While phenomenologists such as Husserl and Maurice Merleau-Ponty take consciousness and bodily motility respectively as specific areas of focus, and while Martin Heidegger explores the universality of existential structures such as death and time as well as the inauthentic and authentic existential possibilities that emerge from them, in this book I offer a critical analysis of the less visible yet no less pervasive roles race, gender, class, age, ethnicity, and ability collectively play in structuring the meaning of everyday experience. My argument is that although these latter are occasionally the specific focus of individual and societal attention, all too often these and other equally real but intangible aspects of a person's identity tend to function primarily as part of the unthematized background context that structures daily life. More precisely, they function as what Husserl calls horizons, which help to situate the meaning of any given experience, albeit in ways that one is often unaware of in the absence of explicit reflection.

Describing the Husserlian concept of the horizon as it is taken up in Hans-Georg Gadamer's philosophical hermeneutics, Linda Martín Alcoff states: "The concept of horizon helps to capture the background, framing assumptions we bring with us to perception and understanding, the congealed experiences that become premises by which we strive to make sense of the world, the range of concepts and categories of description that we have at our disposal" (Alcoff 2006: 95). In *Truth and Method*, Gadamer discusses what he calls the "fusion of horizons," a process according to which past horizons are indissolubly linked to present horizons, complicating but also enriching the process of interpretation. Although Gadamer focuses particularly on how this fusion of horizons is accomplished by the historian, who delves deeply into the study of past cultures, bringing her own contemporary perspective to bear on a particular historical reality, it is evident that his account also applies outside an academic context insofar as individuals weave together, on an ongoing basis, disparate memories, cultural traditions, present experiences, and future expectations into a meaningful existence.[1]

Many other contemporary continental philosophers either explicitly discuss the concept of the horizon in their work or, at the very least, turn our attention to the "background, framing assumptions" that Alcoff claims respectively constitute the horizon for different individuals. While Gadamer emphasizes how our own and others' horizons are fused together when we study different cultures, and views this as an enriching process that expands interpretive possibilities, Simone de Beauvoir examines cases where an individual's horizons can be severely restricted, thereby limiting the possibility of exercising one's freedom in a meaningful way. Frantz Fanon's discussion of a racial epidermal schema in *Black Skin White Masks* supports Beauvoir's analysis of oppression, revealing how the background assumptions of others collectively constitute a "historico-racial schema" that structures both black and white perception and black and white body images.

Through a close examination of how the jurors in the 1992 Simi Valley, California, trial of the police officers in the Rodney King case "read" the videotape of King's beating, Judith Butler demonstrates that "seeing" is never neutral but always involves a process of interpretation that occurs within an existing social and political context. Just as one's utterances always take place, as Wittgenstein observes, within a particular language game, so too, seeing always takes place within a particular cultural framework that helps to define the limits of perceptual intelligibility. A vital component of this process involves determining who possesses the ability to constitute what counts as intelligible. As Alcoff observes, only those who are seen as possessing "legitimate" perceptions (or who are seen as capable of legitimizing the perceptions of others) are viewed as possessing "epistemic authority" (Alcoff 1991, 2006).

If, as Butler argues, seeing is not a purely individual, subjective process but always emerges within and is made meaningful through a broader cultural context, the question becomes, how can one "read against the grain," that is, how can one develop new ways of seeing that break away from the racist and sexist patterns that have formed part of human beings' collective historical horizons for centuries? To respond to this question requires that one take seriously the perils of clinging to old habits as well as the promise of forming new ones. For while it is clear that habit plays a powerful role in reinforcing the status quo, one must also acknowledge what Merleau-Ponty calls the "plasticity of habit," that is, the ability of individuals and societies to form new ways of engaging the world of their concern.

Within contemporary continental philosophy this question concerning the possibility of experiencing the world differently has often taken an agonistic form and is usually cast in terms of the possibility of exercising agency in resistance to oppressive hegemonic norms and social practices. While I am also very interested in overcoming oppressive ways of viewing and responding to those who society deems "other," the problem with the debate when it is framed in this way is that it pits the individual (or minority community) against society and makes it seem as if the issue is primarily a matter of enabling individuals to break free of societal restraints so that they can determine the meaning of their existence on their own terms or in terms defined independently by their own particular community.[2]

Even for existentialists such as Jean-Paul Sartre who celebrate individual freedom, one is never merely a "being-for-itself" but always, at the same time, a "being-for-others," and this means that one cannot fulfill one's responsibility for one's own existence without also acknowledging one's responsibilities to others and to society as a whole. Alcoff argues that identity itself should be conceived as an "interpretive horizon" that is neither a purely individual accomplishment nor a function of social imposition from the outside. In her words, "identity is not merely that which is given to an individual or group, but is also a way of inhabiting, interpreting, and working through, both collectively and individually, an objective social location and group history" (Alcoff 2006: 42). Identity, on this view, is never fixed once and for all but is continuously constructed and reconstructed out of past, present, and future intersubjective experiences. In short, as Seyla Benhabib asserts, the self is always situated. Or, as Sartre and Simone de Beauvoir would claim, "the self" is constantly in a state of becoming because our situation and the demands it places upon human beings, both individually and collectively, are always changing. Moreover, if one argues, as Alcoff and others have, that each individual has multiple identities, each with their own unique histories, aims, possibilities, and restrictions, then these interpretive horizons become even more complicated and, at the same time, all the more imperative to investigate.[3]

If identity is indeed an "interpretive horizon" that is socially (and physically) constituted through concrete everyday experiences, and if one's horizons are never the sole "possession" of any given individual but are also shared by others, then this demands a rethinking of the traditional dichotomy between the self and the other that continues to play a central role in the Western philosophical tradition.[4] Despite acknowledging that human beings always inhabit a social situation, the existentialist tradition has tended to understand the authentic individual as someone who relies on herself and her own interpretations rather than on those of others.[5] But this presupposes that these interpretations are separable in the first place. This is precisely the point I am challenging by emphasizing the constitutive role played by shared horizons of significance in determining what counts as "ordinary" experience.

Sonia Kruks claims that by "retrieving experience" as a primary level of critical analysis, we can "retrieve an account of a self that is embodied and socially situated, a self that can never leap out of its skin. But although this is a self that cannot exist independently of its facticities, it is not reducible to them" (Kruks 2001: 51). I agree with Kruks that (re)turning directly to experience, and more particularly, to the familiar but often invisible horizons that define the parameters of mundane existence, is essential. More specifically, I am arguing that only by interrogating the "ordinary" dimensions of experience is it possible to arrive at an understanding of the dynamic forces that give meaning to individual lives and that are both the obstacle and the vehicle to achieving lasting social change.

It is impossible to take up the question of how "ordinary" experience is constituted in and through particular horizons of significance without acknowledging that for some people, ordinary experience (rather than its disruption) is itself defined by extreme suffering and misery. Indeed, for those people for whom deprivation and degradation is a way of life, the disruption of the ordinary can be a hope, a fantasy, or even a prayer. Thus, one must always be cognizant of the fact that the sedimentation of everyday experience into recognizable patterns can serve to codify oppression as readily as it can promote a reassuring sense of existential stability.

To avoid the complacency that all too often arises in response to the familiar, one must be attentive to the continual possibilities for transformation offered by those aspects of the world that cannot be rendered intelligible within established horizons, and that therefore demand new ways of thinking, feeling, and being. Discussing this process in explicitly temporal terms, Elizabeth Grosz suggests that the indeterminacy and inexhaustibility of the past (including, therefore, the familiar) is precisely what opens it up to new futures:

> Instead of the past being regarded as fixed, inert, given, unalterable, even if not knowable in its entirety, it must be regarded as inherently open to future rewritings, as never "full" enough, or present enough, to propel itself intact into the future. The past is never exhausted in its virtualities, insofar as it is always capable of giving rise to *another* reading, another context, another framework that will animate it in different ways. (Grosz 2004: 254)

According to Grosz, achieving change in the future requires not breaking with the past (as if this could ever be done in any absolute sense) but reanimating the past so that its latent possibilities can be realized and acted upon. *Refiguring the Ordinary* takes up this project by (1) drawing attention to and (2) offering new readings of familiar horizons that have all too often escaped serious philosophical attention but that collectively help to define and structure the "ordinariness" of daily experience as such. Such horizons may or may not be shared, but, even if shared, they are always lived in their own way by particular individuals. No two people construct, understand, and respond to the familiar in exactly the same manner, even when they inhabit what may appear to be virtually identical situations because, as I argue in *Body Images: Embodiment as Intercorporeality*, following Merleau-Ponty, their experience is differentiated from the start by the distinctiveness of their own bodily engagement with the world.

The horizons I explore in the pages that follow range from the body, death, and city-life, to less accessible but no less powerful horizons such as race, class, gender, ability, ethnicity, and age. Regardless of the respective roles these horizons play in one's ordinary experience, as horizons they are, as Edmund Husserl first noted, indeterminate and inexhaustible. To re-figure the ordinary as I seek to do here involves a critical examination of what counts and doesn't count *as* ordinary through an examination of the horizons that establish the parameters of the ordinary as such; it is to (re)turn to the familiar as the site of individual, social, and political possibility, recognizing that the sedimentation of experience is not the obstacle to, but the very condition for, personal as well as cultural transformation.

In part 1, "Figuring the Ground," I offer conceptual definitions of several of the key terms that I use throughout the text, such as context, perspective, horizon, ambiguity, absurdity, and reversibility, and I show how these terms have their own complicated genealogies, their own horizons of significance within continental philosophy, pragmatism, and Gestalt psychology. Part 2, "Narrative Horizons," explores the ways in which meaning emerges "between the lines" of a text, and how the body itself serves as the ongoing "narrative horizon" through which human beings actively make sense of their lives. The focus of part 3, "(Re)Grounding the Figure" is on how sexist, racist, classist, and other oppressive ways of understanding and responding to both individuals and societies become sedimented over time, forming bodily habits of perception that are exceedingly difficult to recognize, much less overcome. Part 4, "Urban Perspectives," turns to the city as an omnipresent horizon of urban as well as rural life, to explore how the "flesh" of the city is embodied in a person's own flesh, offering crucial limits to as well as avenues of possibility for everyday existence. In part 5, "Constraining Horizons," I offer some explicit challenges to the assumption that it is always possible to break out of the constraints posed by narrow or rigid horizons and the inflexible meanings that seem to result from them by multiplying our perspectives and the horizons out of which they are constituted. As the opening quote from Joan Didion and the tragic events of September 11, 2001, amply attest, all it takes is an instant for the familiarity of one's world to come tumbling down, and at these times, even the multiplication of perspectives may only intensify the recognition of the enormity of the losses that have been sustained.

Whether the disruption of the ordinary is experienced as a curse or a blessing, it is evident that it is the permanent possibility of such disruption that defines the structure of human experience. If one takes seriously the ways in which class, race, gender, ethnicity, age, and ability no less than death and the body itself serve as overlapping, albeit indeterminate, horizons of significance that collectively contextualize individual as well as group experiences, one can understand how the meaning of these experiences becomes over-determined and thereby resistant to change. And yet, recognizing the continual interplay of these horizons in relation to one another as one's situation itself continually changes over time and across space helps to explain the improvisational nature of human experience from one moment to the next. Thus, to affirm the indeterminacy of these multiple horizons as a constitutive feature of experience allows one to understand why the familiarity of the ordinary can always be refigured in extraordinary ways.

PART 1

Figuring the Ground

1

Context and Perspective

While contemporary cognitive scientists continue to grapple with what is commonly referred to as the "frame problem," namely, the integral role played by contextual features of any given situation that influence how that situation is understood and responded to, because the very intangibility and indeterminacy associated with these contextual features makes them resistant to quantifiable analysis, continental philosophers working in the phenomenological and hermeneutical traditions have long recognized that it is impossible to separate the perspective through which an individual grasps a given situation from the context(s) in which that situation emerges.[1] And yet, even continental philosophers who acknowledge from the outset that the indeterminate horizons that accompany any given experience are precisely what provide the indispensable (albeit changing) context that helps to shape the meaning of that experience often stumble a bit when asked to define more precisely the ongoing role that these horizons play in everyday life.

The lack of theoretical clarity that frequently accompanies even the rich descriptions of the horizon provided by Husserl in *The Crisis of European Sciences and Transcendental Phenomenology* stems not only from the horizon's unbounded quality or from the difficulty of understanding how it intersects with other horizons that help to "frame" how an individual grasps a given situation, but also from the fact that, in the attempt to understand the role of the horizon qua horizon, it is transformed into the focus of inquiry in addition to functioning as a necessary part of the background that drives inquiry itself.[2] The elusiveness of the horizon becomes even more apparent when one attempts to distinguish it from the term with which I am closely associating it above, namely context.

In order to lay the conceptual groundwork for my own discussion of the multiple horizons that help to establish the parameters of ordinary experience for any given individual, I will begin by examining the relationship between context and perspective, two phenomena that are directly influenced by these horizons and that, in turn, are capable of altering these horizons themselves. In the discussion that follows I will distinguish carefully between these three terms, although, from an experiential point of view, it is not always possible to separate the horizon from the context since, in an important sense, a horizon functions as an ongoing (though changing) context from which an individual draws in constructing her own unique perspectives. However, although I will treat the horizon as a context and often refer to it as such throughout this book, here I reserve the expression "context" for a more general context of significance that includes a number of different horizons and that operates across different situations, helping to link those experiences together in a more or less unified way.

"Horizon" is often understood as playing the role of a ground within the figure-ground relationship that, as Merleau-Ponty and Gestalt psychologists maintain, actively structures perceptual experience. Like Merleau-Ponty, I am arguing for the extension of the findings of the Gestalt theorists regarding the figure-ground relationship beyond perception itself to encompass all aspects of bodily intentionality. The claim that I am making, following Merleau-Ponty, is that human experiences more generally (and not merely perceptual experiences) are organized in terms of a more or less determinate figure that is set over and against a more or less indeterminate ground.[3] And, as Husserl has shown, this ground is not univocal but consists of many different horizons that are not reducible to one another and yet overlap in all sorts of interesting ways. While Husserl and Merleau-Ponty focus primarily on spatial and temporal horizons, failing ever to acknowledge the ways in which complicated phenomena such as race, class, gender, sexuality, religion, ability, ethnicity, and age can themselves function as overlapping horizons of significance, it is their recognition that the constitutive role played by the horizon tends to be rendered invisible insofar as one focuses on the specific object of one's intention/attention, that makes it possible to see how these horizons can be omnipresent in one's experience without their collective influence being explicitly registered. A central argument I will be making throughout this text is that it is impossible to achieve genuine social, political, or even psychic change, that is, to transform or "re-figure" what is taken to be "ordinary" experience, without grappling with the constitutive role these indeterminate horizons play (or fail to play) in any given individual's or community's daily existence.

An important philosopher to bring into this discussion is the American pragmatist George Herbert Mead, because he offers such a rich account of how perspectives are themselves intersubjective in origin insofar as they arise directly out of an individual's interactions with other people. Indeed, Mead's entire discussion of perspective is based upon the social relations that one sustains in an ongoing way with others. By following his argument that perspectives are socially constituted, one can in turn see how the social constitution of perspective depends upon shared horizons and shared social contexts. For Mead, it is in and through everyday participation with others in what he calls a "conversation of gestures" that perspectives as well as selves are constructed. These conversations allow for a variety of meanings to emerge precisely because of the differences in gesture, horizons, context, and perspective that the various interlocutors contribute to the conversation, thereby revealing multiple sources for the ambiguity that both Merleau-Ponty and Beauvoir identify as an essential feature of human experience. Moreover, an important implication of Mead's analysis of the social constitution of the self, as Alcoff argues, is that "the rich and complex texture of what we think and experience as our inner lives is frequently beyond our individual intention and understanding" (Alcoff 2006: 121).

To claim that a context, horizon, or perspective is socially constructed does not mean that all individuals who share that context, horizon, or perspective experience these latter in the same way. Indeed, as Husserl, Merleau-Ponty, and Sartre have all persuasively argued, and as the overlapping but distinct experiences of identical twins reared together demonstrates, the individuality of each person's body is sufficient to guarantee that no two individuals will occupy the same perspective or bring the exact same horizons and/or contexts to bear upon their experiences. Before one can arrive at a better sense of how overlapping horizons such as race, gender, and class are experienced differently by different people, however, one must first achieve a deeper understanding of the interdependency of perspectives, horizons, and contexts and of the respective roles each plays in establishing the meaning and structure of "ordinary" experience.

Michel Foucault's opening account in *The Order of Things* of the importance of perspective as it is revealed in the complex relationships among the people and objects depicted in Velasquez's painting *Las Meninas* suggests that perspective is an auspicious place to start. Drawing upon the history of aesthetics, Foucault show how perspective both constructs and reveals the parameters of the world of human concern. In accordance with Mead as well as Merleau-Ponty, Foucault maintains that perspective is not a stable entity comfortably ensconced *within* an individual psyche. Rather, Foucault depicts perspective as a shifting set of relationships that is articulated in the Velasquez painting through the painter's gaze as it is responded to and transformed through the gaze of his model and in turn the viewer:

> From the eyes of the painter to what he is observing there runs a compelling line that we, the onlookers, have no power of evading: it runs through the real picture and emerges from its surface to join the place from which we see the painter observing us; this dotted line reaches out to us ineluctably, and links us to the representation of the picture. (Foucault 1970: 4)

And Foucault continues:

> In appearance, this locus is a simple one; a matter of pure reciprocity: we are looking at a picture in which the painter is in turn looking out at us. A mere confrontation, eyes catching one another's glance, direct looks superimposing themselves upon one another as they cross. And yet this slender line of recipro-cal visibility embraces a whole complex network of uncertainties, exchanges, and feints. . . . No gaze is stable, or rather, in the neutral furrow of the gaze piercing at a right angle through the canvas, subject and object, the spectator and the model, reverse their roles to infinity. (Foucault 1970: 4–5)

This rather dense and provocative passage from Foucault highlights some of the most crucial points I will be addressing and contesting throughout this book. While Foucault successfully captures the fluidity of both context and perspective insofar as they are manifested through a dynamic, complex inter-change between the painter and any number of possible viewers, he describes the site of this exchange as a "neutral place," a claim I am specifically challeng-ing. Neither context nor perspective (nor the horizon for that matter) is ever neutral. As Kaja Silverman, Luce Irigaray, and Beauvoir all persuasively argue in different ways, this allegedly neutral gaze has been historically predicated almost exclusively upon the experiences of men.[4] Indeed, the ongoing influ-ences of race, gender, sexuality, class, age, ethnicity, ability, historical time pe-riod, and so on in the lives of the painter, his model, and the audience argue against the possibility of a neutral place out of which perspectives emerge and are exchanged. Moreover, in his subsequent analysis, Foucault demonstrates that the ways things are ordered imposes a non-neutral structure on the per-spectives one develops toward them. Insofar as the "painter is observing a place which, from moment to moment, never ceases to change its content, its form, its face, its identity," the alleged neutrality that undergirds this experience is always already belied (Foucault 1970: 5).

An additional problem occurs when vision is depicted as the primary or even the only way of constructing a perspective and/or discerning the influence of perspective (e.g., in the audience's response to a work of art). In *Downcast*

Eyes: The Denigration of Vision in Twentieth Century French Thought, historian Martin Jay offers a critical analysis of the "ubiquity of visual metaphors" in describing the functioning of perception and language and claims that "[d]epending, of course, on one's outlook or point of view, the prevalence of such metaphors will be accounted an obstacle or an aid to our knowledge of reality" (Jay 1993: 1). More recent work by disability theorists has emphasized the dangers of assuming vision to be the dominant sense for all human beings since it is clear that those who are not sighted organize their perceptual field perspectively without relying on vision. And, as Merleau-Ponty argues in *Phenomenology of Perception*, even for those who are sighted, vision is part of a larger, dynamic, kinesthetic perceptual system in which it is impossible to isolate the contributions of one sense from those of another except through very artificial (e.g., experimental) means that disrupt the unity of the original experience. Bearing these important concerns in mind, I would like to turn now to consider Mead's original account of what perspectives are (and are not) and how they function in everyday experience. His emphasis on how perspectives combine to form what he calls a "community perspective" offers, I suggest, an especially promising means of combating accounts of perspective that tie it exclusively to a given individual's experience and/or that describe perspective as if it is a private feature of perceptual experience.

Perspective

Regarding the notion of a perspective, Mead says that it is "absurd to place the perspective inside of the organism" (Mead 1938: 111). This is because the perspective does not *belong* to the organism, but reflects and incorporates aspects of the situation with which the organism is confronted. According to Mead: "If we wish to regard it metaphysically, there are an infinite number of possible perspectives, each of which will give a different definition to the parts and reveal different relations between them. Which of these particular perspectives is the right one, metaphysically? There is no answer to the question" (Mead 1939: 99).

In Mead's account, there is no one "right" perspective that cancels out the rest because the situation can be organized and understood in a number of different ways.[5] This means that different perspectives are themselves relative to one another insofar as they serve as alternative means of grasping the present situation that are not independently constituted. A single perspective is not divorced from other perspectives and does not separate one individual from other individuals, precisely because the social framework of the present is not created by any one individual, but reflects a network of social relationships and social systems. Moreover, Mead suggests that different perspectives are capable of being organized within a single perspective, and this is what makes it possible for a gesture to retain the same meaning across different perspectives.

Ultimately, for Mead, individual perspectives become socially organized into a "community perspective" that allows objects to "exist in their relationship to the group," therefore making possible "common characters which exist for all the members of the group, though they exist also within the perspective of each individual" (Mead 1938: 203). This community perspective does not supersede the individual's own perspective, but is synonymous with what Mead calls the generalized other: a set of accepted attitudes and responses that have been internalized by members of the same social community. The community perspective, then, is incorporated into the individual's own perspective, and this is what makes universality of meaning possible since different individuals each possess and make reference to the community perspective in their gestures and conduct.

Unless I am directly appealing to the perspective of the generalized other when I am acting in a given situation, however, the community perspective provided by the generalized other seems to function more as a context within which a perspective arises rather than constituting the perspective itself. Mead's emphasis on the manner in which one perspective can be incorporated into another is helpful in revealing the varying social standpoints that are brought together within a single perspective, but it becomes less and less evident on his account what constitutes the perspective itself and what constitutes a more general context of significance that underlies a given perspective. As I will show, Merleau-Ponty also fails to distinguish adequately a perspective from a context, and this makes both accounts of perspective somewhat problematic. Before we can differentiate a context from a perspective, it will be helpful to examine what Merleau-Ponty has to say about perspective.

Although Merleau-Ponty discusses the notion of perspective at some length in the *Phenomenology of Perception,* the nature of perspective and the role it plays in perceptual experience remains somewhat unclear. On the one hand, Merleau-Ponty asserts that "I am not tied to any one perspective but can change my point of view, being under compulsion only in that I must always have one, and can have only one at once" (Merleau-Ponty 1962: 407). Even while acknowledging the uniqueness of perspective, however, Merleau-Ponty also warns that "I do not have one perspective, then another, and between them a link brought about by the understanding, but each perspective *merges into* the other and, in so far as it is still possible to speak of a synthesis, we are concerned with a 'transitional synthesis'" (Merleau-Ponty 1962: 329).

If, as Merleau-Ponty claims, I can have only one perspective at a time, but am also unaware of the precise point at which one perspective ends and another begins, this can occur only because the perspectives I have appealed to in the past or will take up in the future serve as the horizon for the present perspective that I have adopted. Indeed, Merleau-Ponty has characterized the continuity of a person's perspectival grasp on the world in terms of a "synthesis of horizons" that "merges with the very movement whereby time passes" (Merleau-Ponty 1962: 330). In so doing, he implies that it is impossible to understand any one perspective without appealing to a variety of other perspectives that I may or may not adopt with regard to the present situation. Some of these perspectives may be available to me through my own past experiences or through the experiences of others; however, it is evident that these alternative perspectives do not often present themselves in a clear, articulated fashion. Instead, I would argue, they constitute the horizon out of which my present perspective takes root and, in its own distinctive way, "seizes the world."

If perspective is defined as the spontaneous organization of a series of gestures (or events) into a meaningful, dynamic whole, one can say that my perspective on any given situation incorporates elements of the past and future, yet is grounded socially, physically, and temporally in the present.[6] Moreover, the future possibilities that inform my present perspective themselves provide a context for the future perspectives I develop. For Merleau-Ponty, the continuity of our temporal experience is thereby assured by the ongoing manner in which "[t]he normal person *reckons with* the possible, which thus, without shifting from its position as a possibility, acquires a sort of actuality" (Merleau-Ponty 1962: 109).

Context and the Figure-Ground Structure

Regarding the notion of context, Merleau-Ponty states that "[i]f we turn back to the phenomena, they show us that the apprehension of a quality, just as that of size, is bound up with a whole perceptual context, and that the stimuli no longer furnish us with the indirect means we were seeking of isolating a layer of immediate impressions" (Merleau-Ponty 1962: 8). While it is evident that all perception takes place within an ever-changing context of significance, and that all perception is perspectival, it is not equally clear how the contexts that situate an individual's experience and the perspectives that structure that experience develop in relation to one another.[7] Furthermore, Merleau-Ponty's claim that perspectives are continually "merging" and Mead's view of perspectives as "nested" within one another also raise the question of whether it is even possible to talk about *a* perspective or *a* context, since an understanding of perspectives and contexts as distinguishable phenomena always seems to come after the fact. In Merleau-Ponty's words: "We do not begin by knowing the perspective aspects of the thing; it is not mediated by our senses, our sensations or our perspectives; we go straight to it, and it is only in a secondary way that we become aware of the limits of our knowledge and of ourselves as knowing" (Merleau-Ponty 1962:

324). Perspectives, then, define the perceptual field insofar as they orient one toward an object, person, or situation, and they are "invisible" to the extent that this object, person, or situation occupies the field of one's concern. Indeed, "[t]he object-horizon structure, or the perspective, is no obstacle to me when I want to see the object: for just as it is the means whereby objects are distinguished from each other, it is also the means whereby they are disclosed" (Merleau-Ponty 1962: 68). Since perspective, for Merleau-Ponty, is a matter of how a particular object reveals itself against a given background, and since an object changes in accordance with changes in its background and vice-versa, the figure-ground relationship must be the starting point for understanding the influence that context and perspective have upon one another.

If perspective is not solely a matter of the object or horizon taken in isolation, but involves the system that is formed out of their dynamic interaction, it may at first glance be tempting to identify a perceptual context with the horizon itself. Thus, one might claim that embedded within every perspective is a context of significance that changes relative to a particular perception, since "[a]n initial perception independent of any background is inconceivable" (Merleau-Ponty 1962: 281). In such an account, the context would be integral to the perspective since it would serve as the background for individual perceptions and would therefore have a ubiquitous function in everyday experience. And yet, the concreteness of the spatial presence of the background in the figure-ground structure can be lost sight of if one too quickly identifies a perceptual background with the more encompassing notion of context. Moreover, by equating context with the background in the figure-ground structure, one runs the risk of subordinating context to perspective, and it is not clear that context is so subordinated to perspective in daily life.

Merleau-Ponty refers to the background for individual perceptions both as being perceptible and as being constituted out of a whole network of past experiences and future expectations that, on principle, are not a part of the sensory field at any given moment. This produces a tension in his discussion of perspective and of the figure-ground structure of perceptual experience since the indeterminacy of the background is twofold: on the one hand it is the obverse side of the perceptual clarity of the figure, which requires a spatial background in order to manifest itself as a distinct entity, and, on the other hand, it is due to the nature of the attitudes, experiences, and expectations that also combine to form the background and that defy explication since they possess a generality that transcends the immediacy of the present situation.

If one views the perceptual background as a primarily spatial phenomenon, then one can understand the indeterminacy of the background in relation to the corresponding determinacy of the figure, and can even explore the influence and extent of this indeterminacy in particular situations. Such an investigation was, in fact, a predominant concern of the Gestalt psychologists, and their experiments along these lines are referred to by Merleau-Ponty and others who have worked on perception. It is once one turns to the second type of indeterminacy, however, that the notion of background itself becomes obscured and that one begins to lose sight of the relation of the background to a specific figure. As mentioned earlier, this second type of indeterminacy is a function of the unthematized fashion in which my former and future experiences "color" my present situation and help to present it in one light rather than another.

While I agree with Merleau-Ponty that previous and anticipated experiences certainly influence the course of a given individual's present action, there is a need to locate this influence at a different *level* of experience than that provided by the figure-ground structure. Just as Merleau-Ponty refers to the varying spatial levels through which we build up our own sense of spatiality, there is a corresponding variety of contextual levels that help to determine the perspectives one takes up toward objects, other people, and the situation as a whole. These contextual levels are constituted out of such diverse perceptual phenomena as memories, expectations, familiarity with the situation, time of day, degree of formality required by a particular social encounter, and the number of people with whom one is dealing, and all of these contextual aspects of the situation are value-laden. Trying to separate out these various influences is problematic, however, for just as the different spatial levels that ground an individual's perceptual experience are unified through a specific physical (or bodily) orientation, the contextual levels out of which a particular perspective arises are themselves often experienced as an unarticulated perceptual whole.[8]

Despite the variety of factors that contribute to the creation of a perceptual context, however, it is evident that memories play a primary role in assessing and evaluating how one can or should act at any given point in time. Hence, the influence of memories cannot be limited to a certain contextual level, but rather permeates all of the contexts that give significance to a particular situation. This is not to say that memories play a fixed role in one's experience, however, since individuals are often unaware of the extent to which their expectations are defined by previous social interactions. Furthermore, as Mead has noted, the specific expectations or goals that individuals want to realize in a given situation directly influence the level of involvement or participation with which they engage that situation.

One might claim, then, that with regard to the varying contextual levels that are operative in any given situation, memories and expectations serve as the parameters within which individual perceptual experiences are defined and understood. And yet, as parameters that are themselves continually *re-constituted* out of a continuous perceptual framework, they are subject to the same ambiguity and indeterminacy that Merleau-Ponty has found to be inherent in all structures of the perceptual world. Clearly, it is the cross-temporal aspect of the varying contexts one brings to one's everyday experiences that allows one to transcend the spatiality of the physical figure-ground relationship with which a person is actively confronted. These contextual levels themselves are a reflection of previous social situations and hence have also taken place within a particular spatial level; however, insofar as the context I bring to a particular situation stems from experiences I have had or will have before or after that situation, it is not as directly tied to the spatiality of the present situation as is the figure-ground structure.[9]

Because Merleau-Ponty fails to distinguish the contribution of a more general context of significance from the immediate spatial situation as it is revealed in the relationship between figure and ground, he is unable to account for the continuity that is revealed across different perspectives, a continuity that derives from similarity of context rather than similarity in the figure-ground structure. That is to say, although all perspectives presuppose the presence of a figure outlined against a ground, these perspectives themselves often attain a type of permanence that is not characteristic of the shifting figure-ground structure. In fact, it is *individual events or individual gestures* rather than *perspectives* that tend to be responded to as meaningful figures manifested against a particular social, spatial, and temporal background; a perspective, on the other hand, can be only indirectly indicated in a specific gesture since the significance of the perspective that in turn situates that gesture derives from a more general context that is never fully revealed.

While gestures are the medium through which people communicate with one another, I am claiming that it is the perspectives that are formed out of different "conversations of gestures" that tie individual gestures together into meaningful wholes. And, since these perspectives are developed spontaneously and not according to a prearranged law, the scope and relevance of a particular perspective will shift over time. Changes in perspective are expressed through modifications of gesture; however, it sometimes happens that one's gestures may change before one is even aware that the change conveys a difference in perspective.[10] Thus, I am arguing that the figure-ground relationship is primarily efficacious at the level of individual gestures since it is these latter that are spatially grounded in the present and that emerge as distinct phenomena that motivate one's action. These individual gestures are not perceived as isolated entities, however, but are integrated into a particular perspective or point of view as they take their place within a broader conversation of gestures.[11]

The Situation

An implication of my analysis is that the context one brings to a particular situation, influenced as it is by a multiplicity of past and future experiences, cannot be expressed as easily in the present situation as can a perspective that is more directly tied to a specific set of gestures.[12] Perhaps the reason it is so difficult to make context the explicit focus of a particular situation is because context is precisely what constitutes the situation *qua* situation for me. It is, in fact, because past and future are also implicated in the present situation (in the form of memories, attitudes, and expectations) that there will always be aspects of the situation that are not revealed in the present moment, but that nonetheless help to constitute a horizon of significance that enables me to adopt a particular perspective toward a given experience. In Merleau-Ponty's words:

> What needs to be understood is that for the same reason I am present here and now, and present elsewhere and always, and also absent from here and from now, and absent from every place and every time. This ambiguity is not some imperfection of consciousness or existence, but the definition of them. Time in the widest sense, that is, the order of co-existences as well as that of successions, is a setting to which one can gain access and which one can understand *only by occupying a situation in it, and by grasping it in its entirety through the horizons of that situation.* (Merleau-Ponty 1962: 332, my emphasis)

It is through inhabiting a situation that implicates past and future as well as the present that I discover the temporal dimensions of perceptual experience, and, furthermore, it is through attending to the horizons that help to constitute each situation that I learn how to transform my situation and change my perspective. The situation and its horizons are, therefore, always already presupposed in the perceptual process since they serve as the framework for the individual gestures that express my own response to the world. Inhabiting a situation means that I am at once "present and absent" because to be immersed in the situation entails taking up a perspective toward that situation, a perspective that relies on a context of significance that projects beyond the facticity of the experience at hand. Self-knowledge also is directly tied to a given situation, for: "I know myself only in so far as I am inherent in time and in the world, that is, I know myself only in my ambiguity" (Merleau-Ponty 1962: 345).

And yet, although Merleau-Ponty acknowledges the importance of the situation for self-understanding as well as for an understanding of temporality, a problem with his account is that he never clarifies the role that context plays in differentiating one situation (and one perspective) from another.[13] Instead, Merleau-Ponty focuses more on the notion of a perceptual field than on the way in which these fields combine to form a unique situation. He discusses how each of the five senses constitutes a field of perceptual activity, but he does not describe sufficiently how these shifting fields bring about continuity in one's perspectives—a continuity that is provided by an ongoing context of significance that helps to determine when one situation has ended and another has begun.

Regarding the function of the perceptual field, Merleau-Ponty asserts that "[w]e now begin to see a deeper meaning in the organization of a field: it is not only colours, but also geometrical forms, all sense-data and the significance of objects which go to form a system. Our perception in its entirety is animated by a logic which assigns to each object its determinate features in virtue of those of the rest, and which 'cancel out' as unreal all stray data; it is entirely sustained by the certainty of the world" (Merleau-Ponty 1962: 313). Here, Merleau-Ponty distinguishes the significance of objects from their color, geometrical form, and sensory properties, and views all of the above as mutually constitutive of a perceptual field. And yet, at the end of the *Phenomenology of Perception* one is still left wondering how all of these aspects of the thing relate to one another and to the individual perspectives one continuously takes up toward new situations. If, on the other hand, one takes context to be the ongoing framework that gives each situation its own peculiar focus, as I have been arguing, one can arrive at a better understanding of why each situation is made up of experiences, attitudes, and half-articulated expectations that are not the property of any one person alone. This is because the indeterminacy and ambiguity that are so characteristic of the perceptual process are themselves located *within* a particular context, and make possible the transition from one situation to another without requiring a corresponding change in one's physical orientation.

Within any given situation, Merleau-Ponty suggests, past, present, and future tend to be incorporated in a fluid totality that achieves its primary determinacy through the immediacy of a spatially-oriented, figure-ground structure. This latter structure, in fact, continually "fills in" the indeterminacy of the situation in the fullness of the present moment, and the perspective that results out of this experience (and, more precisely, out of the individual gestures out of which it is composed), in turn becomes part of the context for one's future experiences. However, by failing to distinguish the contribution of a more general context of significance from the immediate physical "presentness" of the situation as it is revealed through the relationship between figure and ground, Merleau-Ponty remains unable to account for why it is that when I recall an earlier social encounter when conversing with a friend, I so frequently begin by recreating the broader interpersonal context that situated the experience, often de-emphasizing the actual spatial setting of the encounter itself (unless there was something unique about this latter that I feel must be conveyed). Moreover, if the context was simply the immediate perceptual horizon or background for a specific experience, it is not clear why, when recounting the incident, I would emphasize the social setting in which a particular encounter unfolded as an indispensable backdrop for understanding the actual content of the discourse. Here, what is deemed especially important is recreating the less visible, contextual features of the situation that gave rise to a particular conversation so that my friend, too, will understand why I acted the way I did at that point in time. That is to say, I look to the context to help supply the *reasons* for my action, and this context, when viewed from a later perspective, incorporates my own responses to others as well as the responses of other people to me.

The importance of context for understanding everyday experiences extends not just to situations that have already taken place, but also to situations that one anticipates will take place in the future. Thus, if I expect a certain letter to arrive by next Tuesday, I concentrate not only on what the letter might or might not say, but also on the attitude and expectations of the person sending the letter, as well on my own possible attitude and response to having received it. While it is certainly the case that these attitudes and expectations form a horizon for the interpretation of the letter when it actually does arrive, they are not rooted in the present situation in the way that the color of the notepaper, the handwriting, and the scent of the paper are. Instead, these attitudes and expectations together form part of the basic context out of which a specific perspective toward the letter develops, and the figure-ground structure, by contrast, refers to the way in which the meanings of the written words themselves form a pattern against the background of the written letter as a whole.[14]

A good example of how perspectives are influenced by the more general context within which action takes place has to do with the way I view drivers when I am a pedestrian and the way I view pedestrians when I am driving. Both pedestrians and drivers have places to go, and each views the other as an occasional obstacle in arriving at a final destination. When I am driving, I resent the sudden appearance of a pedestrian cutting across the street in front of me *even though* I myself always cut across the same street whenever I see an opening in the stream of traffic. I silently curse the smug street-crosser and am angered when he or she causes me to miss my timing on the next light. When I, as a pedestrian, am waiting to cross the street, however, and a car speeds up to prevent me from crossing in time to avoid a whole onslaught of vehicles arriving from the previous light, I am furious at the driver's impatience and can become quite haughty about the respect due me as a pedestrian. After all, I am simply a fragile human being, without the protection of a honking mechanical monster at my disposal to make others jump to do my bidding. The second I step into a car, however, the situation changes, and I am the one angrily wondering what the hell those people are doing calmly crossing, crossing, crossing the street long after my light has turned green and they no longer have the right of way.

Just as the phenomenal field is capable of displaying a high degree of continuity even as it changes over time and across space, "ordinary" experience itself is characterized by continuity in the contexts an individual brings to different situations; as Merleau-Ponty so often notes, it is the continuity (or lack of continuity) of the world and of human bodies as physical entities within the world that is responsible for the unity (or lack of unity) one finds within one's daily life. On the other hand, the contexts that one brings to situations themselves emerge only through those situations; the context that is invoked when I am driving differs from the context that is involved when I am a pedestrian. More specifically, the difference between these two contexts and the different perspectives to which they give rise has to do with the specific nature of the task at hand. Driving a car is a different type of activity than walking and hence carries with it a different set of attitudes and expectations, which I implicitly make use of to isolate my own perspective as driver from that of the pedestrian. And, as long as I am driving, I can successfully maintain a division between my own perspective and that of the pedestrian despite those features of the situation that we share in common. If my car breaks down, however, or if I reach my destination, my own perspective as driver immediately gives way to a new perspective that is in turn related to a new activity. Moreover, the context that underlies my perspective is not merely a reflection of my spatial situation, but instead, serves to motivate the particular spatial organization that I give to the field of my concern. To a driver, the pedestrian cutting in front of the car is an *obstacle*; to a pedestrian, the over-anxious driver is a *threat*.

Although a context of significance cannot be said to precede the individual perspectives that give it its content, a given context is always already operative within each person's experience, and, if one wants to change one's perspective on a given issue or problem, one must first come to terms with the context that has helped to present this issue or problem in a certain light. Context, I am suggesting, provides the measure of one's perspectives, and perspectives provide access to the broader contexts of significance within which human beings give meaning to their lives. Moreover, it is in the interaction between context and perspective that one must seek to locate the significance of individual gestures. As Merleau-Ponty notes, this can be accomplished by recognizing

> around our initiatives and around that strictly individual project which is oneself, a zone of generalized existence and of projects already formed, significances which trail between ourselves and things and which confer upon us the quality of man, bourgeois or worker. Already generality intervenes, already our presence to ourselves is mediated by it and we cease to be pure consciousness, as soon as this natural or social constellation ceases to be an unformulated *this* and crystallizes into a situation, as soon as it has a meaning-in short, as soon as we exist. (Merleau-Ponty 1962: 450)

If as Merleau-Ponty suggests, a person's relationship to her own gestures and to her own identity is already mediated by "a zone of generalized existence and of projects already formed, significances which trail between ourselves and things," then it is clear that it is impossible to definitively separate the horizons that collectively provide a generalized context for one's ordinary experiences from the perspective an individual takes up toward those experiences. Indeed, it is this inseparability of context (and the many horizons that constitute it) and perspective that I have been emphasizing throughout this analysis. Rather than viewing the indeterminacy of the multiple, overlapping horizons that situate a given experience (an indeterminacy that belongs not only to each of them individually but also to their interaction) as an obstacle to determining the meaning of that experience, I am arguing that it is impossible to describe even the simplest and most ordinary experiences without recourse to the horizons that contextualize them. Thus, to understand what counts as ordinary for any given individual requires that one directly consider the horizons that help to structure the everyday world of that person's concern. Even when these horizons are shared, the fluidity of the intersubjective experiences out of which they are composed, as well as the fact that they are experienced and taken up by different individuals in all sorts of unpredictable ways in response to sudden changes in the situation, suggests that even the most rigid or limited perspective can almost always be supplanted by an alternative perspective on oneself, on others, and on one's situation as a whole.[15]

2

Ambiguity, Absurdity, and Reversibility: Three Responses to Indeterminacy

From the time of the pre-Socratics, philosophers have struggled to explain the essential indeterminacy of human experience. Rationalists, most famously René Descartes, have tended to see it as a type of epistemological defect, and have sought ways to eliminate it altogether.[1] Even empiricists, who are directly confronted with the pervasiveness of indeterminacy in everyday existence, tend to be confident that the collection of more data and a corresponding refinement of theory will ultimately lead to the diminishment of those aspects of human experience that seem to resist straightforward inspection or analysis. For both rationalists and empiricists, indeterminacy has historically taken the form of a *problem* that needs to be resolved in order for knowledge to progress.

The phenomenologist Edmund Husserl is a notable exception in this regard. Indeed, Husserl's understanding of phenomenology requires that one be true to the phenomenon one is investigating. If the phenomenon is itself essentially indeterminate, then this indeterminacy must itself be acknowledged and described on its own terms rather than seen as an obstacle to be overcome. And yet, Husserl himself, at times, seems to be uncomfortable with the implications of his claim that there is a "zone of indeterminacy" that accompanies each and every act of consciousness. I will argue that his own determination to establish philosophy, and phenomenology in particular, as a "rigorous science" is largely responsible for his ambivalence regarding the role played by indeterminacy in daily life. My claim is that there is a deep tension Husserl never satisfactorily resolves between (1) his drive to secure the scientific rigorousness of phenomenological inquiry through comprehensive descriptive analysis and (2) his recognition that indeterminacy is an indispensable feature of human experience within the life-world and that therefore some phenomena cannot be known rigorously.

In maintaining the ineradicability of indeterminacy as a structural feature of perceptual (and conceptual) experience while simultaneously claiming that "philosophy as rigorous science" is still possible, Husserl initiated a lively philosophical discourse about the nature and significance of indeterminacy that is still going on today.[2] Although many thinkers have been influenced by Husserl's discussion of indeterminacy as a pervasive feature of human existence, I would like to explore the varied ways in which Husserl's notion of indeterminacy gets taken up by three French philosophers in particular, Simone de Beauvoir, Albert Camus, and Maurice Merleau-Ponty. I have chosen these three to focus on in part because all three explicitly acknowledge at various points in their work their indebtedness to Husserl. Second, the fact that these three thinkers were contemporaries who received similar philosophical training makes it especially interesting to see how the notion of indeterminacy gets taken up and differentially addressed in their respective works. Third, their individual ways of foregrounding the indeterminacy of existence have significantly advanced Husserl's original discussion of indeterminacy to encompass the ways in which indeterminacy is corporeally lived (Merleau-Ponty), functions as an ambiguous ground for ethics (Beauvoir), and is an absurd source of value (Camus). By examining how these three philosophers develop the ontological, ethical, and metaphysical implications of indeterminacy, it is possible to see indeterminacy not as a threat to philosophical inquiry, but rather as an ongoing challenge that keeps inquiry fresh and alive insofar as it encourages the multiplication of perspectives for making sense of one's life.

Husserlian Indeterminacy

In the first volume of *Ideas Pertaining to a Pure Phenomenology and to a Phenomenological Philosophy*, Husserl claims that the perceptual field is surrounded by an infinite "zone of indeterminacy," a "misty horizon that can never be completely outlined" but "remains necessarily there" (Husserl 1982: 92). Although the project of science, broadly conceived, can be understood in terms of its effort to make this zone smaller and smaller, Husserl maintains that there will always be a "residue" that resists complete determination, a residue that is infinite in scope insofar as it extends both temporally and spatially beyond what is immediately given. Husserl's emphasis on the necessary presence of this zone of

indeterminacy poses a challenge not only to science but also to his own phenomenological project insofar as this "misty horizon" surrounds each of the
individual phenomena included within the perceptual field as well as the perceptual field as a whole.

Quantum mechanics takes up this challenge by positing indeterminacy as
constitutive of the phenomena it investigates, and Husserl also includes this zone
of indeterminacy within his eidetic description of the natural attitude, discussing
how indeterminacy itself serves as a necessary ground for the determination of
distinct perceptual objects.[3] To comprehend fully the philosophical richness of
Husserl's understanding of indeterminacy, however, one must examine its specific influence upon a generation of scholars who followed him. This is because
despite the fact that the notion of indeterminacy is repeatedly evoked in Husserl's
thought, he never explores its ramifications for his own phenomenological project in sufficient depth. Perhaps this is due, above all, to the challenge that an
emphasis on indeterminacy poses for Husserl's eidetic reduction. The challenge
involves the successful negotiation of a double-bind: to discuss the phenomena
in their givenness as phenomena requires a corresponding discussion of the indeterminate ways in which they are given, and yet, it is this very indeterminacy that
seems to threaten an understanding of the essential manner and mode in which
they appear. In Husserl's own work, he frequently circumvents this double-bind
by pursuing the former approach at the expense of the latter, namely, by systematically discussing the various ways in which intentional objects are presented to
consciousness through a "zone of indeterminacy." This zone of indeterminacy
becomes very closely identified with the horizonal nature of our everyday experiences, as in the following passage from *The Crisis of European Sciences and
Transcendental Phenomenology* when Husserl asserts that

> the particular object of our active consciousness, and correlatively the active,
> conscious having of it, being directed toward it, and dealing with it—all this is
> forever surrounded by an atmosphere of mute, concealed, but cofunctioning
> validities, a *vital horizon* into which the active ego can also direct itself volun-
> tarily, reactivating old acquisitions, consciously grasping new apperceptive
> ideas, transforming them into intuitions. Because of this constantly flowing
> *horizonal character*, then, every straightforwardly performed validity in natu-
> ral world-life always presupposes validities extending back, immediately or
> mediately, into a necessary subsoil of obscure but occasionally available reacti-
> vatable validities, all of which together, including the present acts, make up a
> single indivisible, interrelated complex of life. (Husserl 1970: 149)

What are these "obscure validities" that cannot be separated from the "single
indivisible, interrelated complex of life"? To call them validities and to emphasize their inextricability in relation to people's everyday experiences indicates
quite strongly the fundamental role that these indeterminate aspects of exis-

tence play in each and every reflective (and pre-reflective) act. Moreover, their indeterminacy, which, as Husserl maintains, can only "occasionally" be made available to intentional consciousness, seems to be primarily a function of their character as possibilities, possibilities not yet or previously chosen, which nonetheless influence the meaning that is given to the present experience. Thus, this indeterminacy can be viewed, to a large extent, as arising out of the temporality of human existence, a temporality characterized by a present that is articulated out of the horizons of the past and the future, temporal dimensions that are by their very nature in flux, and therefore indeterminate.

And yet, to understand the indeterminacy that underlies human experiences merely as a function of temporality would be an oversimplification of Husserl's own complex understanding of the horizonal nature of those experiences. For it is important to remember that there are two horizons that Husserl claims must be taken into account when one seeks to understand what it means to perceive a thing, the "internal" horizon and the "external" horizon, both of which have their own significance, their own possibilities, and their own indeterminacy.[4]

Husserl distinguishes the internal and the external horizon and the role that they play in the perception of things as follows:

> For consciousness the individual thing is not alone; the perception of a thing is perception of it within a *perceptual field*. And just as the individual thing in perception has meaning only through an open horizon of "possible perceptions," insofar as what is actually perceived "points" to a systematic multiplicity of all possible perceptual exhibitings belonging to it harmoniously, so the thing has yet another horizon: besides this "internal horizon" it has an "external horizon" precisely as a thing within a *field of things*; and this points finally to the whole "world as perceptual world." (Husserl 1970: 162)

The internal horizon, then, refers to the multiplicity of possible perceptions I can obtain of a given thing, and these perceptions as well as this thing are located within a perceptual field that includes other phenomena and the possible perceptions I may have of them.[5] This perceptual field constitutes an external horizon that in turn is grounded within the *world* that serves as the continuous horizon for all of my actual and possible experiences. Indeterminacy appears in and through all three of these horizons (internal horizon, external horizon, and world horizon), and, to the extent that any particular thing or aspect of that thing is rendered determinate, other things that are co-present, their aspects, and the perceptual field itself will necessarily remain more or less indeterminate.

Despite the presence of indeterminacy as a factor to be reckoned with in all of my experiences on several different levels, in *Ideas* Husserl is optimistic about the potential for making more and more aspects of experience determinate. Nonetheless, he also implies that determinacy can be achieved only against a background "fringe" that is more or less indeterminate:

> [A]n experience that has become the object of a personally directed glance, and so has the modus of the deliberately looked at, has its own fringe of experiences that are not deliberately viewed . . . a fringe of background inattention showing relative differences of clearness and obscurity, as well as of emphasis and lack of relief. (Husserl 1982: 220)

Husserl sees this "indeterminate fringe" as a source of eidetic possibilities that are actualized by bringing "what is not the object of a personally directed look within the focus of pure mental vision, raising the unemphatic into relief, and making the obscure clear and ever clearer" (Husserl 1982: 220). What is especially significant about these passages is that they reveal Husserl's methodological commitment, namely, to render the indeterminate aspects of experience as determinate as possible. This project is a familiar one that Husserl has himself inherited from the Cartesian tradition. The transition from Descartes to Husserl in the conceptualization of this project includes Husserl's recognition that in order to make some aspects of experience determinate, other aspects of experience will, as a direct consequence of this determinacy, remain indeterminate.[6] Moreover, Husserl views this indeterminacy positively precisely insofar as it is against these indeterminate horizons that objects can be brought into relief. And yet, Husserl holds out the hope that an individual can (perhaps at some future time) concern herself with these indeterminate aspects of experience, making them determinate through the deliberate focus of her attention, which in turn suggests that the indeterminacy is primarily a function of attention (that is, results from the very nature of intentional consciousness) rather than an essential aspect of the phenomena themselves.

What is so distinctive about the ways in which Camus, Beauvoir, and Merleau-Ponty invoke and develop Husserl's notion of indeterminacy in their own work is their transformation of indeterminacy from being more of a *consequence* of intentionality to being a fundamental feature of human existence, one that extends beyond an individual's intentional awareness of her situation, characterizing the situation as such. For Beauvoir, indeterminacy is explored through the notion of ambiguity, an irreducible ambiguity that characterizes human existence and that demands a response through concrete human actions, actions that can in no way dispel or diminish the ambiguity, but that allow a person to *live* this ambiguity in meaningful ways. Camus interprets indeterminacy as existential absurdity, an absurdity that threatens the attempt to give meaning to one's life and that therefore makes suicide the "one truly serious philosophical problem" (Camus 1983: 3). Finally, Merleau-Ponty investigates the *corporeal* significance of indeterminacy through the phenomenon of reversibility: a phenomenon that is revealed through the constant, mutual interaction between the flesh that is my body and the flesh that is the world.

Indeterminacy as Ambiguity

"From the very beginning," Beauvoir asserts in *The Ethics of Ambiguity,* "existentialism defined itself as a philosophy of ambiguity" (Beauvoir 1976: 9). This ambiguity she traces back to Kierkegaard and his opposition to the Hegelian dialectic, which ultimately surpasses ambiguity through the *Aufhebung* reconciling thesis and antithesis. Indeed, Beauvoir suggests, without ambiguity, without "failure," there can be no ethics. Instead of focusing on the ethical ramifications of ambiguity that she explores in this text and that I have discussed elsewhere, I will instead address the following two questions: What does this ambiguity consist of precisely, and why can it be understood as a type of failure?[7]

Elaborating on the Sartrean claim that "man is a useless passion," Beauvoir states that "man, in his vain attempt to *be* God, makes himself exist *as* man, and if he is satisfied with this existence, he coincides exactly with himself. It is not granted him to exist without tending toward this being which he will never be. But it is possible for him to want this tension even with the failure which it involves. His being is lack of being, but this lack has a way of being which is precisely existence" (Beauvoir 1976: 12–13). The ambiguity of existence, as Beauvoir describes it here, refers to a tension that arises through making oneself what one is (an existing being whose existence is defined as *lack*) by trying to be what one is not (God, or absolute coincidence of the Sartrean in-itself and for-itself). Insofar as what one is cannot be reconciled with what one is not, the tension is maintained, and it is the ongoing negotiation of this very tension that resists resolution that Beauvoir identifies with the failed project of human existence. The tension involves failure because it allows one to coincide with what one is precisely when one fails to coincide with what one is not since what one *is* turns out to be a *lack* that defies coincidence. And it is this failure that reveals the essential ambiguity of human existence, namely, the co-existence of two different ways of inhabiting one's situation, which must be simultaneously lived through without either of them ever being fully attained or reconciled with the other.

This fundamental, ontological ambiguity that is tied to the Sartrean duality and incompossibility of for-itself and in-itself is not the primary ambiguity that Beauvoir is concerned with in this text, however. Instead, it provides the basis for her call for an "existentialist conversion" that, she claims, occurs when each person acknowledges rather than avoids the ambiguity of her own existence, and actively seeks to realize this ambiguity in her everyday life. Realizing this ambiguity, Beauvoir maintains, involves refusing to posit one's ends as absolutes, that is, refusing to believe in "unconditioned values." And it is by recognizing the relativity of the ends that one nonetheless attempts to arrive at absolutely in one's actions, that one confronts another type of ambiguity, namely, the ethical ambiguity that arises when one is faced with the perpetual dilemma of having to perform actions that require absolute commitments without ever being able to attain absolute justifications for them. Finally, it is because there are no un-conditioned values that one can be forced to choose between two mutually in-compatible but mutually compelling alternatives, and this gives rise to ethical ambiguity in the fullest sense of the word, an ambiguity that *must* be decisively reckoned with, but that cannot ever be satisfactorily resolved one way or the other.[8]

Interestingly, Beauvoir compares this existentialist conversion, this recognition and embracing of the ambiguity of existence, to a Husserlian reduction whereby one "brackets" one's "will to be" in order to be made conscious of one's "true condition" (Beauvoir 1976: 15). For, she asserts,

> just as phenomenological reduction prevents the errors of dogmatism by sus-pending all affirmation concerning the mode of reality of the external world, whose flesh and bone presence the reduction does not, however, contest, so existentialist conversion does not suppress my instincts, desires, plans, and passions. It merely prevents any possibility of failure by refusing to set up as absolutes the ends towards which my transcendence thrusts itself, and by con-sidering them in their connection with the freedom which projects them. (Beauvoir 1976: 14)

The "true condition," which the Husserlian reduction allows one to be made conscious of, involves consciousness of the interdependency of noesis and no-ema, of the intentional act that identifies a given phenomenon as such, and of the intentional object that orients and gives meaning to the intentional act. To recognize the fundamental connection between noesis and noema is also to deny the existence of absolutes; it is to deny the presence of meaning indepen-dent of consciousness and consciousness independent of meaning. Moreover, Beauvoir's association of the existentialist conversion with Husserl's phenome-nological reduction also points toward the close link between the indetermi-nacy that is revealed in and through the reduction and the ambiguity that she claims is an essential feature of human existence. While Beauvoir is adamant that the ambiguity of even the most ordinary experience deepens its meaning rather than rendering it meaningless or absurd, it is fascinating to see how Camus arrives at the latter intuition by beginning with a similar insistence upon Husserlian indeterminacy.

Indeterminacy as Absurdity

In his essay "An Absurd Reasoning," Camus credits Husserl with opening "to intuition and to the heart a whole proliferation of phenomena, the wealth of which has about it something inhuman" (Camus 1983: 20). It is striking that Camus associates the richness of the phenomena Husserl opens up for phenomenological investigation with "something inhuman," because, for Husserl, insofar as the phenomena are capable of being grasped as such, they are tied inextricably to human (intentional) activity. And yet, what Camus is appealing to with this notion of the "inhuman" is that which is foreign to human affairs and, more importantly, human comprehension. Indeed, Camus identifies Husserl as one of those "men who vie with one another in proclaiming that nothing is clear, all is chaos, that all man has is his lucidity and his definite knowledge of the walls surrounding him" (Camus 1983: 20–21). Although I sincerely doubt that Husserl would have been comfortable with this evaluation of his project, what Camus is suggesting here is that a primary contribution Husserl has made to the phenomenological and existentialist traditions has been to open up for investigation a range of phenomena that are, on principle, incapable of being articulated fully. Moreover, Camus suggests in this passage that the inability to arrive at a comprehensive description of these phenomena that together constitute the life-world is due to the very nature of the things themselves that resist human "lucidity."

Although I would argue that Husserl does not posit such a poignant conflict between the phenomena and the human effort to grasp their essences, the grounds for such a reading of Husserl are established in part through Husserl's emphasis on the "experience-fringe," or the indeterminate features of each experience that are not deliberately focused on and whose presence leads Husserl to formulate "the eidetically valid and self-evident proposition, that *no concrete experience* can pass *as independent in the full sense of the term*" (Husserl 1982: 221). Husserl's awareness of the "walls" surrounding attempts to render particular experiences lucid can also be found in his subsequent claim that each concrete experience "'stands in need of completion' in respect of some connected whole, which in form and in kind is not something we are free to choose, but are rather bound to accept" (Husserl 1982: 221).

Camus interprets being compelled to accept aspects of the situation that one has not chosen as evidence of the irrationality (incomprehensibility) of the human situation. He claims that each person has a "longing for happiness and for reason" that can be understood as a longing to break down the barriers that bar the way to human lucidity, thereby attaining the happiness that comes from conquering this "alien" or irrational territory and expanding the domain of reason. This kind of happiness, however, can never be attained; indeed, as Camus famously proclaims, "the absurd is born of this confrontation between the human need and the unreasonable silence of the world" (Camus 1983: 21). Rather than trying to negate or avoid this absurdity by either denying the need for lucidity (which can be understood as a demand for Cartesian clarity and distinctness) or refusing to confront it with what cannot be understood, Camus asserts that absurdity "must be clung to because the whole consequence of a life can depend on it" (Camus 1983: 21).

This longing for happiness attained through reason and the impossibility of satisfying it is most poignantly reflected in Camus's own myth of Sisyphus. In his retelling of this Greek myth, Camus argues for the *compatibility* of the longing, the recognition of its absurdity that arises out of the irrationality of the situation, and the possibility of a new kind of happiness when he calls Sisyphus the "absurd hero" and concludes that "we must imagine Sisyphus happy" (Camus 1983: 120, 123). Sisyphus's "defiant" happiness is happiness in the face of the longing, happiness that refuses to give up the human need out of which this longing is born. For Camus, it is the recognition and embracing of this need and the simultaneous acknowledgement of the impossibility of satisfying it that is the truly affirmative act.

While Beauvoir suggests that indeterminacy gives rise to a proliferation of meanings, guaranteeing that no one meaning will ever provide the definitive interpretation of a given situation, Camus argues that the essential indeterminacy of human experience renders it meaningless, but nonetheless worth living. Despite this crucial difference in their respective understandings of the implications of indeterminacy for living life meaningfully, Camus, like Beauvoir, sees indeterminacy as a crucial point of departure for understanding the possibilities as well as the limits of human existence.

Indeterminacy as Reversibility

In his commemorative essay to Husserl, "The Philosopher and His Shadow," Merleau-Ponty sets himself the task of evoking the "unthought-of element in his [Husserl's] works which is wholly his and yet opens out on something else" (Merleau-Ponty 1964a: 160). Merleau-Ponty identifies this unthought-of element with those aspects of human experience that are not graspable through the constituting activity of intentional consciousness. Regarding this constituting activity, Merleau-Ponty asserts that "[o]riginally a project to gain intellectual possession of the world, constitution becomes increasingly, as Husserl's thought matures, the means of unveiling a back side of things that we have not constituted" (Merleau-Ponty 1964a: 180). This unthought-of element, not surprisingly, refers especially to the indeterminate aspect(s) of experience that cannot be made determinate; it is the "experience-fringe" that forms the horizon for each of one's perceptions. Merleau-Ponty implies, moreover, that it is unthought-of in at least two different senses: it is unthought-of insofar as it does not get developed in Husserl's own work, and it is unthought-of insofar as it is *incapable* of being constituted by thought.

In Merleau-Ponty's last unfinished work, *The Visible and the Invisible*, he takes up the challenge of thinking the un-thought by investigating some of these "syntheses which dwell this side of any thesis" (quoted in Merleau-Ponty 1964a: 163). One of these "syntheses" is the phenomenon of reversibility, a corporeal "synthesis" that is continually being played out in the daily experiences of touching and being touched and that is described eloquently by Merleau-Ponty through the example of one hand touching the other. It is a strange kind of synthesis, however, because although it is continually enacted it is never completed. The hand that touches is the hand that is touched; the two experiences occur simultaneously but are not perceived simultaneously. One can feel oneself touching or being touched, and can "reverse" one's attention from the one experience to the other, but, just as in the famous duck/rabbit gestalt, it is impossible to experience both sensations at once. Moreover, there is no thesis here insofar as this "synthesis" unfolds, for the most part, pre-reflectively; it occurs independently of the constituting activity of consciousness and even when one attempts to grasp it reflectively, it proves elusive to further analysis.

In one of his final, untitled Working Notes, Merleau-Ponty makes a schematic reference to Husserl's desire to analyze that which resists analysis through "disentangling" or "unraveling" what is entangled, and he notes that "the idea of chiasm and Ineinander is on the contrary the idea that every analysis that *disentangles* renders unintelligible" (Merleau-Ponty 1968: 268). Reversibility cannot be "disentangled" because it involves a chiasmatic intertwining of the flesh in which the touching and touched are indeed "Ineinander." It is because I touch that I can be touched, and if I am not touched, then I will not be able to touch; neither experience is reducible to the other, and yet each makes the other possible.

The duality of touching and being touched is a paradigm for Merleau-Ponty's discussion of reversibility, but the corporeal phenomenon of reversibility also characterizes temporality itself, giving the latter a bodily dimension insofar as "past and present are Ineinander, each enveloping-enveloped—and that itself is the flesh" (Merleau-Ponty 1968: 268). To say that the chiasmatic relationship between past and present is the flesh suggests that time and being must be understood together, not apart from one another. And, to deepen an understanding of this relationship in a manner that will avoid disentangling that which is entangled, Merleau-Ponty claims that what is required is a "a new kind of intelligibility (intelligibility through the world and Being as they are-'vertical' and not *horizontal*)" (Merleau-Ponty 1968: 268).

What is this new type of intelligibility that Merleau-Ponty was seeking toward the end of his life? While his unexpected death in the middle of his work on this text in many ways seems to foreclose an answer to this question, it is evident that it is an intelligibility that does not seek a wider and wider sphere of determinacy, that does not progress along a linear temporal path, but rather, one that descends into the depths of the phenomena, in a vertical dimension that has no absolute "top" or "bottom" but that allows movement in both directions at once. And perhaps through this descending/ascending, reversible movement, one may uncover that "fungierende or latent intentionality" that Merleau-Ponty suggests Husserl only begins to reveal, an intentionality that encompasses the non-human as well as the human, an "intentionality within being" (Merleau-Ponty 1968: 244).

Indeterminacy Reconsidered

At the conclusion of the "Philosopher and His Shadow," Merleau-Ponty states that "[w]illy-nilly, against his plans and according to his essential audacity, Husserl awakens a wild-flowering world and mind" (Merleau-Ponty 1964a: 180–181). Merleau-Ponty, Camus, and Beauvoir are only three of the many philosophers who have responded to this call. What is so distinctive about their own responses to Husserl's legacy is that they have managed to open up this wild-flowering world and mind that defies straightforward analysis to the gaze, to touch, to activity—in short, to our participation. Each of them seeks a path within this chaotic turbulence without destroying or denying the fundamental indeterminacy that is its "subsoil." And yet, the meaning they find (or, in Camus's case, fails to find) and explore is not the same; the notions of ambiguity, absurdity, and reversibility cannot be reduced to one another as different names for the phenomenon of indeterminacy.

Beauvoir's discussion of the ethics of ambiguity focuses on the non-categorical imperatives that compel human beings to define themselves through their actions, actions that continually address but cannot resolve an essentially ambiguous situation. Camus searches for happiness through an absurdly defiant affirmation of the insurmountable barriers that are ranged all around human lucidity, an affirmation that can and must say "yes" to life. Finally, Merleau-Ponty explores the reversible interplay between the visible and the invisible dimensions of the flesh, an ongoing dynamic that uncovers new realms of indeterminacy and, therefore, new possibilities for phenomenological investigation.

The different directions taken by Beauvoir, Camus, and Merleau-Ponty indicate how rich indeed is the subsoil of this wild-flowering region. Moreover, their work collectively demonstrates a central claim I am making throughout this text, namely, that the indeterminacy of the horizon should be understood as operating not solely on the "fringes" of experience, but at its center.

PART 2

Narrative Horizons

3

Reading/Writing between the Lines

"Reading/Writing between the lines," as I am using the expression here, involves examining how literature opens up a text to new interpretations that cannot be foreseen by the writer in advance insofar as these interpretations are generated by unknown readers who in turn come to constitute an anonymous community. These multiple interpretations draw directly upon the ambiguity and indeterminacy of the text itself, that is, its ability to signify in more than one way and to bring different horizons into play for its respective readers. The ability to generate these interpretations is dependent upon what Husserl calls the "free variation" of the imagination, and, I will argue, these interpretations in turn lead to a co-responsibility for the text on the part of both the reader and the writer. In *Toward a Phenomenology of Sexual Difference: Husserl, Merleau-Ponty, Beauvoir*, Sara Heinämaa describes what Husserl calls "free variation in imagination" and the need for it as follows: "To find the essential features of experience, the philosopher must compare particulars that are most different from each other. He cannot contend with what is familiar or common, but has to extend his study to exceptional cases and fictional modifications" (Heinämaa 2003: 14–15). According to Heinämaa, Husserl's "idea of philosophy as a radical inquiry that proceeds with the help of imagination and fiction" was a formative influence on Beauvoir's writing, allowing her to bring philosophy and literature together in her work rather than seeing the latter as mutually exclusive enterprises

(Heinämaa 2003: 15). Drawing from Beauvoir's own comments about writing in her autobiographical texts, Heinämaa observes that "[w]hen reflecting on her aims as a writer, she [Beauvoir] argues that memory, dreams, and imagination are weak and limited resources when compared to the power of literature. It is only written fiction that opens to us fields of experience that overcome what we can see and remember" (Heinämaa 2003: 15). Although Heinämaa, following Beauvoir, distinguishes the lesser powers of memory, dreams, and the imagination from the greater power of fiction in the passage above, it seems clear that the ability to "overcome what we can see and remember" through fiction depends to a large extent upon the ways in which fiction engages memory, infiltrates dreams, and stimulates the imagination. This means that one cannot talk about the power of fiction without also referring to the various imaginative faculties that it calls into play.

Acknowledging the ways in which fiction directly engages the imaginative capacities of both writers and readers, however, does not mean that these capacities are necessarily enlarged or expanded by what is read. Toni Morrison, for instance, argues that precisely insofar as "[t]he imagination that produces work which bears and invites rereadings, which motions to future readings as well as contemporary ones, implies a shareable world and an endlessly flexible language," it is essential that one examine closely the nature of the world that is being shared (Morrison 1992: xii). More specifically, Morrison maintains that historically American writers have tended to presuppose the whiteness of (themselves and) their audience, thereby producing a legacy of "literary whiteness" that unconsciously circumscribes the parameters of an imaginatively "shared world" not only for white writers and readers but for readers and writers of color as well.[1] The stakes of this process are poignantly revealed in her subsequent question: "What happens to the writerly imagination of a black author who is at some level *always* conscious of representing one's own race to, or in spite of, a race of readers that understands itself to be 'universal' or race-free?" (Morrison 1992: xii).

The search for a genuinely shareable language, Morrison suggests, requires that writers and readers confront and take responsibility for the racialized (as well as gendered) assumptions that occupy often invisible places in their own literary imaginations, since "[t]he world does not become raceless or will not become unracialized by assertion" (Morrison 1992: 46). To the extent that allegedly race-free fiction in the United States has historically presupposed that its readers and writers are white, the American literary imagination is itself racialized and racist, depending, she argues, upon the exclusion of the African other. And, as Morrison maintains, it will therefore take more than just assertion to produce new literary imaginations that can contribute to the creation of more truly shareable worlds.

Traveling Messengers

In her foreword to Maurice Natanson's posthumously published book, *The Erotic Bird: Phenomenology in Literature,* Judith Butler describes how, for Natanson, the reader is a "traveler" in the fictive universe of the text, a universe that always moves beyond the text itself as well as the world that is known. "This kind of traveling," Butler claims,

> is not always linear or exegetical, but it returns, faithfully, to that moment of immediacy, dense with time past and future, in which the ordinary suddenly becomes strange, and that strangeness is exposed as the condition of possibility of the ordinary. Importantly, the fictive domain irrealizes the world, but it does not deny its reality; neither does it escape the world. Literary works perform this irrealization of the world, and this is their peculiar intentionality: they provide the suspended occasion for considering any given configuration of the ordinary as something yielded by the world as one of its possibilities. Although no example can quite capture the strange and wondrous occasion of its own possibility, the moment in which the example nevertheless illuminates what it cannot capture is the moment of phenomenological insight. (Butler 1998: xv–xvi)

Butler hails Natanson for his ability to irrealize the world for his readers, his moments of phenomenological insight in which the ordinary reveals its extraordinary possibilities. Natanson, in turn, uses as literary examples authors who have guided his own traveling in the world of the irreal. Chief among them is the famous Danish philosopher, Søren Kierkegaard. Inspired by Natanson's lifelong passion for the philosophy in literature and the literature in philosophy, I too would like to turn to Kierkegaard because his work beautifully reveals both the possibilities and the obligations that stem from "reading/writing between the lines."

Søren Kierkegaard's *Fear and Trembling* begins with the end of a parable by Hamann:[2] "What Tarquinius Superbus said in the garden by means of the poppies, the son understood but the messenger did not" (Kierkegaard 1983: 3). To discover the context for this epigraph, the reader must go outside Kierkegaard's text; neither he nor the pseudonymous author, Johannes de Silentio, ever supplies the rest of the parable, nor do they attempt to show the relevance of this enigmatic statement to the "dialectical lyric" that follows. It is significant that before entering into the text, the author demands that the reader extend her knowledge beyond the text. That is, if one is to grasp the nature of the message understood by the son but not by the messenger, one will need to discover the "missing pieces" of the parable. Only then will the reader be in a position to determine the relevance of this epigraph to the text that follows.[3]

My initial acquaintance with the parable arrived secondhand via my own teacher, Maurice Natanson. This indirect account has satisfied me, perhaps because it fits so well with Kierkegaard's mode of indirection and because Kierkegaard was himself acquainted with the parable through an essay by G. E. Lessing. In the version that I was told by Natanson, Tarquinius Superbus was an emperor fighting a battle with his fellow countrymen far away from his kingdom, leaving his son to rule in his stead. The emperor discovered while he was away that his ministers were plotting against his son and were planning to take over the kingdom. Since he could not leave his troops to warn his son of the impending danger, he sent a messenger instead. Since he could not be sure that the messenger was trustworthy or that the messenger would not be waylaid by the councillors themselves, he chose an indirect means of letting his son know what was going on. He asked the messenger to find his son, lead him into the palace garden and cut off the heads of the tallest poppies. The son, "reading" the message correctly, promptly authorized the death of the "heads" of state, and the kingdom was saved.[4]

Being given the missing pieces of the story, however, does not resolve the questions raised by the parable and by its placement at the gateway to *Fear and Trembling*. How did the father know what message to send? How was the son able to "read" the message? If the reader is to read this tale as an allegory for Kierkegaard's own method of indirection, then should Kierkegaard himself be understood as the father, the messenger, or even the son? Where does the ostensible author of the work, Johannes de Silentio, fit in? And what about Abraham and Isaac, another father and son whose relationship provides the central focus of the pages that follow? Lastly, where does the reader of the text fit into the picture? Is the reader merely a silent witness to the unfolding of the work, or is she somehow implicated in it?

These questions are raised between the lines of the text. They arise in that non-space between the epigraph, the missing tale that precedes it, and the multifaceted text that follows. Undoubtedly, the text itself gives us clues about how to understand the broader relevance of messengers who never "get" the message, senders of messages who can never be sure that their messages will be properly understood, and recipients of messages who must perform the labor of interpreting the message and who may or may not "get it right." Nonetheless, if one seizes upon an "obvious" application of the parable to *Fear and Trembling*, namely, that God is the Father/Emperor, that his messenger is the clergy whom Kierkegaard chastised again and again in his writings for passing on a message to which they themselves were not spiritually committed, and that the readers/audience are in the position of the son who must decipher the message through the intermediary of a mimetic messenger who knows not the significance of what he is imitating, then one is still left in a quandary as to the role played by the author(s) of the work itself.

For isn't the author also a messenger, one who relays to the reader a message about messages? But since Johannes de Silentio is merely a pseudonym, perhaps he serves as a (silent) messenger for another messenger, that is, for the "real" author, Søren Kierkegaard. What kinds of distortions might arise when messengers don't receive their messages directly? Is it possible for the reader/audience to establish any criteria to distinguish between "false" and "true" messengers? Would a "true" messenger be one who follows her instructions faithfully and does not attempt to enrich the message with her own interpretation?[5] Is there room in this account for the messenger to take on the labor of understanding the message?

This last question parallels, in interesting ways, the question of the role of the "midwife" that Plato so often identifies with Socrates in his dialogues. Thus, one might ask, what is the nature of the "assistance" that the midwife gives to the laborer? Isn't the work of the midwife itself a certain kind of labor, one whose significance all too often recedes into invisibility as the "product" of that labor (i.e., the child) becomes the universal focus of attention?[6]

The Freedom (Not) to Send Messages: On Poetry and Prose

By inquiring about the crucial, facilitating role played by the anonymous messenger, perhaps I am deflecting attention away from the message itself. This may be so. Certainly, if one accepts the allegorical reading I have offered above and views the messenger as analogous to the clergy that Kierkegaard was so critical of during his lifetime, Kierkegaard's own view seems to be that messengers of God, at least, may be better dispensed with altogether since they seem to dilute and even distort God's message through their translations. But the messenger in the parable cited by Hamann and recited by Kierkegaard through Johannes de Silentio seems to be a more faithful messenger insofar as he dutifully repeats to the emperor's son the very gestures the emperor shows him. And yet, to characterize this messenger as faithful is also problematic, since the messenger, by all accounts, does not seem to exhibit any particular kind of passion for the message itself, a commitment that is essential for Kierkegaard if his actions are to be identified with faith.

These complications make it difficult to make sense of the role played by the messenger in communicating the message. They are compounded when one steps back from this allegorical reading and explores what is overlooked in the complex processes of writing and reading if they are characterized in terms of messages sent and received. For, it seems evident, the model of writers as senders of messages and readers as recipients of those messages, recipients who may interpret the message correctly or incorrectly, seems woefully inadequate in capturing the "essence" of these processes and how they are co-implicated in one another. What happens to style, for instance, on such a model? Given Kierkegaard's own idiosyncratic style, a style that maintains its strange consistency both within and across the numerous pseudonymous authors he utilizes in his early works, questions of style do not seem easily separable from questions regarding the content of the work itself. The emperor's mimetic messenger, by contrast, appears to have no style of his own; at the very least, his style is invisible to the reader and in no way seems to interfere with his straightforward communication of his peculiar message.

Pondering these conundrums leads me once again outside the text, both Kierkegaard's text as well as this text, to engage the assistance of one of Kierkegaard's own philosophical "offspring," Jean-Paul Sartre, a "son" who was certainly not as loyal to his "father" as the emperor's son, but one to whom Kierkegaard's honorific title, "father" of existentialism, was indeed passed on. Indeed, many newcomers to existentialism view it as originating with Sartre himself, and therefore unwittingly contribute to the replacement of the "father" by his "son."[7]

In his famous essays on writing, "What Is Writing?" "Why Write?" and "For Whom Does One Write?" Sartre also employs the language of messages to describe the communication that takes place between writer and reader. While he concedes that style "makes the value of the prose," Sartre also argues that "it should pass unnoticed. Since words are transparent and since the gaze looks through them, it would be absurd to slip in among them some panes of rough glass" (Sartre 1988: 39). Style, on this account, plays a necessary, and very important, role in communicating the writer's message, but it has no intrinsic significance: "The harmony of words, their beauty, the balance of the phrases, *dispose* the passions of the reader without his being aware and order them like the Mass, like music, like the dance. If he happens to consider them by themselves, he loses the meaning; there remains only a boring seesaw of phrases" (Sartre 1988: 39).

Although Sartre believes that the writer's "message" takes precedence over all else, he also makes a distinction between those writers who are responsible for conveying messages to their readers, messages that should reflect and communicate the writer's own political commitments, and those who are absolved of this responsibility. More specifically, both Kierkegaard and Sartre distinguish the "labor" of the poet, that individual who, as Kierkegaard claims, lyrically sings the praises of others, from the prose writer, whose labor is supposed to reflect a moral commitment, a commitment that is performatively enacted in his or her words.[8] Unlike the poet, Sartre claims, whose words "name nothing at all," and who therefore cannot be understood as a messenger, the prose writer "knows that words are action. He knows that to reveal is to change and that one can reveal only by planning to change. He has given up the impossible dream of giving an impartial picture of Society and the human condition" (Sartre 1988: 37).

For Sartre, the task of the prose writer is to disclose an aspect of the world in order to change it, but this change cannot be accomplished by the (words of the) writer alone. Issuing from the freedom of the writer, the writing, Sartre claims, addresses the reader in her own freedom in the form of a question that demands a response. Without an audience, Sartre suggests, there can be no writing, for there can be no questions if there is not someone or something that is questioned or, to use Heidegger's language, placed in question by the question (Heidegger 1993: 93). And what writing places in question is not simply the complacency of a being who is content to live in the world without shouldering responsibility for his existence, but human being as such, a radical contingency that continually transforms its existence through its own questioning. "The function of the writer," Sartre tells us, "is to act in such a way that nobody can be ignorant of the world and that nobody may say that he is innocent of what it's all about. And since he has once committed himself in the universe of language, he can never again pretend that he cannot speak. Once you enter the universe of meanings, there is nothing you can do to get out of it" (Sartre 1988: 38).

Writer and reader are inextricably related within and through this "universe of meaning," for each serves as the condition for the possibility of the other. Here, freedom addresses freedom, and, as Thomas Busch points out, Sartre offers in "What Is Writing?" a much more satisfying picture of the rich possibilities for a genuine intersubjective dialogue/relationship than he provides in *Being and Nothingness*.[9] For Sartre, the goal of the writer is to call the reader to responsibility for the situation that has been disclosed through the (reading of the) writing, and the goal of the reader is to respond responsibly to the writer by freely participating in the world that the writer has disclosed and thereby altered. In short, the reader must assume responsibility for the writing and the writer must assume responsibility for the reading—a genuine co-responsibility that extends across both time and space.[10]

What is one to make of Sartre's and Kierkegaard's respective claims that the poet does not share this responsibility for his or her writing? In *Repetition*, Kierkegaard claims that the "poet is ordinarily an exception," an exception who marks the transition to but is not one of the "religious exceptions" (Kierkegaard 1983: 228). In *Fear and Trembling*, Kierkegaard hints at what is exceptional about the poet's status as an exception, "for with his little secret that he cannot divulge the poet buys this power of the word to tell everybody else's dark secrets. A poet is not an apostle; he drives out devils only by the power of the devil" (Kierkegaard 1983: 61). The "word-dance" of the poet, for Kierkegaard, closely mirrors the heavily encumbered yet light-footed step of the tragic hero whose travails it is the poet's task to describe. What is this "little secret" the poet possesses that buys the "power of the word," and what kind of magical power does this turn out to be? And, to return to the musings with which I began, what is the status of the poetic parable that begins *Fear and Trembling*, a work that is itself characterized by its silent/secretive author(s) as a "dialectical lyric?"

Sartre is much clearer on the difference between the prose-writer and the poet than is Kierkegaard. For Sartre, the poet's words themselves become "things," with all of the opacity and resistance that characterizes the world of the in-itself. The prose writer's words, by contrast, should transparently indicate the things they are disclosing, and, as has been shown, even style should "pass unnoticed" in order to allow the writer's message (which expresses his or her political commitment) to "shine through." According to Sartre, "poets are men who refuse to *utilize* language." Moreover, he adds,

> since the quest for truth takes place in and by language conceived as a certain kind of instrument, it is unnecessary to imagine that they aim to discern or expound the true. Nor do they dream of *naming* the world, and, this being the case, they name nothing at all, for naming implies a perpetual sacrifice of the name to the object named, or, as Hegel would say, the name is revealed as the inessential in the face of the thing which is essential. They do not speak, neither do they keep silent; it is something different. (Sartre 1988: 29)

Sartre elaborates this difference by stating that words are in the "wild state" for the poet, whereas they are "domesticated" for the prose writer. Notice, however, that this account itself is delivered through a prosaic writing. That is, Sartre's own prose gives an account of itself and its difference with poetry *in* prose. Would a "poetic" perspective offer another account of the differences between poetry and prose? That is, to what extent does the medium in which the "message" is delivered affect the type of message that is sent?

While Sartre in this essay radically distances (with a poetic flourish here and there) his own prosaic, political writing from the apolitical work of the poet, sculptor, painter, and musician, Kierkegaard has a much more ambivalent relationship with poetry and with prose. This ambivalence, I would argue, reflects Kierkegaard's awareness that poetry's indirect methods are potentially more powerful for delivering certain kinds of messages than the direct methods associated with prose. The "power of the devil" commanded by the poet is, I believe, none other than the power of language itself, a seductive power that goes all the way back to the snake's tempting words to Eve in the Garden of Eden.

It is no coincidence that Faust himself haunts the text of *Fear and Trembling*; his "spiritual" pact with the devil is performatively enacted through language, quite poetic language at that. If, as Sartre suggests, prose writing is "transparent," turning the reader's attention to what the writing is about rather than the writing itself, then perhaps poetry, which makes words into things that can be explored in their own right, and which collapses in the process hard and fast distinctions between form and content, is the more suitable medium for conveying the message of faith. For faith, on Kierkegaard's view, is not something one should use as a stepping stone to something else, but is simultaneously method and goal, means and end.

If one is unable to distinguish, at least for certain kinds of messages, what is said from how it is said, the potential for "misreadings," including missing the message altogether, or just plain getting it wrong, seems to multiply infinitely. To use Sartre's analogy, if there are too many "rough panes of glass," one's attention will be distracted from what can be seen *through them* to the texture and patterns exhibited in the panes themselves. Going back to Kierkegaard's epigraph to *Fear and Trembling*, the reader is told that the son *understood* his father's message, though the messenger did not. This "perfect" (non-linguistic) understanding may be comforting, but the comfort is taken away almost immediately in the *Exordium* that follows, where Kierkegaard reveals the constant potential for "misreadings" of the father by the son and of the son by the father. God alone, it seems, is a father incapable of "misreading" his son, and yet this does not in any way guarantee that the son will be able to (spiritually) "read" the father. A transparent reading is out of the question, for both father and son, because the faith is not genuine until it is tested and the son is transformed by the test and so has to be known/"read" afresh.

And where, as Luce Irigaray might ask, do the daughter and the mother appear in this transaction; what role are they permitted to play in this reading/writing? They could be construed as that which is written upon, the invisible material that makes both writing and reading possible. Or, if they are merely absent from this exchange, one might well wonder whether they will have their own way of sending, receiving, and understanding messages. Will their role parallel that of Diotima, the wise woman who "speaks" indirectly to her audience through Socrates in Plato's *Symposium*, and if so, does the fact that a man is designated to speak for her change the nature of her speech?[11]

"Faithful" Teachers and Committed Readers

The challenges faced by Kierkegaard's reader(s) are formidable, but they fade in comparison to the challenges faced by one who wishes to guide students in a reading of Kierkegaard as a "professor." What is one to "profess" here? If the professor is herself a committed reader in the Sartrean sense, and if the writing one is committed to precludes sharing the commitment in a Kierkegaardian sense (for each must undertake this process individually), then how can the "professor" responsibly facilitate the message without determining, in advance, the significance it should have for the reader? That is, the task of the professor would seem to be to communicate her *commitment* to the text in a manner that does not privilege a certain "reading" of the message offered by the text; the professor must allow the reader the opportunity to participate actively in the labor of interpretation. The serious nature of these commitments to teaching, to reading, and to writing, which I do take to be political commitments, should however, discourage uncommitted readings; indeed, if, as Kierkegaard suggests, no less than the reader's own life is at stake in the reading/writing, it is better not to read/write at all than to do so irresponsibly.

For both Kierkegaard and Sartre, commitment and responsibility go hand in hand, and both presuppose the freedom of the reader as well as the freedom of the writer. To be either an uncommitted writer or an uncommitted reader is to fail to exercise one's freedom to commit oneself to a given situation, and therefore is to be irresponsible. The reader can express her commitment to the situation created through the writing by vehemently disagreeing with how it is depicted, but to refuse to take a stand at all reflects a lack of commitment that is not an act of freedom but, for both Sartre and Kierkegaard, a failure to assume it in the first place.

For Sartre, the reader is free not to read the book and to leave it untouched, but the moment the book is opened, the reader has a responsibility to the writer to read *faithfully*. Faithful reading is not a reading that is dictated by the intent of the author any more than it is a reading dictated by the intent of the reader. Reading/writing cannot ever be a matter of dictation at all, for this latter, mechanical activity ignores rather than addresses the freedom of those who submit or are submitted to it.

In his essay that responds to the question "Why Write?" Sartre states:

> [S]ince the one who writes recognizes, by the very fact that he takes the trouble to write, the freedom of his readers, and since the one who reads, by the mere fact of his opening the book, recognizes the freedom of the writer, the work of art, from whichever side you approach it, is an act of confidence in the freedom of men. And since readers, like the author, recognize this freedom only to demand that it manifest itself, the work can be defined as an imaginary presentation of the world in so far as it demands human freedom. The result of which is that there is no "gloomy literature," since, however dark may be the colours in which one paints the world, one paints it only so that free men may feel their freedom as they face it. (Sartre 1988: 67)

Significantly, the earlier, careful separation Sartre makes between painting and prose in his previous essay, "What Is Writing?" is abandoned in this passage. The writer "paints the world" through an "imaginary presentation" that "demands human freedom." The "secret power" of poetry that Kierkegaard alludes to manifests itself once more, undercutting prose's faithful attempts to give its own accounting of itself. Here the poet-artist and the prose-philosopher seem to come together, in a movement that also unites the reader and the writer in a fateful alliance, fateful because the stakes for both Kierkegaard and Sartre are no less than life or death. For, just as the poet and the philosopher, while not reducible to one another, cannot ultimately be separated from one another insofar as they communicate and share responsibility with one another for the intersubjective existence they are respectively addressing, so too, reader and writer are brought together in a relationship that is characterized as much by its tensions, ruptures, and divisions as by mutual recognition and respect. Moreover, this mutual recognition and respect, insofar as it is founded on the irreducible freedom of reader and writer, is not threatened by, but makes possible, these schisms.

On Authors, Readers, and Texts

Roland Barthes further complicates an understanding of this fateful alliance between reader and writer in the famous conclusion of his essay "The Death of the Author" when he declares that "in order to restore writing to its future, we must reverse the myth: the birth of the reader must be requited by the death of the Author" (Barthes 1989: 55). Rather than offer a picture of freedom encountering freedom, of messages offered and received, Barthes suggests here that the reader takes the place of the Author, that the reader is the one who both gives and receives the message, and, moreover, that this message refers not to an Author who initiates it and/or to a state of affairs that persists outside of language, but to "language itself, i.e., the very thing which ceaselessly calls any origin into question" (Barthes 1989: 52).

Barthes, in fact, would wholeheartedly reject the very term "message" because it seems to restrict the significance of the text to the conscious intentions of the author; this is a persistent danger in Sartre's understanding of the message conveyed by the text in the passages I cited above. Responding to this concern, Nikki Sullivan argues, in *Tattooed Bodies: Subjectivity, Textuality, Ethics, and Pleasure*, following Barthes, "that reading and writing are not simply functional tools with which to discover or represent meaning or truth, but rather that these open-ended processes are both affective and intersubjective or intertextual"[12] (N. Sullivan 2001: 151). Yet, despite Sartre's own emphasis on the constituting role played by the writer's intentions in establishing the terms of the discourse that unfolds between writer and reader via the text, he does not view the writer as a univocal subject who remains self-identical before, during, and after the writing. Nor, for that matter, does Kierkegaard.

What is striking about both Kierkegaard's and Sartre's understandings of reading and writing is that they require an assumption of responsibility that is not grounded upon a fixed (or known) identity. To take responsibility for one's reading and/or writing does not presuppose in any way that one is an ultimate authority on what one has read or written. Indeed, as is known from their own personal histories, both Sartre and Kierkegaard were rather uncomfortable with the heavy mantle of authorship. Sartre turned down the Nobel Prize for Literature and Kierkegaard used one pseudonym after another, finally claiming a rather diffident "authorship" of his early writings in an appendix that appears in the middle of the *Concluding Unscientific Postscript to Philosophical Fragments*, bearing the rather innocuous and impersonal title "A Glance at a Contemporary Effort in Danish Literature."

Although Barthes has been heralded for offering an "erotics of reading," the death of the author in no way implies that the writer is completely absent from the text.[13] Displacing the author in favor of the writer in *The Pleasure of the Text*, Barthes expresses what I would perversely call the "indispensable dispensability" of the writer to the text (and to the reader): "The writer is always on the blind spot of systems; adrift, he is the joker in the pack, a *mana*, a zero degree, the dummy in the bridge game: necessary to the meaning (the battle), but himself deprived of fixed meaning; his place, his (exchange) *value*, varies according to the movements of history, the tactical blows of the struggle: he is asked all and/or nothing" (Barthes 1975: 35). For Barthes, the writer is both essential and inessential. The writer is "necessary to the meaning" of the text without being able to guarantee the meaning of her own existence. In writing, Barthes maintains, "I write myself as a subject at present out of place, arriving too soon or too late (this *too* designating neither regret, fault, nor bad luck, but merely calling for a non-site): anachronic subject, adrift" (Barthes 1975: 62–63). Not only does writing fail to "secure" the subject, but reading fails to do so as well. Rather than "find oneself" through the text, Barthes claims that the subject loses herself in the "tissue" of the text: "lost in this tissue—this texture—the subject unmakes himself, like a spider dissolving in the constructive secretions of its web" (Barthes 1975: 64). Only the text itself seems to escape this undoing, through a generative process that Barthes likens to the spider's web, which "is worked out in a perpetual interweaving" (Barthes 1975: 64).

Paradoxically, just as the spider's web secures its victims in order to "undo" them, the text also secures writer and reader, allowing them to come into existence not as substantive subjects, but as those who give meaning and purpose to the web's existence by being woven within it and who are necessarily destroyed in the process. Desire plays a key role in this entrapment. There is the desire of the reader for the writer, the desire of the writer for the reader, and the desire of the text for both.[14] "The text," Barthes maintains, "is a fetish object, and *this fetish desires me.*" Barthes reconciles his affirmation of the writer in *The Pleasure of the Text* with the death of the author in his earlier essay, I would argue, through this interplay of desire. For, while the author is dead "as institution," Barthes suggests that he is erotically resurrected through the desire of the reader, a desire that emerges in and through the text: "in the text, in a way, I *desire* the author: I need his figure . . . as he needs mine" (Barthes 1975: 27).

Writing without Readers or Writers

While Barthes emphasizes the reader at the expense of the author in "The Death of the Author," his emphasis on the undoing of both in *The Pleasure of the Text* paves the way for Derrida's suggestion in "Signature Event Context" that *both* reader and writer are absent in the text. To return to the image of the "fateful alliance" between reader and writer that I invoked a short time ago, Derrida argues that, in an important sense, the reader and the writer, or, to use his terminology, scribe and subscriber, are fundamentally in the same situation. "All writing," he asserts, "in order to be what it is, must be able to function in the radical absence of every empirically determined addressee in general. And this absence is not a continuous modification of presence; it is a break in presence, 'death,' or the possibility of the 'death' of the addressee, inscribed in the structure of the mark" (Derrida 1982a: 315–316). And he goes on to add:

> What holds for the addressee holds also, for the same reasons, for the sender or the producer. To write is to produce a mark that will constitute a kind of machine that is in turn productive, that my future disappearance in principle will not prevent from functioning and from yielding, and yielding itself to, reading and rewriting. . . . I must be able simply to say my disappearance, my nonpresence in general, for example the nonpresence of my meaning, of my intention-to-signify, of my wanting-to-communicate-this, from the emission or production of the mark. (Derrida 1982a: 316)

To recognize writing as production, for Derrida, is to recognize writing as an "iterative structure cut off from all absolute responsibility, from *consciousness* as the authority of the last analysis"; it is to acknowledge that writing is "orphaned, and separated at birth from the assistance of its father" (Derrida 1982a: 316). As a child without a father (a son, perhaps?), writing is cast adrift, lacking the authority of the paternal name to ground its citationality. Here Derrida rejects absolute responsibility for writing because, for him, it is indelibly associated with "consciousness as the authority of the last analysis." And yet, Derrida's own emphasis on acknowledging the constitutive role played by that which is excluded leads me, as his reader, to look more carefully at this dual rejection of "absolute responsibility" and "consciousness as absolute authority" to see whether or not there is a "remainder" of responsibility and/or consciousness that survives in the writing itself.

Specifically, my question is whether or not a sense of responsibility can be salvaged in this analysis of writing; if not, I fear that the child (writing) will not only be orphaned (having lost both its parents: the all-too-visible Father/Author and the invisible mother), but that, to speak in a psychoanalytic register, the child will have succeeded in castrating/sacrificing himself.[15] For in what sense can the writing be responsible for itself unless writing itself becomes Writing and is granted a form of agency that has hitherto been associated most closely with that transcendental, self-caused being, God? Such a move (one that Derrida himself is careful not to make but that might be made by less scrupulous scribes) does not solve the issue of responsibility but cuts off an inquiry into responsibility from the outset, since God, by definition, is not responsible to anyone, and it is not clear how one can be responsible without being responsible to others.

In a critical vein, Foucault follows the implications of Barthes's and Derrida's respective emphases on writing in the absence of the writer (and for Derrida, in the absence of the reader as well). He notes in his essay "What Is an Author?" that "[g]iving writing a primal status seems to be a way of retranslating, in transcendental terms, both the theological affirmation of its sacred character and the critical affirmation of its creative character" (Foucault 1984: 104). According to Foucault, to focus on the writing in the absence of the writer and the reader is not to get away from absolute authorities, but rather to elevate writing itself to an a priori status, thereby removing it from its own discursive context. It is interesting that Derrida himself invokes the a priori structure of iteration (and, more specifically, forms of iteration) in the following passage: "[G]iven this structure of iteration, the intention which animates utterance will never be completely present in itself and its content. The iteration which *structures it a priori* introduces an essential dehiscence and demarcation" (Derrida 1982: 326, my emphasis). On the surface this is a rather strange claim, since the very notion of iteration seems to be at odds with its providing an a priori structure to writing and to the intentions that may or may not underlie it. And yet, there is indeed a logic to Derrida's argument that makes it clear why he assumes the risks involved in invoking and appropriating the rationalist notion of an a priori. To claim that iteration structures intentions (and utterances) in an a priori fashion is to argue that there is no extra- or non-discursive context one can appeal to, to "explain" the writing itself, that is, to determine its significance. Rather than privilege any one form of iteration, Derrida is arguing that iteration (or, to use the more active tense, iterability) itself supplants the metaphysics of presence that glorifies the a priori. Since writing is itself always already citation, iteration is indeed the a priori structure of writing. And yet, to pursue Foucault's critique, doesn't the elevation of iteration into an a priori structuring end up giving writing the "transcendental," even onto-theological, status that Derrida is attempting to deconstruct?

Toward the end of "Signature Event Context," Derrida states rather too suc- cinctly that "[w]riting is read, and 'in the last analysis' does not give rise to a her- meneutic deciphering, to the decoding of a meaning or truth" (Derrida 1982a: 329). To ponder the significance of the fragment of the parable at the beginning of *Fear and Trembling* is not, I think, an attempt to "decode" its meaning, for what it offers its readers is, among other things, a meditation on what it means for messages to be coded. Indeed, the coding of Kierkegaard's pseudonymous writ- ing is not "decoded" by the reader's discovery of the "real Author" of the text. Nor is the fragment of the parable "decoded" by being supplied with its missing con- text. And yet, despite the explicit citationality and iterability that is so well marked in *Fear and Trembling*, an iterability that defies more "direct" attempts to grasp the phenomenon of faith firsthand, despite the lack of clarity regarding the author's own intentions regarding the text, and despite the lack of clarity in the reader's own intentions that the text sets out again and again to frustrate, I am claiming that there is nonetheless a strong sense of responsibility that emerges from the work, a responsibility that is shared, in the Sartrean sense, between reader and writer, one that demands that faithful/fateful response of one to the other.

Responsibility without Subjects

In his book *Fables of Responsibility: Aberrations and Predicaments in Ethics and Politics*, Thomas Keenan claims that coming to terms with responsibility

> requires breaking with the horizon of subjectivity—decision, choice, agency— to a constitutive alterity that precedes it and that it cannot comprehend. We can call this "elsewhere" language—rhetoric, text, literature, or fable—not to distinguish it from some would-be empirical reality or history but to underline that others and their traces are always working within us already, in a space and time that cannot be reduced to that of consciousness or self-presence. (Keenan 1997: 66)

Keenan implies in this passage that there is no such thing as "my" responsibility because "my" signifies a responsibility that begins and ends with an individual consciousness or agency. On his account, subjectivity is unsustainable as such; it is simultaneously established and undermined through language, which is it- self "a constitutive alterity that precedes it and that it cannot comprehend."[16] For Keenan, rhetoric, text, literature, and fable are indistinguishable from one an- other as well as from any empirical reality that may seek to establish itself out- side the traces of language; the distinction between poetry and prose that is so important to Sartre, Keenan renders untenable. The prose writer is no more in control of a message than the poet lacks a message. And if one can no longer understand writing in terms of messages sent or unsent, or reading in terms of messages received or unreceived, indeed, if one can no longer separate writers from readers or either from writing itself, everything is up for grabs.

Paradoxically, responsibility is all that remains for Keenan precisely because language, subjectivity, and reality are all indifferent to human beings' attempts to justify (themselves through) them. He suggests that neither language, subjectivity, nor reality can serve as a transcendental ground for the others and that there is no "outside" that can found all three. In a surprisingly Sartrean passage, Keenan explains why responsibility persists in the face of this radical contingency. Both reading and politics, he argues,

> have their necessity in the withdrawal of security. These fields, because they expose us to events that cannot be calculated, programmed, "settled by experts or machines," demand responses (in another vocabulary, decisions) that cannot be referred to anywhere else, to something we know or mean. Our freedom is defined by this responsibility, not that of a subject who knows what it does. . . . If what we did could be authorized by something we knew (nature, truth), doing it would have nothing of the political or of reading about it. . . . Indeed, the possible impossibility of reading makes politics—freedom and responsibility—ineluctable. (Keenan 1997: 95)

Responsibility and freedom themselves seem to *precede* the subject on this account; they demand the interpellation of the subject who assumes them. Although the "ineluctability" of freedom and responsibility is presented from within a Derridean framework, this particular passage echoes Sartre's own explanations of how the radical contingency of the situation compels those who inhabit it to take responsibility for it. For Sartre, however, freedom and responsibility can never precede the subjects who assume them. They are meaningless until they are exercised. On the other hand, this does not mean that the subject precedes freedom and responsibility either. All three emerge in one and the same "upsurge" of human existence in the world.

To return to the tale of Tarquinius Superbus, what I find striking in this story is that the emperor, his son, and the messenger all bear a certain (and differing) responsibility for the message that is neither fully conscious nor mutually exclusive—phenomena associated with traditional conceptions of absolute responsibility that both Derrida and Keenan are (rightly, I think) rejecting. In the case of the messenger, his responsibility for the message cannot be grounded in the authority of his consciousness since he himself has no understanding of the message. Retrospectively, we might argue that his conscious intention is to carry the message faithfully from its sender to its receiver, but this intention has little if any bearing on the significance of the message itself. Given the indirect nature of the message, one might be tempted to say that the "true" significance of the message is determined through the intentions of its sender, the emperor, thereby falling into the "trap" of privileging the author at the expense of the writing and the reader, a move that Barthes, Derrida, Keenan, and I myself are trying to avoid. Such an interpretation, moreover, clearly fails to do justice to the crucial role played by its receiver, the one who transforms the message into concrete action.

Despite Keenan's persuasive suggestion that "[r]eading, like politics, if it is still possible, must be unavoidable, allowing no opting out and requiring no commitment (in the sense of cognitive decidability and intention)," questions of responsibility and commitment (and perhaps these ultimately are the "devils" Kierkegaard leaves his readers to contend with) remain. Is *no one* responsible for the killing of the ministers who were themselves plotting to kill the son? Although the issue of responsibility poses some rather difficult questions, and may indeed ultimately be undecidable in an absolute sense, Kierkegaard suggests that it is anything but a matter of indifference; for both Kierkegaard and Sartre responsibility cannot exist without agents that are responsible.

In Kierkegaard's depiction of the knight of faith, the reader is indeed offered a picture of absolute responsibility, but here it is an absolute responsibility that is born of conflicting (ethical and religious) passions, rather than conscious intentions. For Sartre, who is much more Cartesian than Kierkegaard, intentions are paramount, but there is no "Authority" who underlies them. And, moreover, intentions in and of themselves are meaningless from a Sartrean perspective, unless they issue in actions whose very nature is to outstrip any and all intentions. Intentions, he makes clear, issue from no-thing, they are themselves non-substantive and derive their meaning from the situation to which they are directed.

Although Kierkegaard proclaims that "truth is subjectivity," subjectivity on his account is also continuously in flux, continuously being remade and intensified through a renewed commitment to it. Without an existential commitment, there is no subjectivity as such. Yet, as has been shown, despite both Kierkegaard's and Sartre's rejection of a substantive self, both thinkers strongly affirm human beings' responsibility for themselves and for their situation. And, as far as reader and writer are concerned, both Kierkegaard and Sartre stress (Kierkegaard more indirectly than Sartre) a responsibility for the text that is *shared* between reader and writer, a co-responsibility that, I have argued, demands the faithful/fateful response of one to the other.

This responsibility shared between reader and writer is enacted, moreover, *in and through* the writing. Whereas Foucault himself contributes to the disembodiment of the (dead) author through the invocation of the "author-function," both Kierkegaard and Sartre view writing as an embodied call to action, one that implicates writer and reader in a shared dialogue that, in its limitless iterability, enhances rather than diminishes their responsibility for themselves, for one another, and for the writing. To take responsibility for one's writing and/or one's reading, I would maintain, is to commit oneself to "read and write between the lines," that is, to resist simplistic interpretations that dogmatically ascribe fixed significances to the words that appear on the printed page. And yet, it is not the case that "anything goes," either; to read/ write responsibly indeed requires a faithfulness to the text that discourages arbitrary or self-interested interpretations. Rather than elevate the author above the writing and the reader (traditional criticism), or the reader above the writing and the writer (Barthes), or even the writing above the writer and reader (Derrida), this notion of shared responsibility that I am proposing and that, I am claiming, is implicit in both Sartre's and Kierkegaard's work seeks to bind writing, writer, and reader into a complex, creative, and often conflicting aesthetic production, one that is produced (and provoked) afresh with each new reading/writing.

And yet, one may argue, how does this notion of co-responsibility fit with Kierkegaard's emphasis on the absolute responsibility of the knight of faith, a responsibility that can be enacted only by a radical dissociation of the knight of faith from everyone and everything that is beloved and familiar? To defend the very idea of co-responsibility as implicit in Kierkegaard's work requires an account of how this co-responsibility can be upheld in the face of the knight of faith's isolation from the universal community that constitutes the ethical realm.

Reconciling Absolute Responsibility with Co-Responsibility: Revaluing Readers, Writers, and Texts

In *The Gift of Death*, Derrida addresses the paradoxes that attend the Kierkegaardian notions of absolute duty and absolute responsibility as they unfold through his paradigmatic example of Abraham's willingness to sacrifice Isaac on Mount Moriah. As Derrida notes, for Kierkegaard, "[t]he absolutes of duty and of responsibility presume that one denounce, refute, and transcend, at the same time, all duty, all responsibility, and every human law. . . . One must behave not only in an ethical or responsible manner, but in a nonethical, nonresponsible manner, and one must do that *in the name of* duty, of an infinite duty, *in the name of* absolute duty" (Derrida 1995: 66–67). In this work, Derrida does not refute but actually affirms the paradox of absolute responsibility and maintains that the responsibility Abraham has to God, a responsibility that is paradoxical because in fulfilling his responsibility to God, he neglects his responsibility to everyone and everything else, is not atypical but actually is "the most common thing." For, Derrida argues, "[a]s soon as I enter into a relation with the other, with the gaze, look, request, love, command, or call of the other, I know that I can respond only by sacrificing ethics, that is, by sacrificing whatever obliges me to also respond, in the same way, in the same instant, to all the others" (Derrida 1995: 68).

By taking up the responsibility of reading this text as an absolute responsibility, you are making the sacrifice of not fulfilling your responsibility to other texts, other people, other activities. By writing this book, I am making the sacrifice of not writing another book, of not helping others who may be illiterate and therefore unable to engage with this text at all. According to Derrida, "[w]hether I want to or not, I can never justify the fact that I prefer or sacrifice any one (any other) to the other" (Derrida 1995: 70). In this sense, Derrida suggests, each reader/writer is like Abraham. Moreover, not only in the acts of reading/writing, but at every moment of life, individuals silently (or not so silently!) make unjustified sacrifices, in the name of responsibility, to an other or others, and expect others to do the same for them.

Although Kierkegaard would almost certainly disagree with Derrida's reading of the paradox of the knight of faith as being comparable to the paradox of every man and woman, Derrida's reminder that sacrifices necessarily accompany absolute responsibility has implications for the notion of co-responsibility I am arguing for as well. To be co-responsible for a situation also involves sacrifices: most significantly, it involves sacrificing my own "author-function" in relation to that situation; that is, I must recognize that I am not the sole author of "my" situation. To the extent that I share the author-function with other participants in that situation, rigid distinctions between reader and writer can no longer be maintained.

Sharp distinctions between reader and writer also break down in the act of writing itself. To write with understanding of what one is writing requires that one be a reader as well as a writer. After completing this sentence, I re-read it to make sure it accurately expresses what I want it to convey to myself as a reader and to other readers. Indeed, to go back and forth between these two roles is essential to any good piece of writing. Not only do writers (hopefully) re-read their own work as they are writing, they may also on occasion be (un)fortunate enough to read responses to their work by other writers and, in doing so, find their initial roles reversed.[17]

This reversal is quite different from the reversal of the look that exemplifies the Sartrean account of being-for-others. Whereas in *Being and Nothingness* Sartre adopts a Hegelian understanding of being-for-others as the pitting of one subjectivity against another (for Hegel this plays out through the master/slave dialectic), in the essays on writing collected in *What Is Literature?*, as noted earlier, Sartre leaves open the possibility of an authentic intersubjective relationship achieved through the reciprocal processes of reading and writing that is not grounded in an antagonistic subject/object framework. What facilitates this more positive encounter between subjectivities in these latter essays may in fact be the pivotal role played by the text itself. More specifically, Sartre emphasizes that both reader and writer engage one another's freedom through their respective encounters with the text. In the model of the look that serves as the paradigmatic example for being-for-others in *Being and Nothingness*, by contrast, glances are exchanged like blows, each dethroning the other from her exalted position as subject of the gaze. And yet, despite this seemingly inevitable conflict with the other, Sartre maintains that each human being is responsible for the other as well as for herself. I am responsible for the other precisely insofar as I am a being-for-others, not merely a being-for-itself, yet clearly in being responsible for others I can in no way take their responsibility for themselves (and for me) away from them.

Thus, Sartre too seems to be positing something that looks very much like absolute responsibility existing alongside an implicit notion of co-responsibility. As a being-for-others I am co-responsible with those others for the situation that has been mutually constituted; as a being-for-itself, I bear an absolute responsibility for my thoughts, attitudes, and actions within that situation, even though these latter are undoubtedly influenced by my being-with- and for-others.

Kierkegaard, like Sartre, has often been criticized for Cartesian solipsism regarding his understanding of subjectivity. Both Kierkegaard and Derrida emphasize the fact that Abraham shares a secret (with God) that requires silence before Isaac, Sarah, and their servants. Thus, in order to fulfill his absolute responsibility to God, to himself, and even, it would seem, to Isaac, Sarah, and future generations, Abraham must refuse to allow them to participate in his ordeal. In what sense, then, can one view Abraham's family and the generations that follow (including contemporary readers of the story of Abraham), as co-responsible for Abraham's situation without in any way diminishing the awesome sense of absolute responsibility that Kierkegaard claims Abraham can and must endure?

Isaac's own role in Abraham's sacrifice is often neglected, and Sarah is barely acknowledged to play a role at all. The test of faith, even in Kierkegaard's depiction, is always a test for Abraham alone. Only in the four imaginary scenarios that appear within the *Exordium* of *Fear and Trembling*, do mother and child play an active role. Here, Kierkegaard grants that any faltering on Abraham's part, in word or deed, will have an effect on Isaac's own faith, and analogously, he implies, the means used by the mother to wean the child will have an effect on future relations between them. In these poetic explorations of what might have been, Kierkegaard affirms the intersubjective bonds that make individuals responsible for one another before God. To have an absolute responsibility to God does not mean that one bears no responsibility for others or for the situation that one shares with them. Indeed, the power of the story of Abraham, as Kierkegaard well knows, consists in its ability to implicate others in the knight of faith's ordeal; the reader is implicated in (and therefore co-responsible for) Abraham's test of faith precisely to the extent that she assumes responsibility for her own existence, an existence that necessarily implicates others.

As Kierkegaard's readers, Derrida observes, we share Abraham's secret. "But," he asks,

> what does it mean to share a secret? It isn't a matter of knowing what the other knows, for Abraham doesn't know anything. It isn't a matter of sharing his faith, for the latter must remain an initiative of absolute singularity. . . . We share with Abraham what cannot be shared, a secret we know nothing about, neither him nor us. To share a secret is not to know or to reveal the secret, it is to share we know not what: nothing that can be determined. (Derrida 1995: 79–80)

For Derrida, the secret that is transmitted is grounded in *nothing*. This nothing he associates with the "gift of death," which is the gift of otherness itself. Rather than turn to the concrete relations that are established in and through the communication of a secret for which human beings come to be collectively responsible insofar as they must take up the labor of interpreting it for themselves, Derrida emphasizes the lack or absence at the heart of the secret, an absence that he associates with an otherness that does issue not (merely) from the other, but from the individual herself.

Kierkegaard, by contrast, does not ultimately dwell on Abraham's alterity; he both marvels at and celebrates Abraham's joyous return to his family. Kierkegaard's Abraham is not left alone before God upon Mount Moriah (where he was never alone to begin with, since Isaac was always present), but renews and reaffirms his relations with others, once again taking up a life in community that, although seemingly repudiated, was never left behind. Just so, I would argue, to be absolutely responsible for one's reading/writing of a text does not preclude but actually strengthens one's co-responsibility for the situation created through that reading/writing. Undoubtedly, tensions will arise between one's absolute responsibility to oneself and to others and one's co-responsibility with these self-same others for the situation that has been mutually constituted. Nonetheless, despite the sacrifices and secrets that may be involved, messages do get communicated and received. Sometimes they are miscommunicated or even intercepted. Sometimes there are no messages at all. In establishing as well as in contesting the meaningfulness of these communications, human beings simultaneously establish and contest the meaning of their own (inter)subjectivity, a process that produces transformations in the very practices of reading and writing, and therefore in the texts themselves.

4

The Body as a Narrative Horizon

The postmodernist claim that "the body is a text" (and this is usually intended to refer to the human body in particular) has become passé. And yet, it is still worth pondering the concrete implications of this expression because to say that the body is not outside of or opposed to discourse, but is itself discursively constructed, is merely a provocation to further discussion. How is the body discursively constructed? What physical, social, political, economic, and psychical forces inscribe themselves as integral features of any given individual's body, intertwining in unique configurations to shape the parameters of her ordinary experience?

Bodily Texts and Textual Bodies

At the very outset of *Bodies That Matter*, Butler takes up the challenge posed by these questions and acknowledges a central obstacle that one faces in trying to address them. For, she informs us, as soon as she tried to take the materiality of the body seriously, she was led immediately "into other domains"; she "could not fix bodies as simple objects of thought. Not only did bodies tend to indicate a world beyond themselves, but this movement beyond their own boundaries, a movement of boundary itself, appeared to be quite central to what bodies are" (Butler 1993a: ix). If bodies indeed "indicate a world beyond themselves," then to understand the body as a text, or as I will be calling it here, a narrative horizon, means that one cannot restrict oneself to the body proper, but one must look at the ways in which the body is always already engaged with (and formed by) other bodies, social and political institutions, language and gesture, indeed the entire habitus that Pierre Bourdieu claims structures any given community or society at any particular point in time. Moreover, as Butler observes, "To claim that discourse is formative [of the body] is not to claim that it originates, causes, or exhaustively composes that which it concedes; rather, it is to claim that there is no reference to a pure body which is not at the same time a further formation of that body" (Butler 1993a: 10).

Viewing the body as a multi-discursive text has the (intended) effect of destabilizing the body and the way the body is ordinarily understood, insofar as it is directly opposed to the Cartesian philosophical tradition that characterizes the body as a purely material, biological organism regarded as quite separate from (and resistant to) cultural influences. By rejecting this traditional dualistic model, one avoids the intractable problem of determining exactly how two allegedly distinct phenomena, the natural and the cultural, interact to comprise a unified sense of self, but, at the same time, when the body is dislodged from one side of this false dichotomy, the "integrity" of the body as a distinctive metaphysical substance appears to be abolished as well. Additionally, while showing that the body does not exist independently of culture, but is cultural through and through, undermines an absolute opposition between the natural and the cultural (meaning that one no longer has the problem of accounting for how nature and culture as ontologically distinct phenomena work together), there is now a new problem, namely, determining whether or not the body has any ontological standing whatsoever. For, if the body is a text, on what basis, if any, is one to differentiate it from other kinds of texts? In what sense can the body be said to "be" at all?

While I, too, find it both philosophically and politically productive to view the body as a text, I am especially concerned about the ethical implications of such a position, implications that are rarely acknowledged and, for that very reason, are all the more urgent to consider. These implications, I would argue, can and must be understood in narrative terms, since understanding the body as a text means that it has its own narrative structure, and any ethics that arises out of this narrative structure must itself be narratively constructed.[1] To say that the body has its own narrative structure is itself a problematic claim, however, to the extent that it once again seems to set the body apart from everything else, from all that is not part of the body. Indeed, one of the virtues of the position that the body is a text is precisely that it emphasizes the intrinsic connection between the body and language, that is, the ways in which the body is part of a larger "conversation of gestures" that Mead claims is so central to human as well as non-human experience. And yet, it is also important not to see the body as simply caught up in particular narratives, for if the body doesn't play a distinctive role in (its own) narrative construction, then on what basis can we claim that bodies have a distinctive moral standing, a moral standing that implies a measure of responsibility (for that narrative) that propositions and stories in and of themselves seem to lack?

Perhaps there are some people who would argue that propositions or stories actually do have moral standing in their own right, that they need not be associated with a particular author or even a Foucaultian "author-function" to have ethical force. I'm not unsympathetic to such a claim, but I would argue that it can be made only on the basis of an appeal to the "body" of the text itself. To account for the moral imperatives that can and do issue from texts, one must recognize not only that the body is discursively constructed, and thus that the body cannot be separated from discourses about it, but also that texts are themselves embodied, which means that they have their own materiality, which is precisely what defines them (and differentiates them from one another) as texts.

My focus will be on how to come to terms with this embodied dimension of texts, for while much has been written on the body as text, not enough emphasis has been placed on understanding the text as body. Correcting this imbalance will, I believe, provide a much more fruitful means of getting beyond the admitted artificiality of the nature/culture divide as well as the equally problematic "solution" that makes the body just one cultural product among others. Recognizing the materiality, or more precisely, the materialities, of texts (including the body as text) is to acknowledge that texts are necessarily embodied just as bodies can be understood textually. What I am especially interested in establishing is not that texts can be reduced to their materiality or that materiality can be reduced to textuality, for embodiment is not reducible either to materiality or textuality in the first place. Rather, I will be arguing that the body serves as a narrative horizon for all texts, and in particular for all of the stories that human beings tell about, and which become indistinguishable from, themselves.

Constellations of Meaning

Insofar as one's body functions as a central horizon that is brought to bear upon one's experience from one moment to the next, and insofar as the body is interpellated into discourse in particular places and times through the numerous intercorporeal exchanges that Mead calls "conversations of gestures," which, as Foucault points out, always unfold within broader "disciplinary regimes," it is clear that human beings' respective corporeal horizons mutually inform one another, and therefore, mutually inform the ways in which each person "configures" her own experiences.[2] One important consequence of this is that, as Alasdair MacIntyre and Mark Johnson argue, the narratives through which individuals construct their lives are always co-authored. In MacIntyre's words:

[W]e are never more (and sometimes less) than the co-authors of our own narratives. Only in fantasy do we live what story we please. In life, as both Aristotle and Engels noted, we are always under certain constraints. We enter upon a stage which we did not design and we find ourselves part of an action that was not of our making. Each of us being a main character in his own drama plays subordinate parts in the dramas of others, and each drama constrains the others. (MacIntyre 1981: 199)

MacIntyre's stage analogy is particularly apt in describing this process since the actors' own bodily presence is precisely what tends to be foregrounded when they appear on stage. Whether one is captivated by an actor's voice calling from offstage or focuses instead, as Proust's Marcel does, on the movement of the stage actress Berma's hands, it is abundantly evident that the distinctiveness of each individual's contribution to the drama in which she is immersed is expressed through her body.

Before examining more closely how the body functions as a horizon in the intersubjective dramas that intertwine human beings in one another's narratives, it is important to discuss more specifically how narratives themselves are constructed. According to Paul Ricoeur: "All narratives combine in various proportions, two dimensions—one chronological and the other non-chronological. The first may be called the episodic dimension. This dimension characterizes the story as made out of events. The second is the configurational dimension, according to which the plot construes significant wholes out of scattered events" (Ricoeur 1991: 106). Ricoeur views both dimensions, the episodic/chronological dimension and the configurational/achronological dimension, to be equally constitutive of human narratives. He argues, however, that both structuralist literary critics and anti-narrativist historians tend to ignore the configurational dimension altogether because it does not obey a conventional chronology. Rather than moving in the straightforward progression from past to present to future that typifies the episodic/chronological dimension, the configurational/achronological dimension works back and forth in time in what might look, from the outside, to be a random or haphazard manner but that, Ricoeur argues, nonetheless elicits a distinctive, tightly woven pattern. As a spontaneous organizational strategy, I would argue, the configurational act can itself be understood as a gestalt, or figure/ground organization, producing what Ricoeur calls a "constellation of meaning."

For Ricoeur, metaphorical statements can themselves be understood as configurational acts, and they provide him with a primary example of how constellations of meaning are formed out of what seem like entirely disparate and even incompatible associations and/or experiences. Metaphors arise, Ricoeur asserts, not ex nihilo, but in response to a "semantic impertinence" or a "clash" between semantic fields. More specifically, he claims that

> Every metaphor, in bringing together two previously distant semantic fields, strikes against a prior categorization, which it shatters. Yet, the idea of semantic impertinence preserves this: an order, logically antecedent, resists, and is not completely abolished by, the new pertinence. In effect, in order that there be a metaphor, it is necessary that I continue to perceive the previous incompatibility through the new compatibility. Therefore, predicative assimilation contains a new sort of tension, one no longer solely between subject and predicate, but between incompatibility and the new compatibility. (Ricoeur 1991: 125)

This understanding of metaphor as a configurational act that preserves the incompatibility between semantic fields in and through its presentation of a "new compatibility" is, I would argue, a promising point of departure for an understanding of how narratives are constructed and reconstructed. In *Fables of Responsibility*, Thomas Keenan makes a similar point about how tropes function and expands upon it through the metaphorical example: "Achilles is a lion." In this example, he asserts,

> "[l]ion" means something new, now, but it only means it to the extent that it preserves its bond to the "primitive meaning." The resourcefulness by which language turns "its own poverty into wealth" in this economy of re-use works on a principle of substitution: words change places, stand in for each other, cross over from one meaning to another. The hegemony of meaning is far from being questioned: on the contrary, rhetoric is designed to exploit the exchangeability of words to expand the horizon of meaning. (Keenan 1997: 143)

Keenan's emphasis on the "economy of re-use" (according to which a word with a fairly "stable" connotation—lion, a large four-legged animal who, among other things, kills and eats its prey, and is popularly known in many cultures as "king of the forest"—both retains its old meaning and takes on a new one expressing Achilles' courageousness, steadfastness, and leadership) shows, moreover, that the process of creating new meanings, and by extension, new narratives, need not involve the creation of new languages. Rather, I would argue, it is the possibility of continually reworking the reciprocal relationship between figure and ground even within one and the same language that reinforces existing meanings even as it creates new ones.[3]

Keeping this reversibility between figure and ground in mind, I would like to reopen my initial inquiry into the body of the text or, more precisely, into the bodily dimension of the process of narrative construction that makes texts readable as such. Ricoeur prepares the way for such an investigation with his claim that "[i]t is as if metaphor *gives a body, a contour, a face to discourse.* . . . But how? It seems to me, it is in the moment of the emergence of a new meaning from the ruins of a literal predicament that imagination offers its specific mediation" (Ricoeur 1991: 124, my emphasis). While Ricoeur turns to the imagination as a site of productive reference in order to explicate this point, I will address the ongoing role that the body plays as a narrative horizon in discourse (a role that it continues to play even in discourses about the body).

By displacing the focus from the imagination to the body, however, I do not mean to deny the primacy of the imagination in the construction of narratives. "Human beings," as Mark Johnson claims, "are imaginative synthesizing animals." Johnson, like Ricoeur, stresses the productivity of human imaginative activity; more specifically, he claims that this activity is precisely what enables human beings to pursue what MacIntyre calls a "quest" for narrative unity, a quest that has as its goal the organization and production of an integrated sense of self. Moreover, in Johnson's words, "In order for us to have coherent experiences, to make any sense at all of what happens to us, to survive in our environment, and to enhance the quality of our lives, we must organize and reorganize our experience from moment to moment" (Johnson 1993: 152).

Intelligible Narratives

MacIntyre argues that this continual organization and reorganization is guided by a particular *telos*, not one that lies outside this process of narrative construction but rather, like Ricoeur's configurational act, one that emerges in and through it. This telos takes the form of what MacIntyre calls an "intelligible" narrative, a narrative that creates its own unity by giving a meaningful structure to a series of experiences that, in principle, could always have been configured differently. Moreover, the ability to produce intelligible narratives (and therefore intelligible selves), is, for MacIntyre, precisely what establishes moral responsibility for those narratives. For, MacIntyre notes:

> Human beings can be held to account for that of which they are the authors; other beings cannot. To identify an occurrence as an action is in the paradigmatic instances to identify it under a type of description which enables us to see that occurrence as flowing intelligibly from a human agent's intentions, motives, passions and purposes. *It is therefore to understand an action as something for which someone is accountable, about which it is always appropriate to ask the agent for an intelligible account.* (MacIntyre 1981: 195, my emphasis)

Intelligibility, as MacIntyre emphasizes here and elsewhere, arises out of the agent's "intentions, motives, passions and purposes." Ultimately, however, motives, passions, and purposes seem to be subordinated to the primary intentions that MacIntyre identifies as the crucial factor in the construction of intelligible narratives. These intentions, he asserts, are manifested in behavior that is directly connected to the particular setting in which an individual finds herself. For, "We cannot . . . characterize behaviour independently of intentions and we cannot characterize intentions independently of the settings which make those intentions intelligible both to agents themselves and to others" (MacIntyre 1981: 192).

Despite the provocative resonances between Ricoeur's account of the constellations of meaning produced by the configurational act and MacIntyre's account of intelligible narrative, I find MacIntyre's understanding of intelligible narrative to be less satisfactory in exposing the intercorporeal horizons that underpin the ongoing process of narrative/self construction. A central problem with his account is that the traditional language of intention and intelligibility that he utilizes suggests a conscious process that arises within a single person's mind, not the more robust notion of bodily intentionality that Merleau-Ponty develops in *Phenomenology of Perception,* a phenomenon that is not restricted to specific acts of consciousness (nor to human beings alone!). For MacIntyre, a narrative becomes intelligible precisely to the extent that it can be seen as arising out of one or more agents' intentions. When a person is incapable of generating an intelligible narrative because her own or others' intentions are opaque to her, he argues, communication breaks down.

Although I agree with MacIntyre that the ability to be accountable for one's actions is directly tied to the ability to ground these actions in specific narrative constructions, I find his claim that the meaning of these narratives stems from the agent's or agents' intentions to be overly reductive and therefore untenable. This is because he seems to reduce meaning to narrative intelligibility and the intelligibility of narratives to the intelligibility of the intentions that allegedly motivate them. These claims appear to me to be problematic on at least two counts. First, I would argue that meaning cannot and should not be equated with narrative intelligibility. As both Husserl and Merleau-Ponty have shown, the horizons that situate human experience are themselves meaningful; however, their very role as grounds for one's experience means that they are often left out of account in the process of narrative construction, even when this latter depends upon these horizons from the outset. Secondly, and relatedly, the intelligibility of narratives (and the same point goes for their unintelligibility) always includes more than the "intentions, motives, passions, and purposes" associated with them. There is, I am suggesting, a tacit organization to our narratives that is due not to cognition or emotion but to the body itself as the ultimate ground of all narrative construction. Whereas for MacIntyre, narratives seem to be either intelligible or unintelligible depending upon the presence or absence of coherent intentions and/or on the ability or inability of the agent to discern coherent intentions, intentions that are in turn rendered coherent to the extent that they can be situated within a unified narrative, I maintain that human bodies themselves contribute, in an ongoing way, to the construction of narrative intelligibility, and that this occurs even and precisely when the kind of coherence MacIntyre is privileging cannot be found.

Finally, MacIntyre's assumption that an action cannot be meaningful unless it is situated within an intelligible narrative is also problematic because, I argue, along with Merleau-Ponty, meaning does not require or presuppose the rationalist notion of intelligibility with which MacIntyre associates it. Ricoeur, as mentioned earlier, observes that metaphors arise out of a clash between semantic fields, and he claims that they do not eliminate this clash but preserve it through the creation of a new meaning that creates a "new compatibility" on the basis of an existing "incompatibility." The very claim that metaphor involves a clash between semantic fields that generates a new compatibility out of an incompatibility poses a challenge to a rationalist conception of intelligibility. To explore this challenge further, one must ask, "How does this clash occur?" "What is the 'semantic impertinence' that brings it about?" For it is clear that the semantic fields themselves must be configured in a certain way for such a clash to be experienced as such.

Unintelligible Narratives, or the Body's Semantic Impertinence

What I would like to propose is that the body is itself a semantic impertinence, that the body (whether this be an actual human body or the body of a text or the body of some other artifact, creature, or event) serves as the site for the production of semantic fields and, accordingly, for the inevitable tensions that arise among them. To make such a claim, moreover, is not to deny the crucial role that Johnson ascribes to the imagination, for this latter, as both he and I understand it, is not a purely cognitive faculty, but an embodied activity. Despite his recognition of this crucial embodied dimension of all narrative activity, however, Johnson also offers far too reductive an explanation for narrative construction. Specifically, he contends that "[a]ll forms of action (from mundane tasks, to large-scale projects, to life plans) can be understood metaphorically as journeys" (Johnson 1993: 168). This "proto-narrative," he holds, is structured by means of two basic imaginative schemas, the "source-path-goal" schema and the "balance" schema. Like MacIntyre then, Johnson privileges coherent narratives. Unlike MacIntyre, he foregrounds the crucial role the body plays in their intelligibility. And yet, at the same time, he tends to understand the body's role in narrative construction primarily in terms of a set of cognitive "image schemas" that emerge out of, and in turn structure, human beings' embodied experiences.

While Johnson recognizes that "our lives are shot through with gaps, disjunctions, reversals, fractures, and fragmentations that constitute what Ricoeur calls the 'discordance' of human existence" and that "[i]n Ricoeur's terms, both narratives and human lives have a 'discordant concordance,' an ineliminable tension that resists our attempts to construct a total unity and harmony" (Johnson 1993: 170), his cognitivist account of this process tends to view the "discrepant" data as meaningless to the extent that it resists incorporation into a coherent narrative. More than anything, I am arguing that the body itself is this very "discordant concordance," that which frustrates attempts at narrative unity, while simultaneously making the quest for narrative coherence possible. One can best see how this is so, I think, by turning to the archetypical site of narrative, namely, literature.

MacIntyre, perhaps not surprisingly, faults Kafka for the unintelligibility of the endings of his stories despite their initial intelligibility. Although Kafka's "failure" is acknowledged by MacIntyre to be deliberate, MacIntyre nonetheless refuses to probe deeper into the source of this failure, contenting himself with the dismissive, parenthetical assertion that "[i]t is no accident that Kafka could not end his novels, for the notion of an ending like that of a beginning has its sense only in terms of intelligible narrative" (MacIntyre 1981: 198). He makes these remarks in the context of Kafka's *The Trial* and *The Castle*, but I would like to respond to them in reference to *The Metamorphosis*. Indeed, I think Kafka is exemplary in this latter novel in showing how the body serves as the quintessential narrative horizon that drives the quest for narrative intelligibility and, at the same time, thwarts it.

The everlasting debate over exactly *what* kind of bug Gregor Samsa becomes, an obsession Kafka anticipated and refused to indulge in by refusing to allow an image of this "monstrous vermin" to appear on the cover of his novella, reflects a desire to achieve narrative coherence by "normalizing," albeit in a manner that accepts its abnormality, Samsa's bodily metamorphosis. The irony is that even if Kafka had given in to this desire for clarity by specifying exactly what kind of creature Gregor had become, neither the metamorphosis itself nor the narrative in which it is configured would be clearer. Indeed, Samsa's changing body (which continues to change in shape, size, and abilities even after his alleged metamorphosis), I would argue, is precisely what constitutes the crucial narrative horizon that continually resists, more than anything else, Samsa's, his family's, and the reader's attempts to persist in the illusion of narrative intelligibility.

To the extent that one reads the ambiguities of Samsa's bodily changes as a metaphor for those "semantic impertinences" that issue from one's own body, one can understand Kafka to be suggesting that the body continually transgresses all attempts to make it or the narratives grounded upon it fully intelligible. And yet, the body can never be dispensed with altogether, for the body is, as I have claimed, the omnipresent horizon for all the narratives human beings tell (about it). As such, it grounds a person's quest for narrative coherence, and in so doing establishes that individual's moral accountability for the quest itself, an accountability that includes the failure to complete the quest.[4] Moreover, I think this failure can best be understood in Merleau-Pontian terms, not as a lack of intelligibility but as a challenge to the very notion of the intelligible, a challenge that one must not try to "solve" but whose very insolubility gives richness, meaning, and depth to one's experience.

To take up this challenge, I would suggest, is not to avoid but actively to affirm the clash between semantic fields (to use Ricoeur's language) that gives birth to new meanings and makes possible the creation of new narratives. The stakes are high. Oppressive narratives of race, sex, age, ability, nationality, ethnicity, and class have been plentiful and have flourished throughout human history. To oppose them requires not merely rejecting these particular narratives but also acknowledging that one will always fail to achieve whatever narrative coherence one seeks. At the same time, I am arguing, following Beauvoir, that this failure is a good thing because it is precisely what preserves the space of narrative possibility, an openness to new narratives that will perhaps be more accommodating of the "incoherences" that are an inescapable feature of everyday life. This latter project is, as Judith Butler suggests in *Undoing Gender*, none other than "The struggle to rework the norms by which bodies are experienced" (Butler 2004: 28).

To struggle against assertions of narrative coherence that render some lives incoherent, or, as Butler terms it, unlivable, does not mean that human beings must refuse the quest for narrative coherence altogether. Instead, as intersex, transgender, and disability activists have all argued, it is crucial to seek new norms (and new narratives) that "contest forcibly imposed ideals of what bodies ought to be like" (Butler 2004: 28). The only way this can be accomplished, however, is in and through the body itself, more specifically, through an openness to, and acceptance of, bodily differences. For, when corporeal exceptionality is affirmed as bodily normality, the parameters of what counts as intelligible or, for that matter, livable are themselves inevitably stretched, and one's narrative horizons are expanded accordingly.[5]

PART 3

(Re)Grounding the Figure

5

Can an Old Dog Learn New Tricks?
Habitual Horizons in James, Bourdieu, and Merleau-Ponty

It is impossible to discuss the multiple horizons that collectively help to constitute a particular individual's (or even a group's) situation without addressing the ways in which these horizons themselves become habitual and thereby increasingly invisible over time.[1] Through the process of habituation, horizons are naturalized, taken for granted as "the way things are," and this, in turn, makes these horizons even more resistant to analysis, much less transformation. Indeed, habituation and naturalization reinforce one another in establishing the parameters of what counts as ordinary and therefore what counts as extraordinary, experience. By emphasizing how horizons themselves become habitual over time, I argue, one can arrive at a more in-depth understanding of how and why specific bodily responses and gestures (and not others) become naturalized through their repetition. In particular, I maintain that the norms human beings appeal to, both individually and collectively, to explain and justify their actions help to constitute the habitual horizons within which they make sense of their lives.

Habit and Habitability

Although human beings are often exhorted to "break" their bad habits, even those who urge humanity to do so realize that it is impossible to dispense with the habitual altogether since it is the realm of the habitual (or, in phenomeno-logical terms, the realm of taken for granted reality that Husserl associates with the natural attitude) that provides a powerful glue capable of linking together otherwise disparate aspects of both individual's as well as group's embodied ex-periences. In *Remembrance of Things Past*, Marcel Proust spends seven massive volumes depicting, but never exhausting, the power of the habitual, offering us an extended meditation on habit, its temporal rhythms, its limits, and its possi-bilities. In his work, habit becomes Habit, possessing an agency of its own that works in and through us. Proust captures the beauty, power, and ambivalence of habit, and marvels at the paradoxical role habit plays in ordinary experience, eloquently depicting the joys and sorrows its presence as well as its absence pro-duces as it both supports and undermines a person's attempts to establish her place within the world of her concern.

In the early pages of volume 1, *Swann's Way*, he offers the first of numerous observations about habit and its paradoxes: "Habit! that skilful but slow-moving arranger who begins by letting our minds suffer for weeks on end in temporary quarters, but whom our minds are none the less only too happy to discover at last, for without it, reduced to their own devices, they would be powerless to make any room seem habitable" (Proust 1981: vol. 1, 9). Here, Proust portrays habit as a phenomenon that operates independently from the mind and that the mind it-self is dependent on in order to "make any room seem habitable." By marking the connection between habit and habitability, Proust draws attention to how habit enables one to *inhabit* a world, or, more precisely, how habit enables an unfamil-iar space to be transformed into a familiar environment. In his depiction of habit as a "skilful arranger," Proust offers an image of habit as an active agency, going about its business without a person's express knowledge or consent, yet nonethe-less playing an indispensable role in his or her everyday life.

This depiction of habit stresses its positive aspects, its ability to make people feel at home in the world, but Proust also hints at the challenges habit poses to the mind because of the latter's dependence upon it. For if the mind needs to draw upon habit to construct a familiar life-world, and if habit, that "slow-moving arranger," performs its function in its own time, this poses a challenge to the modern philosophers' view of the mind as a self-sufficient entity and sug-gests that habit has its own temporality, its own rhythms, and its own signifi-cances that invisibly leave their traces on all aspects of psychic life.

Ultimately, Proust himself is quite ambivalent about habit throughout the seven volumes of *Remembrance of Things Past*. Continually personifying habit as in the earlier quote, both his narrator and the main character, Marcel, often decry its negative influence on a person's life. In a parenthetical comment to-ward the end of volume 7, *Time Regained*, Marcel laments the power of habit, "which cuts off from things we have witnessed a number of times the root of profound impression and of thought which gives them their real meaning" (Proust 1981: vol. 3, 775). In contrast to the earlier passage, at this point in the narrative habit seems to be at odds with meaning, dulling rather than enhancing the significance of mundane experience.

In the course of his magnum opus, Proust seems to seesaw back and forth between positive and negative views of habit.[2] On the one hand, he suggests that habit provides individuals with a sense of familiarity and security that is essential for daily life, and on the other hand, he just as frequently portrays habit as stultifying, as condemning these same individuals to mindless repetition, and, equally importantly, as reinforcing social conventions that long ago lost their utility. How is one to reconcile these two conflicting views of habit? Can habit keep "an old dog from learning new tricks?" Or is habit precisely what provides a necessary foundation for new meanings to emerge? Proust's texts raise these questions again and again, and he leaves it up to his readers to ponder their answers.

The Social Utility of Habit

Over the years, habit has been ambivalently depicted not only in literature by authors such as Proust, but also in philosophy and psychology. These accounts range from a purely negative view of habit as the bane of human existence, condemning people to repeating the past without learning anything from it, to descriptions of habit as a class-based phenomenon, varying not only from one social class to another, but also from one culture to another, and, finally, to more positive understandings of habit as a source of comfort, as expressive of an ethics, and as a creative bodily experience that makes innovation possible. These various portrayals are strikingly intermingled in the following passage from the chapter on habit in William James's *The Principles of Psychology* (volume 1). "Habit" he declares,

> [i]s thus the enormous fly-wheel of society, its most precious conservative agent. It alone is what keeps us all within the bounds of ordinance, and saves the children of fortune from the envious uprisings of the poor. It alone prevents the hardest and most repulsive walks of life from being deserted by those brought up to tread therein. It keeps the fisherman and the deck-hand at sea through the winter; it holds the miner in his darkness, and nails the countryman to his log-cabin and his lonely farm through all the months of snow; it protects us from invasion by the natives of the desert and the frozen zone. It dooms us all to fight out the battle of life upon the lines of our nurture or our early choice, and to make the best of a pursuit that disagrees, because there is no other for which we are fitted, and it is too late to begin again. It keeps different social strata from mixing. Already at the age of twenty-five you see the professional mannerism settling down on the young commercial traveler, on the young doctor, on the young minister, on the young counsellor-at-law. You

> see the little lines of cleavage running through the character, the tricks of
> thought, the prejudices, the ways of the "shop," in a word, from which the man
> can by-and-by no more escape than his coat-sleeve can suddenly fall into a
> new set of folds. (James 1950: 121)

And he dramatically (ominously?) concludes: "On the whole, it is best he should
not escape. It is well for the world that in most of us, by the age of thirty, the
character has set like plaster, and will never soften again" (James, 1950:121).
"Better for whom?" one may well ask. Indeed, James's attention to the relationship between habit and class in the above passage is striking not only because he
notes the crucial, yet largely invisible, role habit plays in the maintenance of
mutually exclusive social classes but also for the classist assumptions he makes
about the desirability of those very structures. Moreover, James does not restrict
his comments to the ways in which habit ties an individual to a particular class;
rather, he also suggests that habit ineluctably forms an individual's character,
and that this has important ethical implications. Specifically, he claims that

> [t]he hell to be endured hereafter, of which theology tells, is no worse than the
> hell we make for ourselves in this world by habitually fashioning our charac-
> ters in the wrong way. Could the young but realize how soon they will become
> mere walking bundles of habits, they would give more heed to their conduct
> while in the plastic state. We are spinning our own fates, good or evil, and
> never to be undone. Every smallest stroke of virtue or of vice leaves its never so
> little scar. (James 1950: 127)

In order to address the rich implications of these provocative passages, it is
important first to understand James's neurological conception of the process of
habituation. According to James, habit is a material phenomenon that is manifested as a set of concatenated nerve discharges that forms a "reflex path." One
might compare such a system to a row of upright dominoes. Once the first
domino is knocked over, the rest follow one after the other, and, apart from any
outside interference with the trajectory, the movement once begun will lead to
a predictable (or habitual) conclusion resulting in the toppling over (firing off)
of all the dominoes (nerve-centers). On his account, each of an individual's
habits has its own nerve path, and, through repetition over time, the path becomes more and more fixed and less subject to change (or interference).

Anticipating later behaviorists' account of the mind as initially a tabula rasa,
James argues that human organisms begin their development in a "plastic" state,
open to any number of possibilities. Over time, as certain actions become re-
peated in a characteristic sequence, such as getting out of bed, going into the
bathroom, showering, brushing one's teeth, then reentering the bedroom to dress,
and so on, specific neural pathways are formed that correspond to these se-

quences. As these routines become both internally and externally ingrained, one finds oneself performing the entire sequence without being consciously aware that one is doing so. Merleau-Ponty calls this "bodily intentionality," a process whereby the body functions in a purposeful, directed fashion without requiring one's explicit attention. If a person's routine is interrupted in media res, however, a conscious adjustment or reminder may be necessary to resume the activity, since, according to James, the ordinary pathway has been disrupted, and must be "jump-started" as it were, by artificial (that is, conscious) means. While most adults can succeed in returning to their previous activity in the face of such disturbances, those who cannot help to reveal how vital this skill is to daily life.[3]

Plasticity and Habit: The Intentional Arc

Schneider, the disabled World War I veteran described by Merleau-Ponty and early twentieth-century Gestalt psychologists, represents an extreme case of lack of plasticity, insofar as his head injuries rendered him incapable of altering his mundane routines in any way, or in resuming them if they were interrupted. His only choice was to begin all over again with the first movement in the sequence in order to bring the action to completion. Merleau-Ponty claims that what Schneider has lost is an "intentional arc," a more generalized awareness of how diverse aspects of one's experience are interconnected. This intentional arc, Merleau-Ponty suggests, provides human beings with an affective sensibility that enables the integration of quite dissimilar experiences into a synthetic whole. Schneider, unlike the "normal subject,"

> can no longer put himself into a sexual situation any more than generally he occupies an affective or ideological one. Faces are for him neither attractive nor repulsive, and people appear to him in one light or another only in so far as he has direct dealings with them, and according to the attitude they adopt towards him, and the attention and solicitude which they bestow upon him. Sun and rain are neither gay nor sad; his humour is determined by elementary organic functions only, and the world is emotionally neutral. (Merleau-Ponty 1962: 157)

The intentional arc, as Merleau-Ponty describes it, subtends a person's specific intentional acts and can endow a set of diverse experiences with an affective unity that gives them a more generalized meaning.[4] Habit itself plays a vital role in linking together a series of actions that, on the surface, may seem to have very little in common except insofar as they become associated with a more generalized project, as in the case of the various activities associated with a morning routine. And while the morning routine example highlights the mechanisms at work in the formation of human beings' physical habits, James's emphasis on character in the quotes cited earlier makes it clear that an individual's habits extend to much more than such mundane matters as which side of one's teeth is brushed first. According to James, a person's choice of novels to read, places to travel, courses to take, relationships to pursue, are also either a product of or at least strongly influenced by habit. Indeed, an individual's entire character, James asserts, is constituted through the integrated functioning of his or her respective habits; on his account, then, human beings are truly "creatures of habit," and whether this constitutes an indictment or a compliment depends upon the specific nature of the habits that a given individual has cultivated over time.

The Moral Implications of Habit

Given the increasing resistance of human habits to change, morally speaking, it becomes crucial on James's account that people form "good habits" that will function automatically as their "second nature." At the same time, care must be taken to nip potentially bad habits in the bud before they can literally take root in the form of a hardened pathway in an individual's central nervous system. Rather than view the automatism that characterizes oft-repeated actions as a non-moral phenomenon precisely because it seems to bypass a person's conscious awareness, James seems to be offering us a very anti-Kantian picture of morality, one that requires volition merely as a preliminary step destined to give way to non-volitional, moral behavior.[5]

From James's distinction between good habits and bad habits and his invocation of the physiological basis of all human habits, it is clear that he understands the moral universe to be coincident with the Husserlian life-world; for James, there is no separable moral domain that would provide a basis for distinguishing from the outset between moral and non-moral actions. Indeed, his moral judgment concerning those individuals who are unable to form decisive habits of even the most mundane sort is abundantly evident in the following passage: "There is no more miserable human being than one in whom nothing is habitual but indecision, and for whom the lighting of every cigar, the drinking of every cup, the time of rising and going to bed every day, and the beginning of every bit of work, are subjects of express volitional deliberation" (James 1950: 122).

One of the most fascinating aspects of James's discussion of habit is the complex relationship he traces between the plasticity of the central nervous system, a plasticity that makes the construction of new habits or the alterations of old ones possible, and the fixity that he simultaneously attributes to human character, and to the social classes themselves. When he emphasizes plasticity, it would seem that individuals have the unlimited potential to develop new habits or revise old ones; on the other hand, when he stresses the fixity of personal likes, dislikes, and habitual routines, human beings seem as far as possible from possessing the freedom and transcendence of the Satrean for-itself and more and more like Skinnerian automatons doomed to respond to a given stimulus with a pre-programmed set of responses.

James seems to resolve the tension between plasticity and fixity by suggesting that human organisms begin their lives in the plastic state, and over time, as specific neural pathways are established and reinforced, this initial plasticity is lost and people become more set in their ways. It might seem as if James would lament this loss of flexibility, but, as the earlier quotes demonstrate, he does not. Rather, in passages that echo Plato's famous statements about the importance of raising youth properly in *The Republic*, James argues that good habits lead to good character and so human beings should seek to form good habits before they are enslaved to bad ones. Ultimately, James exhorts his readers to increase the domains of everyday life that are governed by fixed, habitual responses, not because he thinks that good habits are an end in themselves, but in order to "free" consciousness to take up more intellectual pursuits such as psychological introspection or other forms of philosophical contemplation. So, just when it seems as if the mind is no more than a bundle of habits, James suggests that these habits actually serve to free the mind to do its "own proper work" (James 1950: 122).

While there is much in the Jamesian account of habit that merits further attention, I have focused in rather broad strokes on the main features of his analysis in order to set the stage for a discussion of the ambivalence that surrounds the phenomenon of habit in more recent authors. Specifically, I would like to address in detail two quite different descriptions of habit that have been proposed by Bourdieu and Merleau-Ponty in order to see how they are both indebted to, and markedly depart from, the Jamesian model. One of the virtues of James's description of habit, as I see it, is his emphasis upon the indispensable role habit plays in a human being's daily life, shaping her character as it shapes the materiality of her world. A negative aspect of his description, on the other hand, is that while James views habit as responsible for establishing moral character, his model of neural plasticity giving way to neural fixity over time also makes it difficult to see how significant individual and social change can ever really occur once the character of the individual or of a particular social class has been firmly established.

The Intersubjective Dimensions of Habit: Bourdieu's Habitus

By turning to Bourdieu's account of habit, or, more precisely, a broader phenomenon he refers to as the *habitus*, it is possible to throw into relief the close relationships that exist between a person's own habits and the habits of others; at the same time, the problem of whether and how individuals are determined by their class-prescribed habits also becomes more pressing. While Bourdieu emphasizes the social dimensions of habit, both Merleau-Ponty and Gilles Deleuze take the bodily dimensions of habit as their point of departure. I will argue that the latters' emphasis on the body is precisely what enables an understanding of how individual and cultural innovation can occur within the context of the habitual horizons that human beings appeal to in order to make sense of their lives. I believe, moreover, that through a critical exploration of these diverse accounts of habit, one can arrive at a deeper understanding of the possibilities habit offers for extending as well as diminishing a person's grasp upon the world.

Bourdieu is well aware of the challenges that habit poses to the traditional freedom/determinism antinomy. If one argues that human beings are responsible for the habits they initially develop, as James suggests, one can uphold a sense of human freedom, but, to the extent that habits function in a largely unconscious manner and are primary determinants of human character, any freedom one might first possess seems to be greatly diminished over time. With his notion of the habitus, Bourdieu attempts to establish what he calls a "conditioned and conditional freedom" that is revealed in human beings' habitual responses to one another and to the world that they (may or may not) share.

Bourdieu describes the habitus as a system of acquired dispositions that are internalized in early childhood. These dispositions, he argues, are first and foremost tied to social class, and are transmitted through the primary agents of socialization: one's family, one's peers, and the educational system. According to Bourdieu, there is no aspect of a person's daily life that is immune to the influence of the habitus. Thus, he maintains that disparate phenomena such as the foods one enjoys, the art one appreciates, the leisure activities one pursues, as well as professional aspirations, political views, and relations with others, are all directly attributable to the specific habitus one has grown up with, whether or not a person recognizes this to be the case. Moreover, Bourdieu states:

> This infinite yet strictly limited generative capacity is difficult to understand only so long as one remains locked in the usual antinomies—which the concept of the *habitus* aims to transcend—of determinism and freedom, conditioning and creativity, consciousness and the unconscious, or the individual and society. Because the *habitus* is an infinite capacity for generating products—thoughts, perceptions, expressions and actions—whose limits are set by the historically and socially situated conditions of its production, the conditioned and conditional freedom it provides is as remote from creation of unpredictable novelty as it is from simple mechanical reproduction of the original conditioning. (Bourdieu 1990: 55)

The habitus, for Bourdieu, is infinite to the extent that it is continually expanding in response to new situations; it is at the same time limited to expressing the specific conditions of existence that define a given class in its past, present, and foreseeable future. Of course, the actual situation may turn out quite differently than a person anticipates, and the disjunction between the expectations an individual formed on the basis of her habitus and the actual situations she finds herself confronting is precisely what defines the habitus as a generative structure, that is, a structure that is capable of what Bourdieu calls "regulated improvisation," or the ability to alter existing schemes to fit new experiences.

The habitus, as Bourdieu describes it, is not an optional framework that is occasionally appealed to in one's daily existence; rather, it provides the basis for making distinctions and arriving at value judgments about the world of one's concern. As he observes, "The *habitus* is a spontaneity without consciousness or will, opposed as much to the mechanical necessity of things without history in mechanistic theories as it is to the reflexive freedom of subjects 'without inertia' in rationalist theories" (Bourdieu 1990: 56). Bourdieu often refers to the habitus as a structuring structure: it consists of a set of structural dispositions that emerge out of social experience that in turn give structure to that experience. There is no such thing as pure perception on this account, that is, perception unaffected by the habitus in which a person has been raised. "The 'eye,'" Bourdieu asserts, "is a product of history reproduced by education" (Bourdieu, 1984: 3).

More specifically, the habitus provides an individual with an internalized system of classificatory schemes through which she interprets new situations by relating them to similar situations she has experienced in the past. This evolving set of structures arising out of, and materialized in, distinctive cultural practices is governed, he suggests, by its own "logic of practice." This improvisational, open-ended logic emerges from and is in turn applied to the concrete situations one encounters. While it lacks the coherence and systematicity of a formal logic that seeks to represent those practices in accordance with the law of non-contradiction, Bourdieu maintains that it has the advantage of being better able to capture both the synchronic and the diachronic dimensions of lived experiences.

For Bourdieu, as I previously asserted, habits are themselves a function of an individual's class habitus. There are even habitual ways of rebelling against the habitus, efforts he sees as doomed to failure. Objectification of the habitus that governs one's practices is, perhaps, one possibility of obtaining some reflective distance from that habitus; however, he argues that objectification is itself a cultural practice whose theoretical distancing cannot remove a person from the habitus once and for all. In his words: "There is no way out of the game of culture; and one's only chance of objectifying the true nature of the game is to objectify as fully as possible the very operations which one is obliged to use in order to achieve that objectification" (Bourdieu 1984: 12). In his early work, *Outline of a Theory of Practice*, Bourdieu explains why this is so: "If agents are possessed by their habitus more than they possess it, this is because it acts within them as the organizing principle of their actions, and because this *modus operandi* in forming all thought and action (including thought of action) reveals itself only in the *opus operatum*" (Bourdieu 1977: 18).

Upheavals in the Habitus: Lessons of 9/11

Although in this particular passage, the habitus seems to be all-encompassing, determining human beings through and through, Bourdieu's Foucaultian emphasis on the generative dimensions of the habitus is crucial to understanding how the habitus itself can develop and change over time. As a dynamic rather than static structure, it does not continually present individuals with ready-made solutions or fixed ways of viewing a given problem. Indeed, as the events of September 11, 2001, in the United States forcibly demonstrated, unexpected events can suddenly occur that were not anticipated from within a given habitus, events that nonetheless have the power to radically affect and even transform the habitus itself.[6]

The failure of ready-made responses in the face of the large-scale devastation and loss of life that took place in both New York City and Washington, D.C., on the morning of September 11, 2001, was immediately apparent even to the politicians from whom responses were demanded. Rather than seeing this failure as an impetus for the formation of a new habitus, most public figures, starting with President George W. Bush, invoked a prior habitus, calling for the end of the current "age of cynicism" and a return to patriotism and unconditional respect for, and loyalty to, the nation. And as civil liberties that Americans have long taken for granted are being revoked on a daily basis in the name of the current "war on terrorism," it has become readily apparent that sudden changes in the habitus (e.g., airport security procedures), even when they are propelled by external events that demand immediate responses, are not always for the better.

Although the example of 9/11 reveals how events themselves can outstrip the capacity of a given habitus to formulate an adequate response to them, an over-hasty, passionate embrace of a previous, more conservative habitus (which has been a common response to challenges to dominant habitus throughout human history) provides ample caution against seeing the breakdown of one habitus as necessarily progressive. In fact, post-9/11 U.S. movement toward a less tolerant society, in which innocent people of Middle Eastern origin face public suspicion as well as the risk of being detained as potential terrorists, makes it abundantly clear why the shift from one habitus to another may make political resistance more rather than less difficult.

Sudden upheavals in the habitus undoubtedly challenge individuals', groups', and societies' abilities to maintain habitual routines. These routines themselves, no matter how mundane, take on new meaning when the very possibility of continuing to pursue them is suddenly in question. In the *New York Times*' daily biographical profiles of the victims who died on 9/11/01, which began to appear as bodies were identified and recovered in the days, weeks, and months after the event, surviving family members invoked again and again the daily habits of their lost loved ones. Whether it was a penchant for working in the garden, walking a dog, swimming in the ocean, listening to music, playing and/or coaching sports, cooking meals for family, driving in the country, working to renovate a house, calling home twice every day, cheering on a beloved team, or encouraging friends when they were down, the victims came to life for the strangers who read about them *through* the repetitive activities that they pursued day after day. Many of the surviving family members pledged that they would carry on their loved one's commitment to these habitual activities to the best of their ability, to honor the memory of who that person was and what that person valued in life.

In these profiles, I would argue, these daily habits themselves took on a higher purpose, serving as poignant reminders that it is precisely in the mundane, intersubjective dimensions of existence that the habitus is most profoundly experienced. Reading about these strangers in the days, weeks, and months after 9/11, I found myself incredibly moved by the descriptions of the simple things in life that they treasured and enjoyed. Some of the pleasures, such as the joy of seeing one's children grow up each day, I also share, and yet, throughout my reading of the profiles, I never lost sight of the fact that this was an evocation of someone else's experience, another life, not my own. In fact, it was often the descriptions of the personalities and activities I least identified with that I discovered to be most compelling.

Bourdieu's Marxist emphasis on how one's social class defines the particular habitus a person internalizes makes it clear how he would account for the emotional power of these short biographical sketches. I resonate to the habitual activities of the victims and their attachment to them, he might well argue, because I myself have enjoyed the same or similar activities and because many of the victims and I are from the same social class. However, it is difficult to see why, on this account, I would feel an equally strong (if not even stronger) emotional response to the descriptions of the victims who occupied a different habitus, for instance those people who were recent immigrants to this country, occupying blue-collar jobs and trying to make enough money to support family members back in their home countries. One way Bourdieu could make sense of this is by appealing to the habitus within which I am immersed and claiming that it prescribes the type of response I should have to others who do not share my habitus and whose situation is worse off than my own. But is this a sufficient account of what I am feeling? Should my visceral, bodily response to the biographies of these 9/11 victims be understood as primarily a function of my class status?

The Limits of the Habitus

Due to the all-encompassing role Bourdieu attributes to the habitus in an individual's life, it is difficult to see what room is left for individual expression that is not reducible to being an expression of our class habitus. This is because Bourdieu, like Marx, presupposes a tremendous degree of commonality in the experiences of different individuals who are members of the same social class. In *The Logic of Practice*, for instance, he maintains that

> [t]he practices of members of the same group or, in a differentiated society, the same class, are always more and better harmonized than the agents know or wish, because, as Leibniz again says, "following only (his) own laws," each "nonetheless agrees with the other." The habitus is precisely this immanent law, *lex insita*, inscribed in bodies by *identical histories*, which is the precondition not only for the co-ordination of practices but also for practices of co-ordination. The corrections and adjustments the agents themselves consciously carry out presuppose mastery of a common code. (Bourdieu 1990: 59, my emphasis)

If this common code is understood on the order of a Wittgensteinian language game, an evolving, yet pervasive language game that encompasses all of one's social practices, the claim that individuals ascribe similar meanings to specific cultural practices because they share a common habitus is quite compelling. What I find problematic, however, is Bourdieu's assertion that this common code is "inscribed in bodies by identical histories," for what two bodies can truly be said to possess identical histories? The supposition of identical histories not only fails to do justice to the specificity of each individual's bodily experiences, but it also leaves out of account the contingencies that give an idiosyncratic flavor to each person's social experiences as well.

Bourdieu binds the individual even more tightly to his or her habitus moreover, when he defines a person's style as "never more than a deviation in relation to the style of a period or class" (Bourdieu 1990: 60). Even the notions of intentionality and subjective experience become a function of the habitus that, in an important sense, produces them insofar as "[t]he fact of collective practice takes the place of intention and can have the effect of producing a subjective experience and a sense of institution" (Bourdieu 1990: 258). The virtue of this subsumption of individual experience and individual history into the social dispositions that comprise the habitus is that the problem of "the Other" that haunts both phenomenology and existentialism never arises; human experience is communal from the outset, and this also establishes the ground for objective apprehension of that experience because intersubjective verification is always possible. On the other hand, when Bourdieu posits that members of the same social class possess the same habitus that has been inscribed in their bodies by their identical histories, one begins to wonder if the price is far too high for a more satisfactory account of the intersubjective foundations for our experience than he claims phenomenology has hitherto provided.

The Habit Body

While Bourdieu's account of the habitus might appear to be much more open-ended than the Jamesian view of human habits and character as hardening like plaster by the time they are thirty, both men, it would seem, have difficulty explaining how radical change or spontaneous innovation can really occur either on an individual or on a societal level.[7] I argue that Merleau-Ponty's understanding of the habit body as "dilating our being in the world," that is, as expanding rather than limiting human possibilities, offers a way of accounting for the creative aspects of habit that cannot be done justice to by either James or Bourdieu. However, James's and Bourdieu's respective understandings of social class as the omnipresent horizon out of which human beings' tastes, aptitudes, and habitual proclivities emerge has the potential to deepen Merleau-Ponty's own discussion of the habit body in crucial ways.

Although Bourdieu continually refers to the primary role the body plays in the materialization of the social practices that contribute to, and are interpreted within, a given habitus, and though he often expresses the primacy of bodily experience in Merleau-Pontian terms, he fails to distinguish, as Merleau-Ponty does, the idiosyncratic ways in which individual bodies and individual gestures express a unique or personal relationship to the world. For Bourdieu, the body is first and foremost the site where the natural and the social are inextricably intertwined in an ongoing process whereby the natural is socialized and the social is naturalized. The basic schemes that differentiate human bodies from nonhuman bodies (e.g., up/down orientation) and male bodies from female bodies (e.g., genitalia and the social domination of one sex by the other) are, he acknowledges, foundational to the development of the habitus and help to bridge the divide between one social group's habitus and that of another. However, the specific properties, aptitudes, habits, and desires that are unique to a given body and that directly affect its mode of engagement with the world are understood as functions of an individual's social class; accordingly, they become meaningful, for Bourdieu, to the extent that they shed light on the latter.

Such a view, I am suggesting, seems patently inadequate in accounting for the power of the brief New York Times descriptions of the lives of the victims of 9/11. For while these condensed biographical sketches certainly reveal the profound influence of a given habitus in each individual's life, reinforcing the pervasiveness of that habitus in the process, they also highlight that particular individual's unique way of *inhabiting* that habitus (in the Proustian sense), of making it her or his own.

Moreover, James's ethical preoccupation with the notion of an individual's character (even if it is destined to become fixed like stone) seems to be quite misplaced if character is itself merely a "deviation from a social norm." The descriptions of variations among individual experiences and specific habitus that phenomenology could potentially offer, Bourdieu rejects from the outset, because he views phenomenology as a subjectivist philosophy ignorant of the social conditions that have enabled the "taken for granted" world to appear as such. Notwithstanding this indictment, I would like to show the usefulness of phenomenology for Bourdieu's project, a project that I believe is seriously flawed unless it can avoid the reduction of the individual to his or her social class. This collapse of the person into his or her social class has the unfortunate effect not only of making the individual subject disappear but also of making social class appear to be much more monolithic and stable an entity than it ever actually is. Challenging the hegemonic functioning of a particular class identification, I believe, is an important first step to challenging the hegemonic functioning of "character" on an individual level, as posited by James. Rather than focusing attention on idiosyncratic experiences or idiosyncratic ways of responding to them as a means of combating the ubiquity of the habitus and/or a fixed character, I would like to turn now to Merleau-Ponty's description of the habit body because I believe it offers a way of affirming both the individual and the communal aspects of human experience without separating them from one another or collapsing them into a single phenomenon.

Bourdieu often critiques phenomenology for limiting itself to describing that which can be rendered an intentional object of consciousness. He sees the Husserlian emphasis on the noetic/noematic relationship as inescapably subjectivist and as trapping human beings within a domain of intentionality that leads to a denial of the meaningfulness of non-intentional aspects of human experience. The habitus, Bourdieu insists, is just such a non-intentional phenomenon that is unwilled and almost never an explicit object of intentional awareness. Indeed, it is precisely the pervasiveness and improvisational character of the habitus, for Bourdieu, that makes it resistant to being grasped intentionally. However, consciousness for Husserl is itself a similarly elusive phenomenon; it is the basis for all human experience without being reducible to one or more of those experiences. And, I would argue, the body plays just such a role for Merleau-Ponty, who describes a bodily intentionality that arises out of bodily movement but does not require a person's explicit awareness. Nor does the bodily intentionality an individual exhibits mark the limit of her bodily possibilities.

Like Bourdieu and James, Merleau-Ponty affirms that habitual activities unfold without an individual's explicitly attending to them: "When I run my eyes over the text set before me, there do not occur perceptions which stir up representations, but patterns are formed as I look, and these are endowed with a typical or familiar physiognomy" (Merleau-Ponty 1962: 144). The immediacy with which these typical "patterns" are grasped by any given perceptual agent belies any appeal to the specific project of an intentional consciousness; rather, this activity is accomplished by what Merleau-Ponty calls the "body-subject." It is not consciousness, Merleau-Ponty observes, but "the body which 'understands' in the cultivation of habit" (Merleau-Ponty 1962: 144). People's habitual responses to the world of their concern, he suggests, rather than restricting the meaning and range of their experiences, actually expand them. As noted earlier, he claims that habit "expresses our power of dilating our being in the world, or changing our existence by appropriating fresh instruments" (Merleau-Ponty 1962: 143).

In contrast to this depiction of habit as a dilation of human being in the world, a view that requires further exploration, Deleuze identifies habit as a contraction, or more accurately, as a series of contractions that draw "something new from repetition—namely difference (in the first instance understood as generality)" (Deleuze 1994: 73). Habit, Deleuze maintains, "concerns not only the sensory-motor habits that we have (psychologically), but also, before these, the primary habits that we are; the thousands of passive syntheses of which we are organically composed" (Deleuze 1994: 74). Despite the striking contrast in the imagery they use to describe habit (a dilation of human being in the world for Merleau-Ponty, and a contraction for Deleuze), both Merleau-Ponty and Deleuze portray habit not as antithetical to innovation but as precisely what enables people to engage the world in new and different ways.

While Deleuze is much more comfortable with the Bourdieusian disappearance of the individual subject, he accomplishes this much differently than does Bourdieu. If the Bourdieusian subject is a particular materialization of a specific habitus, the Deleuzian subject dissolves altogether into its molecularity, the "thousands of passive syntheses of which we are organically composed." The Merleau-Pontian subject, however, while expanded by her acquisition of new bodily habits, at the same time is never reducible to them. Each of these habits offers, for Merleau-Ponty, a different way of inscribing oneself in the world and of inscribing the world in one's body. In his words: "To get used to a hat, a car or a stick is to be transplanted into them, or conversely, to incorporate them into the bulk of our own body" (Merleau-Ponty 1962: 143). Rather than a self-sufficient consciousness or even a self-contained body, Merleau-Ponty offers a view of the body as an open system of dynamic exchanges with the world, exchanges that, in their habituality, ground the body ever more firmly within the world, and, in the process, offer human beings new ways of engaging and transforming it. If a cane can become an extension of our arm, if a car can become a motor extension of our entire body, and if the typist's familiarity with the keys represents "knowledge in the hands" rather than a conscious acquisition of a particular skill, then it becomes possible to see the acquisition of habits as a primary means of establishing the *relationality* of the body-subject, that is, its process of defining itself through the reversible relationships it sustains with its world.

In response to the concerns I raised earlier about the loss of individuality and resistance that attends Bourdieu's understanding of the habitus, Merleau-Ponty's emphasis on the singularity of each and every body-subject makes it clear that each person will find her own habitual ways of negotiating and thereby extending the parameters of his or her world. The specific bodily knowledge exhibited in the blind man's use of his cane or the typist's familiarity with the keys cannot be adequately grasped through their class affiliations, though this latter may help us to understand why he uses a cane rather than another visual prosthesis or why she is a secretary rather than a corporate executive. For Merleau-Ponty, the development of habitual ways of being in the world is precisely what shows us that: "[M]y body must be apprehended not only in an experience which is itself instantaneous, peculiar to itself and complete in itself, but also in some general aspects in the light of an impersonal being" (Merleau-Ponty 1962: 82). As a specificity that possesses through its habits the power of generality, the body, according to Merleau-Ponty, "is my basic habit, the one which conditions all the others, and by means of which they are mutually comprehensible" (Merleau-Ponty 1962: 91).

Whereas Bourdieu sees an individual's immersion in her class habitus as limiting her ability to grasp it as a whole, Merleau-Ponty, like James, argues that a person's habitual responses to her world can actually provide her with the means of gaining a fresh perspective on it. "Thus," Merleau-Ponty asserts, "it is by giving up part of his spontaneity by becoming involved in the world though stable organs and pre-established circuits that man can acquire the mental and practical space which will theoretically free him from his environment and allow him to *see* it" (Merleau-Ponty 1962: 87). Habits, on this account, do not mire human beings in the world or even in a given habitus; rather, they allow, in Deleuzian terms, new syntheses to be established between the body and its world, syntheses that are passive to the extent that they don't require one's explicit awareness, but active to the extent that they express a dynamic engagement with the world. As Merleau-Ponty observes, "habit has its abode neither in thought nor in the objective body, but in the body as mediator of a world" (Merleau-Ponty 1962: 145).

Altering the Habitus: The Transformative Potential of Habit

That this world is always a social world, as Bourdieu argues, cannot be denied. However, significant changes in the habitus have implications at both the individual and the community level. Even Kant, who sees the individual's rationality and autonomy as the defining feature of her humanity, also recognizes in his political writings the crucial role the community plays in all aspects of the individual's life.[8] Although, as the events of 9/11 illustrate, the impetus for significant change in the habitus may occur from without, the form that the changes themselves take as well as their effects are always worked out on an intercorporeal level, that is, through alterations in the daily interactions between bodies as well as within one's own.

Merleau-Ponty's work highlights the importance of the specific bodily aims and projects that demarcate one person's habits from those of another. And the *New York Times* profiles remind us of how one person's absence can completely undo the habits of so many others. Indeed, one of the most powerful and unforgettable images from the media coverage of the World Trade Center towers after they were hit and before they collapsed on September 11, 2001, was of individual bodies falling to the ground after people had hurled themselves out of the windows to escape from the suffocating smoke and fire in the upper levels of the buildings. As collective witnesses to this final, horrifying exercise of individual freedom in the face of inevitable death, millions of people experienced the power of other bodies to affect their own bodies, a communication of the incommunicable.[9]

Taken together, Merleau-Ponty and Bourdieu set the stage for a deeper understanding of the complex relationship continually unfolding between the individual and the larger social community to which she belongs (or even fails to belong).[10] I've focused on habit, in particular, because I believe, with Merleau-Ponty, Bourdieu, and James, that it is at the concrete, material level of ordinary experience, experience that is defined by habit, that human beings can best assess personal and communal commitments to genuine social change. For, if James is correct that an individual's character becomes "set" like plaster by the time she is thirty, this is not the fault of the habits she has acquired, but rather is due to a failure to seize upon the possibilities those habits offer for transforming the givens of one's world.

On Corporeal Generosity

James's work on habit illustrates its power in maintaining oppressive hierarchies based on class, and, through his neurological account, he shows how habitual ways of responding to others and to one's own situation are grounded in the body. Moreover, I argue that the phenomenon of habit, as discussed by Merleau-Ponty, Bourdieu, and James, is absolutely crucial to consider if one seeks to understand why efforts to transform an oppressive status quo are so often unsuccessful, even when the parties involved realize how this status quo provides unearned privileges to some while guaranteeing a lack of access to these privileges to others. James's work, in particular, seems especially useful in this regard, despite its seeming legitimation of a classist social structure, because of his acknowledgement that corporeal plasticity is necessary to form new habits and his simultaneous acknowledgement that these very habits, once formed, have a tendency to rigidify, becoming extremely resistant to change.

The question of plasticity that James asserts is essential in forming new habits and giving up old ones has more recently been taken up by Rosalyn Diprose, though she expresses it slightly differently, namely, in terms of human beings' openness to that which is other, to the alterity that is always present within intercorporeal existence. Addressing the tension between plasticity, or what Diprose calls openness to alterity, on the one hand and rigidity, which produces what she terms ontological closure, on the other hand, Diprose argues that people's "freedom to give" themselves to and learn from others "is limited by the habits and capacities we have developed as well as those of the bodies with whom we dwell, limits guided by the social significance of the corporeality in question" (Diprose 2002: 55). According to Diprose, human responsiveness to what is radically other and the tendency to rely upon habitual modes of relating to that which is other are equally primordial, with all of the tensions that this coexistence implies. In her words: "Both openness toward the other that transforms meaning and its closure through sedimentation of imaginaries are prereflective and corporeal, both are part of the ambiguity of subjectivity, its perceptions, acts, and gestures, that have me and that I am, not by choice but by the grace of the other's alterity" (Diprose 2002: 185).

Following Friedrich Nietzsche as well as Merleau-Ponty, Diprose is much more optimistic than James that new ways of existing and of giving meaning to both individual and collective existence are possible. Nonetheless, she also acknowledges that people who have become habituated to enjoying unearned social privilege have strong incentives to resist social change: "While the possibility of being led by the flow of alterity is already there in perception and in every act and gesture, to make good this possibility would require a break with old habits, an unsettling of sedimentation, particularly by those who benefit from existing social imaginaries" (Diprose 2002: 186–187).[11]

James's work, I have shown, also poses the question of whether human beings are indeed capable of effecting such a radical "break with old habits," and he ups the ante considerably by pointing out that it is not only those who have the most to gain by retaining sedimented cultural practices who seek to preserve them but also those who have the most to lose by keeping them in place. Diprose rejects the possibility of completely liberating oneself from reigning discourses that define who one is and what place one occupies within a socially accepted hierarchy. Nonetheless, she also argues, with Nietzsche, that human beings participate, from one moment to the next, in a continuing project of self-fabrication, a temporal and temporalizing project that introduces difference into all aspects of one's existence. Drawing from several of Nietzsche's texts, Diprose steers a clear course between the Scylla of conformity (or what she often refers to, using Nietzschean terminology, as the "assumption of the same") and the Charybdis of radical individualism, a view of the autonomous individual as free from the weight of social and political traditions. Paraphrasing Nietzsche, she asserts that "[t]he history that conformity disavows is the process of incorporating new experiences and shedding the old, reconciling conflicting impulses, the ongoing process of corporeal self-fabrication, according to concepts that one has inherited and cultivated" (Diprose 2002: 27).

Diprose stresses that this "ongoing process of corporeal self-fabrication" can be undertaken only "according to concepts that one has inherited and cultivated," and yet she nonetheless maintains that individual resistance to and social transformation of sedimented structures are possible. Rejecting the Foucaultian move of locating the refusal of conformity in the failure of disciplinary mechanisms to produce docile bodies because these bodies themselves generate their own resistances to normalization, Diprose argues that the possibilities of innovation and transformation are due to the *generosity* of intercorporeal existence.

The operation of generosity, Diprose asserts, is the "irreducible production of possibilities for existence inherent in body intersubjectivity" (Diprose 2002: 57). She provides further definitions of this phenomenon in several passages. Corporeal generosity, she claims, is "the nonvolitional, intercorporeal production of identity and difference that precedes and exceeds both contractual relations between individuals and the practices of self-transformation figured in some postmodern aesthetics of the self" (Diprose 2002: 75). Later, she maintains that "the generosity of intercorporeality is where politics (the organization of society for the improvement of human survival) takes place" (Diprose 2002: 173). And, she concludes, "corporeal generosity is a writing in blood that says this body carries a trace of the other, so this body and its cultural expression are not finished, and neither you nor I have the final word" (Diprose 2002: 195). If one was to define this concept of corporeal generosity in its simplest terms, one might identify it as a fundamental openness to that which is other, to that which is different or unfamiliar. Diprose's claim, as mentioned earlier, is that this openness to alterity does not come as an a posteriori response to established patterns of relating to others (Nietzsche's "eternal recurrence of the same"); rather, she argues, following Merleau-Ponty, that my responsiveness to the alterity of the other is an ontological feature of my own intercorporeality insofar as my bodily existence is always already produced in and through the bodies of others.[12] For Merleau-Ponty, she states, "[t]his lending to and borrowing from the bodies of others is a generosity lying not just at the core of the erotic encounter but at the heart of existence itself. I am not just a singular body, because I am for-myself by being first of all with and for other lived bodies. The relation between these bodies is one of prereflective intertwining of body schemas. It is in this intertwining of flesh that Merleau-Ponty finds the ambiguity of existence" (Diprose 2002: 89).

Diprose repeatedly uses two terms to describe this ambiguity of self and other that lies at the heart of intercorporeality, namely, "system of indistinction" and the Merleau-Pontian term "syncretic sociability." A system of indistinction, she claims,

> is established between my body as I live it, my body as the other sees it, and the other's body as I perceive it. This tripartite system is one of "syncretic sociability": that is, the self is produced, maintained, and transformed through the socially mediated intercorporeal "transfer" of movements and gestures and body bits and pieces. Just as through the look and the touch of the other's body I feel my difference, it is from the same body that I borrow my habits and hence my identity without either body being reducible to the other or to itself. (Diprose 2002: 54)

This system of indistinction, she suggests, blurs the boundaries between self and others, making it impossible to establish hard and fast distinctions between others' contributions and my own contributions to the perceptual process. Thus, these indistinct corporeal connections are precisely what link human beings together in a dynamic, syncretic sociability, and, Diprose elaborates, "[i]t is by this ambiguity of intercorporeality, where alterity is maintained and existence is transformed through 'syncretic sociability,' that I affect and am affected by others, that I engage in projects and am open to possibilities" (Diprose 2002: 90).

Despite this emphasis on the power of syncretic sociability, Diprose also embraces Emmanuel Levinas's emphasis on the radical alterity of the other. For Levinas, the absolute alterity of the other establishes the profound ethical dimensions of one's encounters with the other, who can never be reduced to the self-same. Drawing from Levinas, she reveals how the alterity of the other is precisely what keeps the sedimentation of meaning from arriving at closure. According to Diprose, Levinas shows that "[i]t is the other's alterity that disturbs me, that difference in proximity generated by his or her own separation, his or her own sensibility. This alterity implies not only that the other cannot be possessed, but that her or his presence contests my possession (not just my possession of things and ideas but my self-possession). The other's strangeness, the feeling that he or she cannot be known, puts my autonomy into question" (Diprose 2002: 136).

Directly citing Levinas, Diprose insists that the absence of autonomy does not threaten my responsibility for myself and/or the other, but rather is precisely what makes these ethical obligations possible: "That responsibility in the face of the other's alterity is an obligation I cannot avoid, rests on the conviction that it is to the other's alterity, his or her teaching, that I owe/give my sensibility, interiority, and 'autonomy' in the first place" (Levinas quoted in Diprose 2002: 139). A primary virtue of Levinas's account, she argues, is his emphasis on the non-volitional or pre-reflective quality of generosity, of an individual's responsivity to the alterity of the other. In other words, "Generosity for Levinas is not a virtue belonging to a volitional subject or an excess of power that, through self-overcoming, enhances the existence of those secure in their form; generosity is the passivity of exposure to the irreducible difference of the other that both bases subjectivity in disturbed sensibility and opens that subjectivity to discourse through which cultural works are given" (Diprose 2002: 168).

Even as she builds upon a Levinasian understanding of how the alterity of the other establishes rather than vitiates my ethical obligation to that other prior to any conscious or deliberate taking up of this obligation, Diprose is also critical of Levinas's insistence on the apolitical character of the ethical domain. For Levinas, ethics, grounded in human beings' non-volitional openness to alterity, always comes before politics, which he identifies as the product of conscious reflection and judgment. Turning once again to Merleau-Ponty, Diprose argues against any attempt to distinguish sharply the ethical from the political dimensions of intercorporeality:

> This separation of politics and ontology from ethics, the said from the saying, implies that the said of language that organizes the social and constitutes our experience in common comes after and does not inform the saying that bears witness to alterity in my encounter with the other. Similarly, the separation of politics and ontology from ethics implies that the realm of the said, conceptualization, knowledge, and judgment comes after, and may be inspired and interrupted by, the affectivity or sensibility characteristic of exposure to the other, but does not inform that sensibility. (Diprose 2002: 170)

According to Diprose, then, subjectivity is always constructed through dynamic encounters between bodies as well as by means of sedimented social and political structures that help to set the terms for (often by limiting) these embodied interactions with others. In Bourdieusian terminology, the interplay between sedimentation and improvisation is constitutive of the habitus and the individuals who live within it; both sedimentation and improvisation presuppose one another because each serves as the ground for the other. Rather than viewing political life as a subsequent response to the syncretic sociability of intercorporeal existence, Diprose argues that "intercorporeality and sociability is where the political begins" (Diprose 2002: 176).

Confronted with the undeniable power of sedimented expectations for and responses to the other, Diprose paradoxically suggests in the following passage that ultimately corporeal generosity is not fully possible. In a rare moment of pessimism she writes: "Not only is corporeal generosity indeterminate and unpredictable, it is also impossible. Unconditional openness to otherness, as the analysis of the clinical encounter suggests, is impossible, given how sedimentation of corporeal style closes off possibilities for existence for both oneself and another" (Diprose 2002: 120). The dynamic interplay between sedimented ways of comporting oneself in relation to others and ethically and politically transformative ways of incorporating and responding to alterity becomes congealed here into a kind of aporia in which habitual patterns of conduct are seen as producing "ontological closure," placing into question not only "unconditional openness to otherness" but any genuine openness to otherness at all. Diprose inherits this tension between sedimentation and transformation from her own philosophical interlocutors, and, as both James's and Bourdieu's work demonstrates, it is difficult to maintain this tension without eventually privileging sedimentation in the form of habitual horizons arising out of specific sociopolitical histories that individuals continually draw upon to make sense of their lives. And yet, to see sedimentation as the enemy of generosity, as limiting people's openness to what is radically other, leads to a conflictual model of intercorporeality that is ultimately unsatisfying because it fails to do justice to Merleau-Ponty's and Diprose's own recognition that even in the most sedimented patterns of conduct, ambiguity and indeterminacy are nonetheless present, guaranteeing that the repetition of old habits will never be a complete repetition of the same.

In contrast to James's emphasis on how human habits become congealed over time, ineluctably forming a person's very character in the process, Merleau-Ponty stresses the ways in which habits allow one to incorporate aspects of the world into one's body (e.g., the typist's keys, the blind man's cane, etc.) and, through this very process, establish an individual's own bodily presence in the world. Rather than presenting transformation and sedimentation as mutually exclusive binaries of openness and closure where each presents a threat to the other, Merleau-Ponty locates innovation at the very heart of sedimentation, and his primary example of how this occurs is through language, more specifically, through the use of ready-made expressions to articulate new experiences. As both Merleau-Ponty and Diprose observe, it is the body's openness to the other, to difference, that makes both linguistic and non-linguistic innovation possible; however, it is the sedimentation of language, social, and political structures, indeed of the human situation as such, that provides the necessary context as well as the means by which acts of corporeal generosity can occur.

If corporeal generosity is to serve as more than a regulative ethical and political ideal, I would argue, then it is essential that this "irreducible production of possibilities for existence inherent in body intersubjectivity" be seen as integral to, rather than opposed by, the process of sedimentation that results in an identifiable habitus (Diprose 2002: 57). If it is indeed the case that these sedimented structures cannot be avoided or eliminated insofar as "my freedom to be open to a particular project, including a particular sexual encounter, is limited by my social history and, in the wake of this, my bodily tolerance to the present situation," then corporeal generosity appears to be impossible only if it is presented as an unconditional openness to the other that is antithetical to the very movement of sedimentation itself (Diprose 2002: 92). Yet, aren't there other ways of conceiving of openness, of innovation, originality, and improvisation, and other ways of conceiving of sedimentation, of habit, of language, of institutionalization, that go beyond oppositional dualisms, that can portray transformation and sedimentation as mutually constitutive phenomena? Diprose is right to emphasize that the process of explicitly holding oneself open to otherness takes work, but it is also the case, as both she and Merleau-Ponty well recognize, that the body's ceaseless encounters with (its own) alterity perform this very labor even when one is most apt to rest content with established patterns of relating to others.

6

Imagining the Horizon

> No more than are the sky or the earth is the horizon a collection of things
> held together, or a class name, or a logical possibility of conception, or a
> system of "potentiality of consciousness": it is a new type of being, a being
> by porosity, pregnancy, or generality, and he before whom the horizon
> opens is caught up, included within it.
> —Merleau-Ponty 1968: 148–149

> The historical movement of human life consists in the fact that it is never
> utterly bound to any one standpoint, and hence can never have a truly
> closed horizon.
> —Gadamer 1982: 271

What, exactly, is at stake, ontologically, perceptually, and politically, in depicting a horizon as closed or as open? For most people, the term "horizon" connotes first and foremost a politically neutral, perceptual phenomenon. Most
commonly it refers to the visual limit of my perception, and it is often identified
with a line that runs across the visual field separating earth from sky. Insofar as
it marks the terminus of the visual field, the perceptual horizon functions to
demarcate the visible from the invisible, that which is present and perceptible
from that which is absent and imperceptible.

In contrast to this familiar view of the horizon as providing closure to the
visual field, Husserl, Gadamer, and Merleau-Ponty emphasize the open-ended

nature of the horizon. All three depict the horizon not as the natural limit of vision but as the indispensable background against which the visible appears as such.[1] Moreover, all three philosophers stress the integral role played by the horizon in all aspects of lived experience. In Husserl's words, the horizon functions as a "zone of indeterminacy" that surrounds each and every human experience, non-visual as well as visual. Merleau-Ponty focuses on the ways in which human beings are "caught up" in the various horizons that situate their experience. As Gadamer lyrically asserts, "The horizon is . . . something into which we move and that moves with us." He reinforces the indispensability of the horizon in ordinary existence when he observes that "[w]e must always already have a horizon in order to be able to place ourselves within a situation" (Gadamer 1982: 271). Although neither Husserl, Merleau-Ponty, nor Gadamer acknowledges, much less develops, the political implications of their respective conceptions of the horizon, I would like to explore the promise of the horizon (insofar as it provides the shifting, yet omnipresent, context for a person's thoughts, perceptions, social attitudes, actions, and even values) for a liberatory praxis.[2]

In the passage cited at the outset, Merleau-Ponty maintains both that the horizon has its own particular type of being and that the person who turns toward the horizon is implicated in that horizon. If these claims are indeed true, then the task of imaging or even imagining the horizon becomes rather complicated. To perform this latter task requires that one interrogate the very nature of the horizon qua horizon and that one must do so not from a detached perspective but from the standpoint of one who is part of that horizon. To make matters even more difficult, one must remember that for Merleau-Ponty, following Husserl, there are not one but many horizons operative for any individual at any given point in time, horizons that are not separate from one another but that overlap to constitute a general framework for one's actual as well as possible experiences. And, for both Husserl and Merleau-Ponty, although many of these horizons are (or at least can be) shared, they always vary from one individual to another.

To take seriously the claim that human beings are part of the horizon that helps to constitute their situation as such requires, I will argue, that one (re)consider the relationship between self and other as it plays out in the horizonal domain of human experience. More specifically, I will suggest that "the problem of the Other" that has dogged both phenomenology and existentialism can best be addressed through an understanding of the Other not as a figure of radical alterity whom I continually confront in my experience, but as someone with whom I am always already engaged on the horizons of each and every one of my experiences.

Shared Horizons

Insofar as the phenomena one encounters in the world are never experienced in isolation, focusing in on any one phenomenon leads inevitably to an exploration of how it is elaborated with respect to other, related phenomena. These are not separate inquiries, moreover, but mutually inform one another. Merleau-Ponty eloquently describes this process as follows:

> In "working over" a favorite problem, even if it is just the problem of velvet or wool, the true painter unknowingly upsets the givens of all the other problems. His quest is total even where it looks partial. Just when he has reached proficiency in some area, he finds that he has reopened another one where everything he said before must be said again in a different way. The upshot is that what he has found he does not yet have. It remains to be sought out; the discovery itself calls forth still further quests. (Merleau-Ponty 1964b: 189)

On Merleau-Ponty's account, the painter expresses the reversible or chiasmatic relationship between visibility and invisibility that characterizes his visual experience on canvas, thereby enabling individual viewers to recognize explicitly how these relationships structure everyday perceptual experience. A primary way in which a viewer participates in the painter's vision, I would argue, is by opening herself up to the horizons indicated in and through the painting. To the extent that she feels herself to be implicated in these horizons, she could be said, perhaps, to have traversed the invisible boundaries that separate her own experience from the experience of others.

Although Merleau-Ponty does not invoke Husserl in this essay, I believe that Husserl's notion of the empathy horizon is particularly appropriate in addressing the intersubjective dimensions of the viewer's and the painter's experience. For Husserl, the fact that human beings live in a world with others means "that even what is straightforwardly perceptual is communalized" (Husserl 1970: 163). Not only do people tend to revise their own perceptions as they attain new perspectives on a given object, but, as Husserl observes, the communalization of perceptual experience guarantees that "there constantly occurs an alteration of validity through reciprocal correction" (Husserl 1970: 163). On his account, each perceiver has, on the one hand, an "original perceptual field opened up through free activity, which leads to ever new perceptual fields . . . within a horizon that can be preindicated through a combination of the determinate and the indeterminate" and, on the other hand, a "horizon of empathy, that of [our] cosubjects, which can be opened up through direct and indirect commerce with the chain of others, who are all others for one another" (Husserl 1970: 255). According to Husserl, it is this latter, empathy horizon, elusive as it is to straightforward analysis, that makes the process of reciprocal correction he describes possible. However, the *coexistence* of an original perceptual field with a broader, empathy horizon makes it impossible to distinguish sharply between individual and communal experiences. Indeed, Husserl asserts that "at the same time . . . within the vitally flowing intentionality in which the life of an ego-subject consists, every other ego is already intentionally implied in advance by way of empathy and the empathy-horizon" (Husserl 1970: 255).

In these descriptions of the empathy horizon, the "otherness" of the Other appears to be radically diminished. Although Husserl continues to maintain a distinction between an individual horizon and an empathy horizon, it becomes less and less clear how these two horizons are to be demarcated from one another. Indeed, the independence of the transcendental ego seems to give way to a subject whose own intentionality is intertwined through and through with the intentionality of others. From the standpoint of what Husserl calls the phenomenological epoché, the process whereby one provides a "pure description" of a given experience without relying upon taken-for-granted assumptions about that experience, these interconnected intentionalities are portrayed as follows: "What remains, now, is not a multiplicity of separated souls, each reduced to its pure interiority, but rather . . . a sole psychic framework, a total framework of all souls, which are united not externally but internally, namely, through the intentional interpenetration [*Ineinander*] which is the communalization of their lives" (Husserl 1970: 255). Although this unified framework that is provided by the empathy horizon breaks down distinctions between one individual and another, I would argue that the very notion of empathy preserves such a distinction. For to experience empathy requires a simultaneous acknowledgement that the other is different from myself (that is, I do not coincide with the other, I empathize with her) but it also implies that there is a way of bridging the gap between the other's perspective and my own.[3]

Despite the ambiguities in Husserl's account of the empathy horizon and the role it plays in the life of each individual, it is clear that his whole account not only of intersubjectivity, but also of subjectivity, depends upon it. For Husserl, what the empathy horizon accomplishes, above all, is the possibility of achieving intersubjective unity in human experience. Perhaps a bit too optimistically, he asserts that, on the basis of the empathy horizon, an "intersubjective harmony of validity occurs, [establishing what is] 'normal' in respect to particular details." Husserl recognizes that "intersubjective discrepancies show themselves often enough," but nonetheless maintains that these discrepancies do not preclude the establishment of an intersubjective unity of experience (Husserl 1970: 163).

In keeping with the title of this chapter, I want to pause at this point, to interrogate further this image of a harmonious, intersubjective experience based upon a shared empathy horizon that Husserl has so eloquently described. In particular, I want to question whether the discrepancies that Husserl acknowledges can arise out of the empathy horizon really do always give way to the intersubjective harmony that, on his account, provides human beings with a sense of inhabiting one and the same world.

To pursue this inquiry, I would like to consider some examples in which the intersubjective discrepancies Husserl mentions above can be understood only if they are seen as emerging from different horizons, horizons that are indeed shared by some, but certainly not by all. If these discrepancies can and often do threaten the intersubjective unity of ordinary experience, then this may mean that rather than inhabiting a single world, or possessing a communal world-consciousness to use Husserl's language, there are limits to empathy that, whether they are self-imposed or socially imposed, lead to the establishment of different (and perhaps even radically incommensurable) worlds.

Horizons of Discourse

The essays contained in Robert Gooding-Williams's edited volume, *Reading Rodney King/Reading Urban Uprising*, offer a series of interpretations of the interpretations made by the police officers, the Simi Valley jury, the black community in South Central Los Angeles, the neighboring Korean American community, and the general public in the aftermath of what has come to be known as "the Rodney King incident." "The Rodney King incident," which took place in 1991, is not restricted to the beating of Rodney King that was captured on videotape and rapidly circulated throughout the world, but also extends to the rioting and destruction that followed the verdict and to the subsequent police officers' trial.[4]

Although the word "incident" suggests a discrete event and therefore may seem to be somewhat of a misnomer in this case, the word still seems to be appropriate insofar as it expresses a definitive experience that has left an indelible mark in the history of race relations in the United States. Like other well-known episodes in recent American history (e.g., Jim Crow laws, the assassination of Martin Luther King Jr., state and federal court rejections of affirmative action policies for college and graduate school admissions in California and Texas, etc.), for better or worse, the Rodney King incident has become part of the historical horizon that grounds a collective American racial consciousness in the early twenty-first century.[5]

In "Endangered/Endangering: Schematic Racism and White Paranoia," Judith Butler argues that the Simi Valley jurors were able to corroborate the policemen's interpretation of the events that transpired on the videotape (specifically the interpretation that Rodney King was and remained a threat to the police before and during his beating) because the video was reproduced for them "within a racially saturated field of visibility" (Butler 1993b: 15). Before discussing her position further, I would first like to examine this expression more closely. The expression "field of visibility" is straightforward enough. It refers to the Gestalt notion of the perceptual field that is organized in reference to a figure perceived against a ground. More specifically, one might understand this field of visibility to consist primarily of those possible objects of perception to which a person is not currently attending but which form part of the background of that individual's current perception (e.g., the objects behind, above, below, or beside the object one is focusing on).

Strikingly, Butler's claim that the field of visibility for the Simi Valley jurors is "racially saturated" seems to refer to an invisible quality of an already indeterminate horizon. For if the field of visibility is indeed racially *saturated*, this means that its racial structure cannot easily be discerned because it is inseparable from the field of visibility itself. And any objects discerned within that field will be discerned through a racially saturated horizon of significance, a horizon that will situate any and all interpretations that arise from it. Alcoff reinforces these points in the following passage from *Visible Identities*, stressing that it is not only the other but also myself who I come to know through a racialized horizon whose very ubiquitousness renders its influence difficult to assess:

> If race is a structure of contemporary perception, then it helps constitute the necessary background from which I know myself. It makes up a part of what appears to me as the natural setting of all my thoughts. It is the field, rather than that which stands out. The perceptual practices involved in racializations are then tacit, almost hidden from view, and thus almost immune from critical reflection. (Alcoff 2006: 188)

The question Butler asks is whether the existence of such a racially saturated field of visibility already privileges racist interpretations. That is, "[i]f racism pervades white perception, structuring what can and cannot appear within the horizon of white perception, then to what extent does it interpret in advance 'visual evidence'? And how, then, does such 'evidence' have to be read, and read publicly, *against* the racist disposition of the visible which will prepare and achieve its own inverted perceptions under the rubric of 'what is seen?'" (Butler 1993b: 15–16). Butler's second question raises the possibility of an alternative, antiracist reading of the Rodney King videotape, one that depends upon an almost invisible shift in this passage from a racially *saturated* field of visibility, in which racist interpretations seem to be almost inevitable, to a racial *disposition* of the visible, which can be "read against the grain" to produce antiracist, counter-hegemonic readings. Aggrandizing the tensions between racist and antiracist interpretations of the King videotape, by reinvoking the notion of a saturated visual field as a constitutive horizon for both readings, Butler claims that these conflicting interpretations produce "a contest within the visual field, a crisis in the certainty of what is visible, one that is produced *through* the saturation and schematization of that field with the inverted projections of white paranoia" (Butler 1993b: 16, my emphasis).

To "win" this contest, Butler suggests that an antiracist reading of the Rodney King videotape must be aggressively promulgated in order to counter the violence and aggressivity of the racist reading. For, she notes, "if the field of the visible is a racially contested terrain, it will be politically imperative to read such videos aggressively, to repeat and publicize such readings, if only to further an antiracist hegemony over the visual field" (Butler 1993b: 17). This "eye for an eye" strategy, however, leaves the reader with two alternative readings whose respective legitimacy seems to rest on little more than whose reading is more violently proclaimed and aggressively established. And, given the current climate in United States racial politics, it would seem that the racist reading would have a distinct advantage in this regard. Another difficulty with this strategy, which reminds me a bit of a shouting match in which whoever shouts loudest dominates the auditory field, is that the two opponents both seem to be competing for complete control over the "correct" interpretation; both are striving for, in Butler's own words, "hegemony over the visual field," a hegemony, it should be noted, that is not restricted to the visual field or even the perceptual field, but extends to the linguistic, cultural, and political domains as well.

Although Butler's strategy of countering a racist hegemony with an antiracist hegemony may be rhetorically and politically effective, I think it is also extremely problematic. I would like to introduce my specific objections to it through asking the following questions: Is aggressivity either necessary or sufficient to promote the viability of alternative readings to the Rodney King incident, and to other equally disturbing events in recent and past U.S. history? And if it is, then is there a way of distinguishing the violence and aggressivity deployed in the antiracist reading from the violence and aggressivity that inheres in the racist one? Last, but not least, is it politically or even philosophically desirable to claim that the goal of the antiracist reading should be to achieve "hegemony" over the visual field (or whatever field is in question)?

The dilemma that motivates Butler's analysis of the Rodney King incident is one that must be grappled with by anyone who adopts a deconstructionist model in which appeals to an extra-discursive truth to adjudicate disputes among interpretations are ruled out from the start. Indeed, in the following passage, Butler challenges the very distinction between "seeing" and "reading," and, in so doing, she rejects any basis for demarcating a direct perceptual truth from "mere" interpretation. Although the Simi Valley jurors were allowed to view the videotape of Rodney King's beating over and over again with their own eyes, Butler argues that "[t]his is a seeing which is a reading, that is, a *contestable* construal, but one which nevertheless passes itself off as 'seeing,' a reading which became for that white community, and for countless others, the same as seeing" (Butler 1993b: 16).

If this seeing is indeed indistinguishable from reading, as Butler suggests, then this means not only that this particular seeing/reading is always contestable, as is true of all interpretations, but also that no straightforward appeal to visual "evidence" will suffice to counter the jurors' interpretation of the video. The dilemma, then, is to determine a basis for privileging one interpretation over another. On what grounds, for instance, can Butler insist on the legitimacy of the antiracist reading of the King videotape over the racist one? Given her own account of seeing as reading, as I have noted, any appeal to the "true facts" of the matter has to be ruled out. To complicate matters further, even to identify these two possible readings as such seems to imply that one is not locked into either of them, and yet, if it is indeed impossible to occupy an extra-discursive position, then it is not clear where the power to name and critique these readings comes from.

One possible strategy that Butler does not employ is to argue that the racist and antiracist readings emerge from different horizons, for instance, one that is racially saturated and one that is not. Then the issue of which interpretation is more accurate could potentially be resolved in terms of which horizon is more appropriate for situating the particular events witnessed on the videotape. However, one would still have to determine which horizon provides the best context for the videotape, and one can do this only from the standpoint of yet another horizon; that is, one cannot appeal to extra-discursive criteria to adjudicate between the respective horizons of significance.[6]

Butler suggests that both the racist and the antiracist readings of the Rodney King videotape emerge out of the same field, a field that is organized "with the inverted projections of white paranoia." How, one might ask, can such divergent readings arise out of the same field? Or, as Alcoff might put it, how is it possible to *see* differently? In another essay from the same collection, entitled "Reel Time/Real Justice," Kimberlé Crenshaw and Gary Peller claim that the jurors' reading of the Rodney King videotape was facilitated by the defense strategy of breaking down the eighty-one-second videotape frame by frame for the court. Instead of the jurors viewing a fast-paced sequence of actions and reactions by the police officers and King, "[e]ach micromoment of the beating of King was broken down into a series of frozen images" (Crenshaw and Peller 1993: 58). And, Crenshaw and Peller argue,

[o]nce the video was broken up like this, each still picture could then be re-weaved into a different narrative about the restraint of King, one in which each blow to King represented, not beating one of the "gorillas in the mist," but a police-approved technique of restraint complete with technical names for each baton strike (or "stroke"). The videotape images were *physically* medi-

ated by the illustration board upon which the still pictures were mounted, and in the same moment of *disaggregation*, they were *symbolically* mediated by the new narrative backdrops of the technical discourse of institutional security and the reframing of King as a threat rather than a victim. (Crenshaw and Peller 1993: 59)

According to Crenshaw and Peller, the jurors' reading of Rodney King as a threat to the police was due primarily to the decontextualization or, in their words, disaggregation of the temporally and spatially contiguous events depicted on the videotape into a set of framed stills. I would argue that one could also describe this process of disaggregation as an attempt to dismantle the unity that ordinarily characterizes the figure/ground relationship. In this particular case, the ground was quite literally detached from the figure and was replaced with a new, allegedly neutral, backdrop, the white poster board.

Replacing the flowing sequence of events captured on videotape with the static poster board backdrop could, to use Gadamer's language, be seen as an attempt to fix or "close" the horizon of significance that the jurors brought to bear on the case. This freeze-frame technique functions to interrupt what Henri Bergson terms the *durée* of human existence, that is, its continual flowing through time. For Bergson, Husserl, Merleau-Ponty, and Gadamer, such a static picture can never yield a living reality but only an artificial and distorted reconstruction of it.[7]

It is also noteworthy that a *white* backdrop was chosen to re-present the events depicted on the videotape. In *Racism, Sexism, Power and Ideology*, Colette Guillaumin discusses the way in which whiteness functions as the unmarked dominant category against which all that is non-white appears as other, as different. Although she is referring to skin color in her discussion, the impact of this hierarchization of color is taken a step further by Frantz Fanon, in *Black Skin White Masks*. More specifically, Fanon talks about the tendency in children's literature to associate the evil character with darkness and ugliness (e.g., "black as sin") and the virtuous hero with light and beauty (e.g., "pure as the driven snow"). In the context of children's literature, then, a direct connection is subtly established between color and moral character, a connection that supports whiteness as both aesthetically and morally superior to blackness.[8]

In the context of these observations, the alleged neutrality of the white poster board must itself be called into question, given that the color of the poster itself can function tacitly to reinforce a racist reading of the videotape. How, for instance, might a black poster board have influenced the interpretation the jurors made of the individual frames?[9] To what extent did the white poster board help to "whitewash" the events portrayed; that is, did it also play a subtle role in legitimizing the white police officers' version of their conduct toward a defenseless black man?[10]

As Crenshaw and Peller note, the still images from the videotape received not only a new visual context but a new narrative context as well. The "technical discourse of institutional security" deployed by the defense team's witnesses symbolically mediated the reception of those reframed images by the jurors and helped to shape the meaning of what they "saw." This decontextualization and recontextualization Crenshaw and Peller describe helps to reveal the high political stakes involved in promoting one particular reading over another. Indeed, I would argue that the deliberate contestation and manipulation of the ground to produce a certain figure (e.g., Rodney King as threat rather than victim), and ultimately to produce a specific set of meanings, powerfully demonstrates the constitutive role the ground plays in defining what comes to be viewed as ordinary reality.

The successfulness of this defense strategy, however, and the acquittal that resulted from it, still came as a shock to many Americans (and to many people who were following the case from abroad). Indeed, the reverberations of that verdict are still being felt in the United States today.[11] If the jurors saw a radically altered version of the events that occurred in South Central Los Angeles that fateful night in 1991, though, why were they faulted for acquitting the police officers on the basis of that reading? For most Americans who deplored the acquittal of the police officers also blamed the Simi Valley jurors for accepting the interpretation of the events that the defense presented to them. The blame heaped upon the jurors for their reading is not so surprising, however, if we remember that for Husserl as well as for Merleau-Ponty, the horizon never *determines* the meaning of the figure, but plays a structuring role in its presentation and articulation. To the extent that the jurors seem to have accepted uncritically a particular interpretation that could not be sustained except through the artificial decontextualization and recontextualization performed by the defense team, the jurors reinforced the hegemony of the racist reading.

If an antiracist reading is possible on the basis of a racially saturated field of the visible, this must be accomplished through a subversive appropriation of this racially organized horizon, one that requires, I would argue, much like the example of the painter for Merleau-Ponty, an awareness of the horizon and the structuring role it plays in everyday perception so that one can render it visible to/for others. By rendering the horizon visible, as Butler and Crenshaw and Peller attempt to do in their essays, one also transforms the horizon itself, making it the critical figure rather than the uncritical ground of one's discourse. Such an enterprise is a risky one, for it generates a whole host of questions. First, are there other aspects of the horizon that one can lose sight of if it is characterized as racially saturated? Isn't the horizon structured by other schematizations aside from racial ones? How might a description of this racially saturated horizon differ if one considers how race always intersects with gender, sexuality, age, class, ability, ethnicity, and nationality? Mustn't one therefore consider the role they *collectively* play in the construction of the visible field to provide an adequate account of the interpretive process? Last, but not least, if this complex horizon is rendered visible, then what new horizons will arise to take its place?

The Limits of Empathy

In her essay "The Problem of Speaking for Others," Alcoff poignantly addresses the issue of what happens when horizons are not shared. Rather than being worried about how a lack of shared horizons can lead to major disagreements in interpretation, such as the racist versus antiracist readings of the Rodney King videotape, Alcoff interrogates the limits of the empathy horizon itself and leads us to question whether any two individuals can and do share the same horizon(s).

As the starting point for her critical analysis, Alcoff considers the possibility that one well-intentioned, empathetic person who decides to speak for a less enfranchised other may, in fact, be led to misrepresent, and therefore fail to do justice to, the interests of that other. This is because the empathetic individual may focus too much on the common ground she shares with the other (the "communalization of their lives" as Husserl puts it) thereby overlooking important differences in the horizons that situate their respective discourses. For Alcoff, it is crucial that both the speaker and those who are spoken for be attuned to the different contexts that distinguish their experiences. Failure to attend sufficiently to the differences between the contexts out of which the speaker's and the spoken-for's voices have emerged (or failed to emerge) can result in misunderstanding and serious misinterpretations. Moreover, because in everyday discourse people often tend to focus on what is said to the exclusion of how and why it is said, the very act of speaking for others has a performative force that can dissuade inquiry into whether the one who is speaking and those who are spoken for share a sufficiently common ground.

Alcoff identifies four "premises" or considerations that a speaker (and I would argue, the listeners as well as those spoken for) must remain cognizant of before, during, and after she speaks. These are: (1) the impetus or motivation for speaking; (2) the location and context for the discourse; (3) the speaker's accountability and responsibility for what she says; (4) the effect the words have on the "discursive and material context" (Alcoff 1991: 24–26). These considerations themselves span the past, present, and future, and together can be seen as requiring the speaker to address those ordinarily invisible features of her discourse that produce visible effects on those about whom and to whom she speaks. The conclusion Alcoff draws from these four premises is that one must try to resist an immediate temptation to speak for others who are less enfranchised than oneself because of the danger of misrepresenting their interests due to one's own interpretation of what those interests are and how they can best be addressed. However, she also argues that individuals cannot always refrain from speaking for others, either, because doing so can lead to an equally problematic abdication of one's responsibility to aid them in improving their situation.

Avoiding the false dilemma of what Alcoff terms, on the one hand, the "reductionist response," which maintains that the differences between the speaker's and the spoken-for's location either automatically validates or automatically nullifies the validity of the speaker's utterance, or, on the other hand, the "retreat response," which maintains that it is better not to attempt to speak at all than to risk doing so inappropriately, she argues that while location itself is epistemically salient, it does not determine meaning and truth. According to Alcoff, "[l]ocation and positionality should not be conceived as one-dimensional or static, but as multiple and with varying degrees of mobility" (Alcoff 1991: 16). Despite the undeniable importance of location in assessing where the speaker and the spoken-for are coming from, she cautions against weighing location too heavily in ascertaining the significance of what is said: "To the extent that location is not a fixed essence, and to the extent that there is an uneasy, undetermined, and contested relationship between location on the one hand and meaning and truth on the other, we cannot reduce the evaluation of meaning and truth to a simple identification of the speaker's location" (Alcoff 1991: 17).

Insofar as Alcoff understands the term "location" to refer to a speaker's social location and not just her physical location, the expression seems quite close to the notion of the horizon as I have been using it here and as Alcoff later uses it in *Visible Identities*. Understanding location in this way leads one to the conclusion that while it is necessary to interrogate differences between the horizons that situate both the speaker's and the spoken-for's discourse, this does not mean that such an investigation will lead one to a final meaning or truth. It may lead one to the conclusion that these horizons are so radically different that one should not attempt to speak for others, or it may lead to a recognition of shared horizons that will provide a common ground for one's discourse. In either case, rendering these horizons visible, despite the pain this effort may entail, is a necessary first step to bridging what may initially appear to be the radical otherness of the other, and hence a necessary first step in building a successful political coalition.

How might one image these structuring horizons, both one's own and those of others? Or, in Merleau-Pontian terms, how can one render visible the invisible ground that makes the visible figure perceptible? Maria Lugones provides one possible strategy, one that she calls, in a well-known essay, *"world"-traveling*. Although Lugones never makes this claim, I would argue that the idea of world-traveling is closely related to Husserl's notion of the empathy-horizon. Both are ways of negotiating the boundaries that separate self and other through opening oneself up to the structural framework that undergirds the experiences of the other. Lugones, however, is more specific than Husserl about what this might entail. Most notably, Lugones focuses on the political implications of world-traveling by concentrating on issues such as who is expected to empathize/relate to whom, for what purposes, and with what consequences.

Lugones maintains that traditionally, world-traveling has not been equally practiced by those who are comfortably within the mainstream of society and those who exist on its margins. That is, the kind of empathetic experience involved in world-traveling is not a natural feature of intersubjective human existence as Husserl has suggested. Rather, Lugones maintains that it, in the United States, is the "outsiders" to mainstream white/Anglo culture who have, as a survival strategy, been expected to become familiar with and accommodate themselves to the interpretations of the mainstream. According to Lugones, "the outsider has necessarily acquired flexibility in shifting from the mainstream construction of life where she is constructed as an outsider to other constructions of life where she is more or less 'at home.' This flexibility is necessary for the outsider but it can also be willfully exercised by the outsider or by those who are at ease in the mainstream" (Lugones 1990: 159).

For Lugones, world-traveling can and should be a "willful exercise" rather than a matter of necessity. It requires, as she notes above, *flexibility* in shifting from a given perspective to another, equally possible one. Doing so, forces one to acknowledge that other interpretations of a particular situation can be just as efficacious as one's own. Most importantly, Lugones suggests that world-traveling provides an indispensable means of relating successfully to others whose interests, needs, and desires are radically different than one's own. She advocates that this become a more reciprocal process than it has been to date. Rather than continuing to expect "outsiders" or, to use bell hooks's language, those on the margins, to travel to the often hostile world of the "center," a world that they are expected to "master" without ever being accepted within it, a similar effort must be made on the part of those in the center to occupy the standpoint of those on the margin. If, Lugones maintains, world-traveling can move from being a compulsory activity practiced by those on the margins to a willful, loving way of bridging the gaps between one individual and another, the "skillful, creative, rich," and "enriching" aspects of this process can be affirmed and celebrated.

Although this is an appealing picture, I believe that Lugones, like Husserl in his discussion of the intersubjective harmony of our communal experience, is too optimistic regarding the benefits of world-traveling. A major difficulty with

Lugones's account, I would argue, is that her description of this process is too one-sided. This is because in her examples only one individual engages in this travel, while the other seems to stay right where she is. One danger of this is that, as Gadamer observes, "[b]y including from the beginning the other person's standpoint in what he is saying to us, we are making our own standpoint safely unattainable" (Gadamer 1982: 270).

In the primary, autobiographical example Lugones uses, namely her relationship with her mother, Lugones's youth, educational level, professional status, and familiarity with English and with "Anglo life" create tensions between her and her mother and make her the more enfranchised of the two. Given these differences in their respective horizons, Lugones feels that it is incumbent upon her to engage in world-traveling in order to relearn to love and accept her mother even while she chooses another path. In Lugones's words:

> I was disturbed by my not wanting to be what she was. I had a sense of not being quite integrated, my self was missing because I could not identify with her, I could not see myself in her, I could not welcome her world. I saw myself as separate from her, a different sort of being, not quite of the same species. This separation, this lack of love, I saw, and I think that I saw correctly as a lack in myself (not a fault, but a lack). (Lugones 1990: 164)

Although Lugones implies that her world-traveling was successful in forging a new, closer relationship between mother and daughter, it is not clear that her mother ever made any effort to travel to her daughter's world in order to come to understand her daughter better. Seemingly acknowledging the problems associated with such a one-sided understanding of the other, Lugones maintains that "[o]nly when we have travelled to each other's 'worlds' are we fully subjects to each other" (Lugones 1990: 178).

To the extent that her mother does not attempt a corresponding journey to Lugones's world, there is a real possibility, as Alcoff shows us, that the daughter's well-meaning efforts to understand her mother will be viewed by her mother (and by others) as patronizing. Instead of viewing world-traveling as a means of identifying with the other that enables us to "understand *what it is to be them and what it is to be ourselves in their eyes,*" as Lugones argues, one may, following Alcoff, conclude from failed attempts to speak for the other that one is *not* the other and that perhaps one may never succeed in seeing oneself through the other's eyes (Lugones 1990: 178).

Despite these weaknesses in her account, Lugones's insight that this process requires flexibility and new ways of "seeing" is invaluable in addressing the issue of how one can break out of hegemonic frameworks that restrict the possibilities for non-hegemonic interpretations. More recently, in *Crip Theory: Cultural Signs of Queerness and Disability*, Robert McRuer argues that the process of opposing oppressive hegemonic perspectives requires more flexible *bodies*, for instance, "gay bodies that no longer mark absolute deviance, heterosexual bodies that are newly on display" (McRuer 2006: 12). Indeed, one might even say that the Simi Valley jurors' inflexible adherence to their own racially saturated horizons (which are geared toward the protection of the dominant white body) helped to guarantee the success of the racist presentation of Rodney King as a threat rather than a victim. On the other hand, McRuer also emphasizes that there is a high market demand for "flexible bodies" who can re-form their desires so that they match the new commodities being offered. Thus, it is important not to be too hasty in celebrating the notion of a flexible body because these are precisely the types of bodies that provide the ideal model for exploitation in the name of capitalist consumption.

Toward a Politics of the Horizon

If an antiracist reading is able to emerge from a "racially saturated field of the visible," such a reading must be capable of transforming not just the figure of the discourse, but the very terms of the discourse itself. If an individual is able to speak legitimately for others who are less enfranchised than herself, without misrepresenting their interests and/or taking away from them their voices and ability to be heard, then, I am arguing, she must become more attuned to the horizons that *differentiate* their experiences from her own, and the empathy-horizon can provide a crucial resource to accomplish this goal.

What I am calling for here is a way of rendering more visible the unthematized framework of both prevailing and historical discourses regarding the other, a "politics of the horizon" if you will, that will restore the dynamic interdependency between figure and ground so that any aspect of the ground can truly be imagined as the figure, or primary focus, of individual and collective concern. Thus, I am suggesting that rather than keeping one's focus exclusively on the figure, the primary event that demands one's attention, such as a particular racist act (e.g., the beating of Rodney King), it is necessary to become more attuned to the less visible, structuring role played by the ground. Moreover, in attending to the ground, to use Merleau-Ponty's words, one can then draw upon the latter's own porosity, its pregnancy, and its generality to open up new ways of seeing. For, I would argue, only if one draws upon the intersubjective richness of the ground out of which the figure has emerged will it be possible to produce new, genuinely shared horizons, horizons that can help to alter the fixity of established discourses about oneself and others.

PART 4

Urban Perspectives

7
City Limits

The broad expanse of the horizon strikingly revealed through an ocean sunset or across large flat plains can give the seer a sense of the horizon as a limit without limit, a condition of infinite possibility. Unless one lives at the ocean's edge, or out in the country, however, these experiences of the horizon tend to be occasional, especially for the millions of people who dwell in cities. While the internet has made such expansive images of the landscape widely and freely available (indeed they often take on a new life as computer screen-savers), many people's daily experience of a spatial horizon is more likely to be the compressed and fragmented horizon that limns the city's own urban fabric, as seen while walking past building after building down a busy street or through an office window.[1] And yet, the romantic image of the ocean sunset persists, capable of displacing the more frequent encounter with radically shifting horizons that urban workers and city dwellers actually experience on a daily basis as they navigate their everyday environment.[2]

In the following pages, I would like to reflect on how the spatial horizon of the city intersects with overlapping horizons of race, class, and gender, those horizons that Husserl, Merleau-Ponty, and the philosophical tradition more generally have not discussed but that I claim are as real as the visual horizon itself. Thanks to the recent work of critical race theorists such as Patricia Hill Collins, bell hooks, Linda Martín Alcoff, Robert Gooding-Williams, David

Theo Goldberg, Robert Bernasconi, and so many others, these horizons are becoming increasingly visible, leading to a growing recognition of their omnipresent, yet shifting influence throughout human experience. Unlike the visual horizon, the impact of these other horizons is less frequently seen but almost always felt. As Simone de Beauvoir observes in her autobiographical journal, *America Day by Day*, and as Toni Morrison poignantly reveals in so many of her novels, the hatred of those deemed to be inferior by virtue of their skin color can be inhaled in the air, breathed in like poison.[3]

Many of the essays in *Reading Rodney King/Reading Urban Uprising* focus explicitly on how people's perceptions of not only Rodney King himself but even the city's horizons are constructed in accordance with racist, sexist, and classist visions. Indeed, I would argue, it is only through the exclusionary logic that is shared by these mutually reinforcing horizons that South Central Los Angeles, with all of its tensions, can be perceived as completely isolated from the rest of the city, a separate world if you will.[4] To support this claim, I will focus on how the city's limits are differentially experienced according to one's sexual, racial, and class privileges, leading to more constrained horizons for those city dwellers who lack such privileges altogether.

Earlier I have argued, following Butler, that seeing is never neutral; interpretation is always going on from one moment to the next in one's everyday existence, and this interpretation takes place not in a vacuum but rather in a culturally saturated context that schematically structures how and what is seen. To understand both what is seen and what is not seen requires that one focus on not only *what* one is seeing but also *how* one sees. And, I suggest, it is only once one becomes more aware of how one sees that one can begin to develop new ways of seeing, thereby disrupting the sedimented patterns that come to typify ordinary experience. For, as Alcoff so poignantly asserts in elaborating a phenomenology of racial embodiment, "[o]nly when we come to be very clear about how race is lived, in its multiple manifestations, only when we can come to appreciate its often hidden epistemic effects and its power over collective imaginations of public space, can we entertain even the remote possibility of an eventual transformation" (Alcoff 2001: 267). The question of exactly how, when, and where to accomplish such a transformation of the "collective imaginations of public space" is, I maintain, contra Irigaray (who focuses on the lack of an adequate understanding of sexual difference as foundational for addressing all other social and political issues), one of the most pressing questions of our time.[5]

Gadamer's notion of a fusion of horizons can be a useful way to conceptualize the overlapping relationships among race, class, and gender if one understands fusion to mean an indissoluble connection among horizons rather than the collapse of one horizon into another. Confident in the possibility of establishing such a fusion across time and space, and even seeing this latter as the very condition whereby history becomes possible, Gadamer argues in *Truth and Method* that bridges can be created across the inevitable differences in cultural horizons that distinguish the experiences of different people living in different places at different times. I would like to explore the power of literature to enact this fusion of horizons between people, to show the connections as well as the disconnections and even ruptures that arise when fusion can not be accomplished.[6] Ultimately, a fusion of horizons is possible, I argue, only because race, class, gender, and other differences are always already interconnected, incarnated, and interwoven in human beings' bodies, in their blood, indeed in their DNA. As this blood gets spilled on city streets, as living bodies are transformed into abandoned corpses that erupt violently within the urban landscape, the city's limits are materialized in one's own flesh, and the urgency, as well as the difficulty, of eliminating oppression becomes more and more evident.

Dead-End Streets

> No one cries when a street dies.
> —Naylor 1982: 191

What does it mean for a street to die? In Gloria Naylor's novel *The Women of Brewster Place*, the manmade wall that separates Brewster Place from the rest of the city turns a once prosperous thoroughfare into a ghetto for African American men and women who have not given up hope that life offers more than is visible on their own dead-end street. In the midst of their experiences of poverty, illness, sexism, alcoholism, racism, homophobia, and drug abuse, the women of Brewster Place cling tenaciously to the relationships that make life meaningful. Despite their best collective efforts, however, Brewster Place does die, and the community established within it is forever dispersed, distributed across other, equally undesirable parts of the city. The death of Brewster Place, a slow demise that affects the very bricks and mortar that constitute its foundation no less than the people who dwell in its run-down tenements, offers a particularly poignant encounter with the city's limits.

While the most traditional ways of understanding the city's limits are in terms of its geographical boundaries and its temporal boundaries (i.e., where it begins and ends, when it was founded, and how it has evolved through time), there are clearly other ways of experiencing urban limits that Naylor's work forces the reader to confront. These latter limits emphasize how different regions of the city circumscribe the horizons for social existence, narrowing the possibilities for achieving understanding and tolerance across what Ruth Frankenberg has called its "racial social geography."[7] It is due to racial social geography, Frankenberg maintains, that someone who lives in close physical proximity to members of another racial group (e.g., a block away) and whose family even employs members of this group as domestic workers on a daily basis nonetheless can perceive these others as absent from her social world. Frankenberg's interviews with specific women from different urban areas complements Naylor's literary depiction of Brewster Place by illustrating how the city can facilitate social segregation even where there is very little physical separation between different people. By focusing so closely on the lives of a few main characters residing on Brewster Place, Naylor is able to foreground the intercorporeal effects of their encounters with different city limits, encounters that indelibly intertwine their bodies with the place in which they reside.[8] To understand these encounters better, it is crucial to examine how the body functions as an ongoing (though changing) horizon through which urban experience unfolds; moreover, the city itself serves as a dynamic horizon for the intercorporeal relationships that are sustained within it.[9]

Intercorporeal Horizons

While in the *Phenomenology of Perception* Merleau-Ponty emphasizes that it is the body in its active engagement with the world that serves as the center of all perceptual experience, contemporary works by feminists, queer theorists, critical race theorists, historical materialists, and disability scholars and activists have amply demonstrated how gender, sexuality, race, class, and ability mutually inform and transform corporeal existence insofar as they collectively influence how one's body is interpreted and responded to by others. Insofar as they function along with age, religion, ethnicity, and nationality as interlocking dimensions of experience, they cannot be disentangled into separate spheres of influence. To the extent that one understands these various dimensions of ordinary experience as mutually constitutive horizons, this means that they are always overlapping and indeterminate, providing fluid rather than static contexts of significance that shift throughout history in response to changing social, political, economic, and material conditions. As a spatio-temporal horizon within which urban existence unfolds, the city, I argue, is an exemplary site for examining how these multiple, overlapping horizons come together, not necessarily in harmony but often in conflict, conflicts that have been most visibly registered on city streets themselves through demonstrations, protests, riots, and even revolutions. The limits as well as the possibilities of these multiple horizons are inscribed into the city; they are part of the urban fabric, though their influence is often concealed by the overwhelming physical presence of the city itself.

Thus, while at first glance the city might seem to be a perceptual horizon par excellence, circumscribed by those ubiquitous signs that proclaim one has reached the "city limits," it is clear that the city also exceeds its material borders, not only through spawning its suburban doppelgänger, the "edge city" described by Joel Garreau and others, but also by functioning as an imaginary or phantas-matic horizon, a site of individual as well as cultural dreams, hopes, fears, and desires. The city, then, is an especially interesting and complex phenomenon to explore because it functions not only as a physical horizon for urban and subur-ban bodies but also as an imaginary horizon for individuals and communities.[10] Indeed, as I hope to show, it is only through an examination of the dynamic in-terplay between the physical and imaginary dimensions of the city that the symbolic and material investments of both individuals and cultures in urban existence can be addressed.

As both a physical and imaginary horizon, a specific materiality with its own spatiality and temporality (what Henri Bergson calls its unique *durée*), and a phantasmatic site of ongoing cultural significance, the city remains a perpet-ual object of fascination, a place where the Lacanian psychic registers of the imaginary, the symbolic, and the real collide. For just as these latter collectively, yet differentially, produce and organize subjectivity according to Lacan (in ways that range from functional to pathological), the city is the fulcrum for multiple horizons of significance that are irreducible to one another and yet cannot be thought or experienced apart from one another. And, I argue, it is the chias-matic intertwining of these material and phantasmatic dimensions of the city that helps to construct not only the limits but also the possibilities of both indi-vidual and collective urban experience.[11]

City Time, City Space

In her essay entitled "Bodies-Cities," Elizabeth Grosz claims that "there is no natural or ideal environment for the body, no 'perfect' city, judged in terms of the body's health and well-being. If bodies are not culturally pre-given, built environments cannot alienate the very bodies they produce." And, she goes on to add, "[t]his is not to say that there are not unconducive city environments, but rather there is nothing intrinsic about the city which makes it alienating or un-natural. The question is not simply how to distinguish conducive from uncon-ducive environments, but to examine how different cities, different socio-cultural environments, actively produce the bodies of their inhabitants" (Grosz 1995: 109). To say that cities "actively produce the bodies of their inhabitants" high-lights the transformative potential of cities, their ability to structure bodily expe-rience in both habitual as well as novel ways insofar as they lay down spatial, temporal, and, I maintain, imaginary coordinates through which human beings navigate and make sense of their world. Even rural areas today receive their ori-entation through their proximity to or distance from larger urban centers. "It's three and a half hours from Chicago," "two hours from Pittsburgh," "an hour and a half from New York City," are all familiar ways of identifying non-urban space. Moreover, because no two cities are alike, the intercorporeal networks established by and within each city also differ in marked ways. As Bergson suggests, the city of Paris has its own temporal and spatial rhythms that one can participate in fully only if one has directly experienced the *life* of the city, physically traversing its city streets, spending time within its public and private spaces. Virtual tours of the city on the web can indeed give me a "sense" of what Paris is like, but they can never substitute for the experience I have when I navigate the city myself. Moreover, as architects and urban planners have always known, the means by which I navigate the city (on foot, by bicycle, car, bus, train, airplane, etc.), will in turn influence the kinds of interactions I sustain with it and the impressions I form of it.

Although Bergson acknowledges the power of narrative descriptions of a city one has never seen to evoke some notion of the unique personality of that particular place, he nonetheless insists that one has to become part of a city to appreciate its specific *durée*. And, while I agree with Bergson that even the best literary depictions of a city never recreate the experience of actually being *in* that city oneself, I nonetheless argue that literature has the power to foreground the less visible horizons of significance that collectively constitute urban experience. The richness of Virginia Woolf's wonderfully condensed description of Harley Street in London on a June day shortly after the end of World War I in *Mrs. Dalloway* reveals that even a single street within a city can convey a wealth of information about both the city and its inhabitants, information that is available to the ordinary pedestrian but that rarely becomes a subject for reflection. By turning one's attention directly to this overdetermined quality of even one small part of the city, Woolf demonstrates how the street can function as a synecdoche for city life itself:

> Shredding and slicing, dividing and subdividing, the clocks of Harley Street nibbled at the June day, counseled submission, upheld authority, and pointed out in chorus the supreme advantages of a sense of proportion, until the mound of time was so far diminished that a commercial clock, suspended above a shop in Oxford Street, announced, genially and fraternally, as if it were a pleasure to Messrs. Rigby and Lowndes to give the information gratis, that it was half-past one. (Woolf 1981: 102)

As the clocks of Harley and Oxford Streets reverberate with the "sense of proportion" that is echoed in the steady rhythms of British bourgeois sensibility, Woolf eloquently reveals how the temporality of the city is taken up by and incorporated within the lives of its inhabitants. The diminishing "mound of time" that audibly courses through the city as the pealing slowly comes to an end reminds Peter Walsh that death is not beyond time but part of the very movement of city life:

Then, as the sounds of St. Margaret's languished, he thought, She has been ill and the sound expressed languor and suffering. It was her heart, he remembered; and the sudden loudness of the final stroke tolled for death that surprised in the midst of life, Clarissa falling where she stood, in her drawing room. No! No! he cried. She is not dead! I am not old, he cried and marched up Whitehall, as if there rolled down to him, vigorous, unending, his future. (Woolf 1981: 50)

Plunging back into the life of the city, Peter Walsh must nonetheless come to terms with his past, his present, and his future: his hopes for a life with Clarissa that were never realized and his fears of not having accomplished enough in his life to make his own mark in time. Though he has escaped London's confines by living in India for many years, the distinctive rhythms of this epicenter of the British Empire continue to claim him. For Peter, like Clarissa, traversing the city on foot and visiting old haunts becomes a means of integrating the various threads of his life, of enacting concretely the fusion of horizons described by Gadamer.

While Peter and Clarissa seek to affirm, albeit in their own ways, the fragile yet durable intercorporeal connections that continue to bind them to one another across their differences, Woolf also suggests that there are some individuals, such as Septimus Warren Smith (and ultimately Woolf herself) who are unable to orient themselves within the city, unable to identify with the inexorable, measured expectations that emanate from the historic city streets, its chiming bells, and, above all, its inhabitants:

"It is time," said Rezia.
     The word "time" split its husk; poured its riches over him; and from his lips fell like shells, like shavings from a plane, without his making them, hard, white, imperishable words, and flew to attach themselves to their places in an ode to Time; an immortal ode to Time. (Woolf 1981: 69–70)

Incapable of engaging in city life, Septimus Warren Smith experiences London as a bystander, not as a participant. He lives in the city but remains even more of an outsider to it than his Italian wife, Lucrezia, who must adapt to the tempo of a new city, a new country, and a new existence as the wife of a man whom she thought she knew but who has since become strange and unfamiliar. First anxiously and then frantically, Lucrezia, the foreigner, seeks to reintegrate Septimus into the current of daily existence—this June day in London in the early 1920s when the war that has forever altered the meaning of space and time has ended, but whose horrors live on in the memories of its victims, providing a new and disturbing horizon that continues to mediate their experience of postwar urban life.

Urban Outlaws

The sense of alienation and resulting pain produced by Septimus's displacement from the city, even as he and Lucrezia slowly wend their way through London's urban fabric, forces Lucrezia to confront the city's imperviousness to those who cannot make its rhythm their own. The general public, however, does not remain impervious to this failure to assimilate; for to be incapable of embodying the "sense of proportion" that Woolf depicts as emanating from the city itself is registered as an affront to humanity, to space, and to time. Through society's refusal to make a place for people like Septimus, Lucrezia recognizes the dangers of proportion, its dark side if you will, namely the pressure of conformity. "Proportion" she observes,

> has a sister, less smiling, more formidable, a Goddess even now engaged in the heat and sands of India, the mud and swamp of Africa, the purlieus of London, wherever in short the climate or the devil tempts men to fall from the true belief which is her own—is even now engaged in dashing down shrines, smashing idols, and setting up in their place her own stern countenance. Conversion is her name and she feasts on the wills of the weakly, loving to impress, to impose, adoring her own features stamped on the face of the populace. At Hyde Park Corner on a tub she stands preaching; shrouds herself in white and walks penitentially disguised as brotherly love through factories and parliaments; offers help, but desires power; smites out of her way roughly the dissentient, or dissatisfied; bestows her blessing on those who, looking upward, catch submissively from her eyes the light of their own. (Woolf 1981: 100)

Hurling himself out of the window of his apartment to the pavement below to escape the doctor who seeks to restore Septimus's sense of proportion by banishing him to the country under a closely supervised regimen of "rest and relaxation," Septimus refuses to pay the price of conformity; through this action he finally finds his place within city life, namely, as one of its casualties. Clarissa, meditating on the life of this man whom she has never met but whose sudden, anonymous death has managed to penetrate even the thick walls of her drawing room in the midst of her party, manages to do something that Septimus could not—she integrates this stranger's death into the meaning of her life:

> The young man had killed himself; but she did not pity him; with the clock striking the hour, one, two, three, she did not pity him, with all this going on . . . the words came to her, Fear no more the heat of the sun. She must go back to them. But what an extraordinary night! She felt somehow very like him—the young man who had killed himself. She felt glad that he had done it; thrown it away. The clock was striking. The leaden circles dissolved in the air. He made her feel the beauty; made her feel the fun. But she must go back.

She must assemble. She must find Sally and Peter. And she came in from the little room. (Woolf 1981: 186)

Unlike Septimus, Clarissa finds the thread that binds her to the world of the living, and this enables her to reconnect with her childhood friends, Sally and Peter, through their shared horizons of memories past. However, I argue, it is precisely Septimus's inability to forge the link between past, present, and future that is part of the very bricks and mortar of the city itself, the fact, as the gratuitous destruction of war itself reveals, that this connection can never be taken for granted but must always be lived afresh, that reveals the fragility of the connection itself. For, as Naylor also emphasizes, cities as well as people can always be destroyed.

Pushing the Envelope

Septimus's death, Clarissa's life; urban decay, urban renewal: the city's limits, as architects have demonstrated throughout history, frequently offer innovative opportunities. Indeed, to take just one example, Peter Eisenman's Wexner Center for the Performing Arts, located on an odd-shaped site, sandwiched between two other buildings on a small section of the main quadrangle on The Ohio State University campus in the city of Columbus, illustrates this alchemical transformation of limit into possibility and of possibility into limit. Rather than attempting to integrate the building seamlessly into its surroundings, Eisenman exposes the seams of the building itself, extending its frame so as to confound the boundaries between inside and outside, boundaries whose ordinary role in ordering our existence is revealed in and through their transgression.[12]

As the ongoing horizon within which urban and suburban experience unfolds and against which rural existence is often extolled, the city continues to manufacture its own constraints, constraints that in turn can become sites of cultural possibility. However, to go back to my earlier quote from Gloria Naylor, streets, like people, do die, and they are not always capable of springing back to life like a phoenix from the ashes. Overcrowding, pollution, racism, poverty, and disease can devour the resources of even the most well-endowed cities. Moreover, one need look no further than the burned-out city streets of Detroit, Michigan, or the ghettos of any major American city to see how the lack of options for the poor can become a developer's playground since he (and it is almost always he, is it not?) can count on the rich to purchase the condominiums that take the place of blighted communities.

"Buildings, like texts," Mark Wigley tells us, "are inserted into the world of dissimulation to speak of an unattainable order beyond it." "The building" he claims, "masquerades as order. Order itself becomes a mask. This mask of order uses figures of rationality to conceal the essential irrationality of both individuals and society" (Wigley 1992: 379). For Wigley then, the very "sense of proportion" that Woolf's London embodies is always illusory. Underlying this order is disorder, and the solidity and stability of the city's buildings serve to quell human beings' anxiety about the shaky foundation of their own existence in the world of their concern. Septimus, as an "urban outlaw" who recognizes the precariousness and artificiality of the social order, seems to have it right. The question then becomes, why don't more human beings, like Septimus (or more recently Gilles Deleuze for that matter), throw themselves out of the windows of tall buildings in order to hasten their inevitable demise?[13] Following these particular "lines of flight," one can perhaps better understand why Albert Camus proclaims that whether or not to commit suicide is the only truly philosophical question and why Jean-Paul Sartre focuses on the unsettling experience of vertigo, the feeling that *nothing* can ultimately keep me from plunging to my death except my resolve not to do so, in order to illustrate the contingency at the heart of human existence that is continually disavowed.[14]

While Wigley, like Jean Baudrillard, sees order as merely a dissimulating mask, with buildings serving as the emperor's new clothes, their ornamentation intended to hide the fact that the emperor is really wearing nothing at all, Grosz moves beyond the binaries of order and disorder altogether, instead privileging what she calls an "openness to futurity." In her words:

> An openness to futurity is a challenge facing all of the arts, sciences, humanities; the degree of openness is an index of one's political alignments and orientations, of the readiness to transform. Unless we put into question architectural and cultural identities—the identities of men and women, of different races and classes, and of different religious, sexual, and political affiliations, as well as the identities of cities, urban regions, buildings, and houses—this openness to the future, the promise of time unfolding through innovation rather than prediction, is muted rather than welcomed. (Grosz 2001: 91)

For Grosz, the innovations arising out of this openness to futurity take place within what she calls the "space of the in-between." The space of the in-between can best be understood, I argue, as a chiasmatic space: a place of possibility where the real and the imaginary are inextricably intertwined; it is the space between buildings, beyond buildings, and the space in which individual and cultural dreams as well as human beings' worst nightmares unfold. In short, I am claiming that the space of the in-between is a way of understanding the notion of the horizon that I have been developing. It is a space where limits can be transformed into possibilities and where possibilities, in the process of actualization, produce new limits.

The Constraints of Convention

As everyone knows, however, some limits remain limits. The openness to the future that Grosz seeks to affirm is always threatened by a tendency to let the pull of gravity carry one backward, not forward. An omnipresent danger, then, is that the space of the in-between could collapse into a repetition of the same. Whether this involves building the same house over and over along a suburban block whose very uniformity and predictability provides the stable pattern that its residents are encouraged to replicate in their daily routines, or a repetition of the racialized and gendered visions of architects and developers who continue to be overwhelmingly white and male, the city's limits must continually be exposed and contested. The space of the in-between is not a spatial and temporal given, then; it can and must be an ongoing achievement, opened up by a persistent effort to unsettle the sedimented structures that form part of the horizon of everyday life. Accordingly, Grosz tells us, "[t]his in-between is the very site for the contestation of the many binaries and dualisms that dominate Western knowledge, for the very form of oppositional structure that has defined not only phallocentrism but also ethnocentrism and Eurocentrism, and the more general erasure of difference" (Grosz 2001: 93).

To preserve the space of the in-between involves, for Grosz, the affirmation of difference—not the oppositional difference that reduces multiplicity to the static dimensions of the same and its other(s), but rather:

> The in-between is what fosters and enables the other's transition from being the other of the one to its own becoming, to reconstituting another relation, in different terms. This in-between is that which is thus shared by politics, by culture, and by architecture, insofar as they are all spaces, organizations, structures, that operate within the logic of identity yet also require the *excess* of subversion, of latency, of becoming that generates and welcomes the new without which the future is not possible. (Grosz 2001: 94)

The excess of which Grosz speaks hovers simultaneously within and beyond the city limits. For if, as I urge, we understand this excess of the in-between *as* a horizon of possibility, then it is clear that the horizon is not simply on the outside, out *there*, but also in *here*, in this text, in buildings, and in bodies, helping to forge the intercorporeal connections and disconnections that comprise the fabric of human life.

To the extent that architecture succeeds in "making" space, transforming the "givens" of the pre-existing landscape, it seems uniquely suited to open up the innovative space of futurity that Grosz is embracing. And yet the fluidity she associates with this in-between insofar as it is "the very essence of space and time and their intrication" is, she argues, "inimical to the project of architecture as a whole" (Grosz 2001: 94). The architectural challenge she poses involves making space that preserves space and time itself, allowing for their endless circulation and negotiation in corridors, in city streets, and in individuals' own bodies. Rising to this challenge will in turn necessitate the creation of new horizons, new ways of living space and time, and new ways of addressing and transforming the city's limits so that they truly have the potential to become sites of possibility. On a concrete level, this will involve reconnecting those dead-end streets such as Brewster Place to the rest of the city in a manner that expands, rather than destroys, the dreams and desires of its inhabitants.

8
Urban Flesh

If one accepts Bergson's claim that each city has its own unique *durée*, its own personality and temporal rhythms, it is at the same time evident that the city is never reducible to any one element but functions as a complicated gestalt, a dynamic, structured whole that serves as an important horizon for social existence for both city dwellers and non–city dwellers alike. The anonymity, ambiguity, and carnality of the flesh, as Merleau-Ponty describes it in his final unfinished work, *The Visible and the Invisible*, are, I believe, especially apropos in conveying the dynamic and turbulent materiality of urban existence, or what I am calling "urban flesh." Merleau-Ponty introduces the concept of the flesh (*la chair*) fairly late in his work, and many commentators prefer his use of this term over his earlier emphasis on the body. Nonetheless, I do not think the concept of the flesh can or should displace discussion of the body altogether. The two terms, while closely related (since the body is, after all, "of the flesh" even if the latter is not reducible to it), are certainly not identical. In an oft-cited passage from *The Visible and the Invisible*, Merleau-Ponty proclaims that the flesh must be understood as an element in the ancient Greeks' sense of the term, namely, as an *incarnate principle* that is not reducible to any one thing yet helps to constitute everything that exists: "The flesh is not matter, is not mind, is not substance. To designate it, we should need the old term 'element,' in the sense it was used to speak of water, air, earth, and fire, that is, in the sense of a *general thing*, midway between the spatio-temporal individual and the idea, a sort of incarnate principle that brings a style of being wherever there is a fragment of being" (Merleau-Ponty 1968: 139). While it might seem strange to view the city as a kind of element since the city itself is composed of the four elements, earth, air, fire, and water, to the extent that the city continually stylizes both individual and collective existence, I argue that it functions as an incarnate principle that serves as an ongoing horizon of significance in human beings' everyday life. As an incarnate principle, it is not indestructible, but must be cared for in order to flourish. For, as the events of September 11, 2001, in the United States poignantly reveal, and as equally devastating experiences in other cities throughout the world continue to demonstrate, sudden tears in the urban fabric can create wounds that reverberate throughout the flesh.

The Violence of Binaries

Through a critical appropriation of Merleau-Ponty's conception of flesh, Irigaray stresses those aspects of the flesh Merleau-Ponty merely hints at when he suggests that the flesh stylizes being, namely, the differentiations of the flesh, how flesh always serves as a mark of difference even as it connects one being to another. In Irigaray's words, "Flesh, the flesh of each one is not substitutable for the other" (Irigaray 1993: 167). She is especially concerned with a very particular form of fleshly differentiation, namely, sexual difference, and she takes Merleau-Ponty to task for failing to acknowledge its *irreversibility*.

Most notably, she argues that women's flesh has historically been understood as a (deficient) mirror of men's flesh, a specular surface that, far from revealing genuine difference, reveals only what men want to see. The danger, on her account, of understanding the flesh as a "general thing" is that the flesh is not pure generality; rather the flesh is always already differentiated, and some forms of differentiation, most notably sexual differentiation, are misrecognized if they are understood through the model of reversibility that Merleau-Ponty famously illustrates through the example of one hand touching the other.

In this example, the hand touched in turn becomes the hand touching, and while these two experiences are distinct, the capacity of either hand to have either experience implies a sameness in difference, a narcissistic cycle that Irigaray identifies with a masculine desire to encompass and master genuine difference. Opposing Merleau-Ponty's "elemental" logic of generality, a generality that she claims is at odds with the ongoing, polymorphous sex-specific differentiation that distinguishes feminine flesh, the sex "which is not one," Irigaray is nonetheless clearly indebted to Merleau-Ponty's insight that the flesh functions as an "incarnate principle that brings a style of being wherever there is a fragment of being."[1] Indeed, I would argue, Merleau-Ponty's provocative understanding of how the flesh stylizes being suggests an ongoing process of differentiation that cannot be reduced to sameness. And yet, insofar as it stylizes, the flesh also unifies, weaving together disparate gestures, movements, bodies, and situations into a dynamic fabric of meaning that must be continually reworked, made, and unmade.

The city itself, with its limits and possibilities, is an excellent example of such a richly textured fabric of meaning. One need only look to the checkered racist and sexist histories of so many American cities to recognize both the fragility and the strength of the ties that collectively produce the varied stylizations (liberatory as well as oppressive) of urban flesh. By emphasizing the corporeal connections and disconnections that differentiate what I am calling urban flesh, I am aligning myself with contemporary feminist theorists, critical race theorists, disability theorists, and others who refuse the reductive violence of a binary logic that would privilege unity over difference or difference over unity. As I will argue, however, such a position should not be construed as an escape from the violence of limitation, for this latter is encountered outside as well as within binary systems.

The focus for this particular discussion is on specific differentiations that produce and are produced by the materiality of the urban, that is, by urban flesh. The very expression "urban flesh" invokes the specter of that which allegedly escapes the urban, namely, nature or natural flesh. To speak of urban flesh, then, requires that we come to terms in some way with the role that nature and the concept of the natural play in circumscribing the possibilities and limits of urban existence.[2] Just as it is no longer fashionable to embrace a Cartesian mind/body dualism, the nature/city divide is also held by many theorists to be passé, an artificial distinction that has traditionally taken the form of reifying the "purity" of nature in contrast to the "polluting" features of urban life.[3] Moreover, just as the gendered connotations of the mind/body distinction have been rendered visible by feminist theorists, so too has the nature/urban distinction been recognized as gendered; even more obviously it is racialized.[4] As a result of the important critical analyses provided by several feminist, critical race, and contemporary urban theorists, romantic invocations of the purity and peacefulness of nature versus the pollution and violence of city life appear naïve at best, and run the danger of supporting sexist, racist, and classist political agendas. Exploring Merleau-Ponty's emphasis on the necessary violence of incarnate existence, the violence of the flesh, is the strategy I employ here in order to arrive at an understanding of urban flesh that does not accept the conventional nature/culture, pure/polluting, feminine/masculine binaries.

Insofar as these binaries themselves help to reinforce social and political inequities that result in violence, violence may seem an unlikely ally in the deconstruction of oppressive binaries that fail to capture the complex realities they seek to circumscribe and contain. However, as Hannah Arendt, quoting William O'Brien, observes, "Sometimes 'violence is the only way of ensuring a hearing for moderation'" (Arendt 1970: 79).[5] Arendt, like Merleau-Ponty, has no intention of glorifying violence. In her words: "[T]he danger of violence, even if it moves consciously within a nonextremist framework of short-term goals, will always be that the means overwhelm the end. If goals are not achieved rapidly, the result will be not merely defeat but the introduction of the practice of violence into the whole body politic" (Arendt 1970: 80). Violence, for Arendt, is a human creation; it is introduced into the world through human activity. She observes that "[n]either violence nor power is a natural phenomenon, that is, a manifestation of the life process; they belong to the political realm of human affairs whose essentially human quality is guaranteed by man's faculty of action, the ability to begin something new" (Arendt 1970: 82). Yet Arendt also asserts that violence is a natural human emotion, and that violence can be the very vehicle through which human beings "set the scales of justice right again. . . . In this sense, rage and the violence that sometimes—not always—goes with it belong among the 'natural' *human* emotions, and to cure man of them would mean nothing less than to dehumanize or emasculate him" (Arendt 1970: 64).

Arendt's claim that violence is not natural because it stems from human rather than non-human activity but that it is nonetheless a "natural" human emotion, whose absence would be dehumanizing and emasculating, is striking.[6] Her appeal to human nature seems to imply that insofar as violence is a "natural" emotion that helps to define human beings, it is ethically justifiable, at least on some occasions. And yet, as Sherry Ortner and others have shown, one must be suspicious of even such well-intentioned invocations of nature (especially when they lead to a further conflation of the human and the masculine) because of the sexist and racist practices that have used the concept of the natural to legitimize oppression.

Turning one's attention to the urban/nature dichotomy complicates these matters further, given the fact that the violence of the city, conceived of as a wholly human creation, has often been contrasted with the peacefulness of the natural, that is, non-human, world. And while hard and fast distinctions between the world of nature and the urban world have often been challenged, the challenges themselves have taken different forms depending on the individual, social, historical, and ideological commitments of the theorists themselves. Eco-feminists such as Carol Bigwood advocate that human beings embrace and celebrate their primordial relationship to a "world-earth-home" that restores nature (and the feminine) to its rightful primacy as the very foundation of experience. Others, such as critical theorist Steven Vogel, argue that there is no such thing as nature insofar as the latter is romantically conceived of as a "pure" domain independent of the city and culture. Both Bigwood and Vogel seek the elimination of arbitrary distinctions between nature and culture; however, they approach this project through opposite paths: Bigwood by claiming that nature is everywhere, even in the heart of the city, and Vogel by claiming that nature is nowhere, that it is culture that is ubiquitous and that has posited nature as its alter ego and legitimizing origin. Whether nature is indeed "everywhere" or "nowhere," it is clear that it functions as an overdetermined, regulative ideal in human beings' very thoughts about culture more generally and urban existence more particularly.

The Violence of Emplacement

The inescapability of nature and the crucial role it plays in establishing individuals' sense of place is also explored by Edward Casey in *Getting Back into Place: Toward a Renewed Understanding of the Place-World*. With regard to the relationship between bodies, buildings, and the natural world, Casey asserts that "[o]nce our bodies are comfortably ensconced in buildings, we simply tend to close out the larger world of nature. Yet the natural world surrounds every body and every building, finally if not immediately. Even if this wider world seems independent of human beings' cherished aims and interests, it *remains around us* as a mute presence tacitly waiting to be acknowledged" (Casey 1993: 147–148). Reinforcing Heidegger's discussion in "The Origin of the Work of Art" of the earth that sustains and supports the world, concealing its active, constitutive presence in the process, Casey affirms that in human beings' relations with cities, nature is always present, yet is rarely registered as such. Rather than remaining within the confines of the Heideggerian tension between a self-concealing earth and a self-revealing world, Casey, in a Merleau-Pontian vein, turns his attention to the lived body that is the very site of this tension, that which grounds individuals' own sense of "emplacement" within the world. For if, as Merleau-Ponty suggests in the *Phenomenology of Perception*, the body is itself a horizon for all possible and actual experience, it is imperative to arrive at a better understanding of how human bodies are themselves situated, or "emplaced," within the world in which they dwell.

The terrorist attacks on the World Trade Center towers in New York City on September 11, 2001, offer one of the most widely circulated contemporary examples of the powerful role the city plays in human beings' sense of their own corporeality. Searing images of the flame- and smoke-engulfed north and south towers shown around the world followed the vertical trajectory of falling bodies as person after person chose to jump to their deaths rather than succumb to an equally certain, but slower and more painful, death inside the burning buildings. Footage from that day shows scores of people hanging out of the north tower from its uppermost floors, frantically breaking through the skin of the building to signal their distress and their hope for assistance that never came from the outside world. Those who witnessed this pain and suffering, however, discovered that their own relationship to those monumental buildings in which so many people were trapped was also transformed. Indeed these victims, and the buildings themselves, have produced a sense of personal, communal, national, and even international vulnerability that is visceral.

"Ground Zero," that non-place where the twin towers once stood, is a reminder of the fragility of human beings' emplacement in the world. Although the Pentagon in Washington, D.C., was quickly rebuilt, no longer revealing the black scars along one of its five faces that put the lie to its alleged impregnability, "Ground Zero" continues to present the destructive power of terrorism for all to see.[7] The collapse of the towers' own bodies was as shocking for many as were the deaths of the thousands of people who were trapped inside. Indeed, although the World Trade Center has always been a controversial presence in New York City—a source of civic and national pride for some as well as an icon to American cultural imperialism for others—its symbolic and material significance has only grown, becoming more complex and even more contradictory, since its destruction. Correspondingly, the bodily identities of those who have been associated with it, including victims, bystanders, residents of New York City and the surrounding metropolitan area, other Americans, allies, enemies, and the terrorists and their supporters themselves, have also been complicated and problematized in unforeseeable ways.

In Husserl's language, the destruction of the World Trade Center towers has disrupted the "natural attitude," the "taken-for-granted" perspective toward their bodily surroundings that Americans have had the luxury of holding onto in a country that escaped the severe physical devastation Europe and Asia suffered in World Wars I and II and other wars of this past century.[8] Indeed, the seeming permanence of a city's building, and of the city itself, has been materially and symbolically significant in anchoring its citizens' own sense of security and stability throughout history. For those in or from countries that have been continually ravaged by war and natural disasters, for those who have been displaced and who have no homes to (re)turn to, including those whose corporeal existence has always been marked by a sense of impermanence, the previous complacency many United States citizens experienced in relation to their own emplacement in the world must truly be incomprehensible. Indeed, ever since the famous fall of Troy, there have been warnings that the city, and therefore its inhabitants, are not as impregnable as they may seem.

If, as Casey suggests, bodies, cities, and nature cannot be understood apart from one another, it should not be surprising that the violent attacks on two of the United States' most symbolically charged sites (the World Trade Center and the Pentagon) in two of its most symbolically charged American cities (New York City and Washington, D.C.), were registered by many as a violent attack on their corporeality, that is, on their bodily sense of well-being-in-the-world. While the horrific violence of these attacks should not be forgotten, there is also the danger that focusing too heavily on their exceptional character and buying into official U.S. propagandistic rhetoric that all that is required in order to live without fear of violence in the future is to "stamp out terrorism" will lead Americans right back into a dangerous natural attitude, namely the belief that dwelling can be accomplished in peace, without violence.

Merleau-Ponty's 1947 volume, *Humanism and Terror*, in its serious attempt to grapple with the violence of the cataclysmic geographical, social, political, and emotional upheavals of World War II, is surprisingly relevant to the unstable and violent times that have continued to characterize human existence in the early twenty-first century. Regarding the omnipresence of violence, Merleau-Ponty maintains, "We do not have a choice between purity and violence but between different kinds of violence. Inasmuch as we are incarnate beings, violence is our lot" (Merleau-Ponty 1969: 109). Although Merleau-Ponty's perspective on the inevitability of violence is hardly surprising given the severe economic deprivation and political unrest that marked post–World War II France as it emerged from years of German occupation, he clearly is making a statement here that extends beyond his own country and his own time, to encompass human (and perhaps non-human) existence more generally. Why, one may ask, does Merleau-Ponty posit a seemingly necessary connection between violence and life as an incarnate being? Is violence characteristic of all incarnate life or just human existence?

At times, Merleau-Ponty seems to embrace the view shared by Sartre, Beauvoir, and Arendt, namely, that violence emerges out of human relationships, specifically from what they all see as the unavoidable conflicts that mark the interactions between different subjects with different projects and a limited amount of resources to pursue them. In the preface to *Humanism and Terror*, however, Merleau-Ponty suggests that it may be possible for societies to at least hope for a time without violence:

> When one is living in what Péguy called an historical *period*, in which political man is content to administer a regime or an established law, one can hope for a history without violence. When one has the misfortune or the luck to live in an *epoch*, or one of those moments where the traditional ground of a nation or a society crumbles and where, for better or worse, man himself must reconstruct human relations, then the liberty of each man is a mortal threat to the others and violence reappears. (Merleau-Ponty 1969: xvii)

Is the hope for a life without violence merely a regulative ideal? Would such a society, in which all citizens presumably acquiesced to follow the established law of a particular political regime, even be an ideal? What if the laws themselves do violence to particular individuals or groups of individuals within that society? More importantly, if, as Merleau-Ponty suggests, violence is the lot of humans as animate, embodied beings, then how can a life without violence ever function as an ideal in the first place?

The Ethics of Violence

Beauvoir, writing at the same time and in the same post–World War II context as Merleau-Ponty, attempts to specify more precisely when violence is morally permissible. Above all, she emphasizes that violence is always enacted in and must be judged through an intersubjective context. In her words:

> [V]iolence is justified only if it opens concrete possibilities to the freedom which I am trying to save; by practicing it I am willy-nilly assuming an engagement in relation to others and to myself; a man whom I snatch from the death he has chosen has the right to come and ask me for means and reasons for living; the tyranny practiced against an invalid can be justified only by his getting better; whatever the purity of the intention which animates me, any dictatorship is a fault for which I have to get myself pardoned. (Beauvoir 1976: 137)

Beauvoir's remarks can make one wonder whether the brief sketch of a nonviolent historical period that Merleau-Ponty offers limits possibilities and leads to a false sense of complacency. In fact, Merleau-Ponty himself suggests that the individual living in an epoch may be regarded as luckier rather than more unfortunate than the individual who lives in a nonviolent regime in which the rule of law is laid down and followed without dissent. The danger of invoking (even if only hypothetically) a historical period in which violence is absent is that the violence of law itself, as an abstract universal whose meaning comes from its forcible application to the particular case, runs the risk of being covered over and thereby disavowed.[9] For, insofar as the power of the law derives its authority performatively to the extent that it is promulgated and enforced by a legislating body, too much emphasis on respect for the law itself qua law can lead to a failure to recognize the disrespectful and oppressive ways in which the law is so often interpreted and administered.

Even if it is possible (if only theoretically) to live nonviolently in a historical period in which the rule of law applies and is acquiesced to by one and all, Merleau-Ponty's account implies that living in an epoch when life is volatile and the torn fabric of human relations must continually be mended presents more possibilities for social and political transformation. However, with this mending comes violence; the activity of reconstruction, whether it takes the form of re-building the environment after a period of destruction or involves repairing fragmented relationships between one individual or even one nation and an-other, produces violent changes that can serve the cause of liberation as readily as that of oppression. Above all, the prospect of reconstruction carries with it the possibility of a new and different future, a future that may well usher in new vio-lence and that may even require new violence to avoid the tragic mistakes of the immediate and distant past. In a particularly prescient passage that seems espe-cially relevant to the United States in a post-9/11, early twenty-first century con-text, Merleau-Ponty suggests that the violence of injustice must be countered with the violence of justice. In his words: "A regime which is nominally liberal can be oppressive in reality. A regime which acknowledges its violence *might* have in it more genuine humanity" (Merleau-Ponty 1969: xv).

From the distance of more than a half century, and for those who did not live through it, the epochal period of World War II often seems restricted to the actual war years themselves, including at most the years preceding the war when Hitler came to power in Nazi Germany. Merleau-Ponty's *Humanism and Terror* offers a reminder that the Cold War between the United States and the Soviet Union was just as terrifying in its potential consequences for many Euro-peans as was the prospect of Hitler taking over the continent. The threat that either the United States or the Soviet Union would resort to nuclear bombs as both sought to gain control over postwar Germany was very real to countries that were still suffering from enormous ecological, economic, and psychologi-cal devastation. Both the United States and the Soviet Union possessed the requisite nuclear technology, and the United States had already revealed its willingness to use the atomic bomb in Hiroshima in response to the Japanese attack on Pearl Harbor. Suspicious of the United States' claim to be *the* cham-pion of democracy fighting against a repressive Stalinist regime in the name of freedom, Merleau-Ponty makes the following observation, one that is uncannily timely as once again the United States leads the fray in a war against an enemy whose very omnipresence makes it seem larger than life, namely, a war on ter-rorism: "Whatever one's philosophical or even theological position, a society is not the temple of value-idols that figure on the front of its monuments or in its constitutional scrolls; the value of a society is the value it places upon man's re-lation to man. It is not just a question of knowing what the liberals have in mind but what in reality is done by the liberal state within and beyond its frontiers" (Merleau-Ponty 1969: xiv). "To understand and judge a society," he adds, "one has to penetrate its basic structure to the human bond upon which it is built; this undoubtedly depends upon legal relations, but also upon forms of labor, ways of loving, living, and dying" (Merleau-Ponty 1969: xiv).

Dwelling in the World

Human beings' forms of labor, and their unique ways of loving, living, and dying, undoubtedly reveal much more than the state of a particular society. They reveal also the ongoing, intercorporeal relations that comprise an individual's situation. This includes the inanimate as well as the animate; indeed, as I noted earlier, the visceral responses of so many Americans and non-Americans to the attacks on the World Trade Center towers and on the Pentagon poignantly illustrate that human relations with the inanimate can be just as powerful, just as violent, and just as disturbing as the relations they sustain with their fellow human beings. The material destruction of the world that is shared by both humans and non-humans, whether it occurs deliberately or spontaneously, forces individuals to contend with the specific, but usually invisible, ways in which the surrounding environment actively shapes the intercorporeal interactions that help to construct their own sense of bodily agency. And, insofar as to be human is to be in as well as of the world, this sense of bodily agency provides the parameters that delimit the very nature of human emplacement, that is, the ability to dwell humanely within the world of our concern.

In his classic essay "Building Dwelling Thinking," Martin Heidegger maintains, "The way in which you are and I am, the manner in which we humans *are* on the earth, is *Buan*, dwelling. To be a human being means to be on the earth as a mortal. It means to dwell" (Heidegger 1971a: 147). A few pages later he states, "To say that mortals *are* is to say that *in dwelling* they persist through spaces by virtue of their stay among things and locations" (Heidegger 1971a: 157). According to Heidegger, Dasein's sense of bodily continuity, or in his words, its "persistence" through spaces, is achieved and reinforced through the continuity of the locations in which human beings are immersed and the things with which they are engaged. That is, it is not merely the physical persistence of the body across time and space, but rather the persistence of the situation as such, that gives rise to the fundamental experience of *dwelling* in the world. In a passage that sounds more Merleau-Pontian than Heideggerian, Heidegger observes, "When I go toward the door of the lecture hall, I am already there, and I could not go to it at all if I were not such that I am there. I am never here only, as this encapsulated body; rather, I am there, that is, I already pervade the room, and only thus can I go through it" (Heidegger 1971a: 157).

In its ek-static projection toward its future projects, the body exceeds its epidermal boundaries to participate in what Merleau-Ponty refers to, in his final works, as the "flesh of the world." Although the body is conventionally understood as occupying discrete coordinates that demarcate it from the place it inhabits, both Merleau-Ponty and Heidegger encourage a rethinking of the body's relationship to its immediate environment. Approaching the lecture hall, anticipating my presence within it, my body is neither "here" nor "there." Indeed, the body, in its chiasmatic, interdependent relationship with its surroundings, inhabits what Grosz, following Derrida and Deleuze, has identified as the space of the "in-between."

For Grosz, the space of the in-between is a space of possibility, the space in which identities are both constructed and deconstructed. In her words: "The space in between things is the space in which things are undone, the space to the side and around, which is the space of subversion and fraying, the edges of any identity's limits. In short, it is the space of the bounding and undoing of the identities which constitute it" (Grosz 2001: 93). While psychoanalytic theory has focused attention on the ways in which identities are undone from the "inside," that is, through the unconscious processes that continually undermine the ego's attempts to establish its own "proper" boundaries, Grosz turns to the outside, to the dynamic interfaces that indissolubly link bodies with the places they inhabit. Just as psychoanalysis has enabled a greater understanding of the rich psychical subsoil that informs and is often in tension with an individual's conscious thought processes, bodily activities, and the idiosyncratic identities continually being constructed both for oneself and for others, Grosz maintains that the space of the in-between "threatens to open itself up as new, to facilitate transformations in the identities that constitute it" (Grosz 2001: 94). This liminal space foils attempts to fix the parameters of any given identity, and, Grosz suggests, the very instability it produces can be utilized creatively to promote a new and different future, a future that is always in the making. This future, she argues, cannot be imagined as a utopia, for "[t]he utopian mode seeks a future that itself has no future, a future in which time will cease to be a relevant factor, and movement, change, and becoming remain impossible" (Grosz 2001: 143).

Rather than cling to utopian fantasies whose ahistoric character reifies one particular vision of the future at the expense of others, Grosz implies that the space of the in-between is precisely what keeps identity mobile and fluid, responsive to the changing interactions between bodies and environments. That this space of possibility can never be taken for granted but must continually be affirmed and protected is poignantly illustrated by the work of feminists and disability activists who have demanded access to spaces from which women and people with disabilities were formerly excluded. Access to these previously forbidden spaces (buildings, men's clubs, etc.), has indeed been transformative, helping to reveal and dismantle the shaky foundations of the stigmatized identities that have historically defined the "inferiority" of both women and people with disabilities, interpellations that have materially, socially, and intellectually constrained the horizons of some in order to expand the horizons of others.

Grosz's earlier work on bodies and cities is relevant here because she emphasizes again and again the power of cities to structure human corporeality. In her words:

> The city is one of the crucial factors in the social production of (sexed) corporeality: the built environment provides the context and coordinates for contemporary forms of body. The city provides the order and organization that automatically links otherwise unrelated bodies: it is the condition and milieu in which corporeality is socially, sexually, and discursively produced. But if the city is a significant context and frame for the body, the relations between bodies and cities are more complex than may have been realized. (Grosz 1995: 104)

The transformative possibilities that emerge from the human body's dynamic interactions with its environment, Grosz suggests, are experienced as threatening only if one resists one's own futurity, that is, if one resists the openness to new experiences that is the very mark of the future as the domain of the "not yet." Casey also affirms the chiasmatic relationship between alterations in the built environment and self-alteration when he states, "In creating built places, we transform not only the local landscape but ourselves as subjects: body subjects become fabricating agents" (Casey 1993: 111). For both Grosz and Casey, human beings' inability to stay in one place and corresponding lack of a fixed identity are positive phenomena because they mean that people can explore new ways of being and, more precisely, new ways of dwelling in the world. To the extent that, as Casey claims, "we tend to identify ourselves by—and with—the places in which we reside" (Casey 1993: 120), the ability to freely and comfortably navigate within one's own built environment has the potential of enlarging "our already existing embodiment into *an entire life-world of dwelling*" (Casey 1993: 120; emphasis in original).

The Fragility of Dwelling

In contrast to the expansive possibilities that are often associated with city life, however, the terrorist attacks of September 11, 2001, on New York City and Washington, D.C., and the daily attacks occurring in cities and villages in Iraq, Afghanistan, Israel, Palestine, Lebanon, the Sudan, and other war-torn countries, are forcible reminders that the restrictions placed on bodies by the places in which they reside can diminish, and in extreme cases even destroy, a positive experience of futurity, and, as a result, radically curtail a sense of bodily agency.[10] Casey maintains that the body itself is a "proto-place" constituting my "corporeal here." "But," he claims, "precisely in its action of proto-placement, my body takes me up against counter-places, including conflictual places, at every moment. In this countering (and being encountered), the body constitutes the crossroads between architecture and landscape, the built and the given, the artificial and the natural" (Casey 1993: 131). While Grosz and Casey tend to valorize the productive dimensions of the tensions between the body and its surrounding environment, homeless activists continually emphasize that we can never take the body's emplacement for granted. Some people, quite simply, have no place to dwell. And, without a dwelling, without a fixed address, their very identity is indeed at risk.

Casey, in particular, lauds the benefits of dwelling both for the individual and for the cherished place in which she dwells: "To dwell is to exercise patience-of-place; it requires willingness to cultivate, often seemingly endlessly, the inhabitational possibilities of a particular residence. Such willingness shows that we care about *how* we live in that residence and that we care about it as a place for living well, not merely as a 'machine for living' (in Le Corbusier's revealing phrase)" (Casey 1993: 174). And he goes on to add, "To cultivate *its* [a domicile's] interior we must cultivate *our* interior; it is a matter of letting one interior speak to another" (Casey 1993: 174). But what if one lives in a slum with limited inhabitational possibilities? What if a person doesn't have a home at all? What if one's own psychic health even requires that a neighborhood park or a rat-infested apartment be viewed merely as a "machine for living?" A danger of overemphasizing the necessity of home for the cultivation of the individual's own identity is that those who lack homes run the risk of having their very humanity placed in question.

For many homeless men, women, and children in urban areas today, the city itself takes the place of home. In one of his few references to homelessness, Casey warns of the threat that the larger city poses to the domesticity of the home:

> Moving about in a city draws us away from the interior depth of a home and into the exterior breadth of a wider urban world. It is hardly surprising that we find homelessness mainly located *in cities*, which are in many respects the antipodes of homes. Cities certainly contain homes, but in their capacity to demand and distract they are continually luring us into the streets. They take us out of our homes and into a more precarious and sometimes hostile extra-domestic world. (Casey 1993: 180)

While Grosz views the city as a space of possibility that can enhance human beings' sense of being at-home-in-the-world, a view that runs the danger of failing to acknowledge the ways in which the city can produce profound feelings of alienation and disidentification, Casey sets up a problematic dichotomy between the city and the home that unintentionally reinforces the stigmatization of those who are homeless. He acknowledges that a home need not be a house and that it is bodily engagement with a given place rather than the length of time one spends in that place that gives rise to the experience of dwelling, but he also implies that it is up to the individual to transform her environment into a home, and he rules out the possibility of the city itself serving such a function.[11]

In her essay "House and Home," Iris Young chronicles in painful detail the tragedy that followed her family's move from apartment life in the city to her parents' "dream house" in the suburbs when she was a young girl (Young 1997). The sudden, unexpected death of her father shortly after the move left her mother completely alone with two children to raise in the midst of strangers without the comfort and support of her urban community. As Young tersely observes, obtaining her dream house in the suburbs became her mother's worst nightmare, since her depression in the face of her husband's death led to her failure to "keep up" the home, a failure duly reported to the police by intolerant neighbors, which resulted in the removal of Iris and her brother to foster homes and to her mother's own incarceration. Thus, the powerful images of Descartes in his study meditating in the privacy of his home, Virginia Woolf's call for each woman to have "a room of one's own," and even Casey's own description of his book-lined study in which he is peaceful and productive, must be balanced by Ibsen's equally powerful image of the home as a prison for Nora in *A Doll's House*, and of Young's chilling description of the home as the site of social judgment and condemnation.

In her book *Family Bonds: Genealogies of Race and Gender*, Ellen Feder, like Young, questions overly positive views of a "home of one's own" by drawing attention to the exclusionary racist and classist strategies operative in Levittown, the first model suburban community in the United States. A "no blacks policy"—unofficial yet rigidly enforced—prevented (and still prevents today) many families from being able to find safe and affordable housing. Moreover, the families that were able to enjoy the "privileges" of home ownership in Levittown found themselves subject to a stringent, Foucaultian disciplinary regime that dictated how often their lawns were to be cut, how many pets they could have, what type of mailboxes they could put up, and where their laundry could and could not be hung.

Rather than leading to the conclusion that home ownership is not a good thing, or that homes do not supply bodies with a sense of comfort and security that can facilitate the development of a positive sense of self, the lessons of Levittown and Young's own experience warn against uncritically embracing the benefits of home in such a way that the failure to have a home or even be at home becomes the fault of the individual rather than a collective failure on the part of the larger community in which she resides (or fails to reside). Young's and Feder's work emphasizes not only the fragility of dwelling but also the privileges and responsibilities that accompany it. The violence of being ejected from one's dwelling, the violence of being displaced from one's home and one's country of origin, may be the very type of experiences Merleau-Ponty had in mind when he wrote that oppressive forms of violence may require violent solutions. Violent solutions need not, of course, involve actual physical violence. Rather, what I believe Merleau-Ponty is suggesting is that the transformation of conservative belief structures that tolerate and legitimize violence requires a genuine up-heaval. This upheaval is violent precisely because it seeks to eradicate not only the experiences of oppression but also the societal structures that support them.

In the final pages of *Humanism and Terror,* Merleau-Ponty affirms that "[t]he human world is an open or unfinished system and the same radical con-tingency which threatens it with discord also rescues it from the inevitability of disorder and prevents us from despairing of it" (Merleau-Ponty 1969: 188). "Such a philosophy," he asserts,

> awakens us to the importance of daily events and action. For it is a philosophy which arouses in us a love for our times which are not the simple repetition of human eternity nor merely the conclusion to premises already postulated. It is a view which like the most fragile object of perception—a soap bubble, or a wave—or like the most simple dialogue, embraces indivisibly all the order and all the disorder of the world. (Merleau-Ponty 1969: 188–189)

Ushering in a new epoch in which the violence of social justice is able to trans-form the conditions, and therefore the possibilities, of what I have been calling urban flesh is itself a collective project whose fragility and volatility guarantee that it is always unfinished, always in the making. Such a project requires that individuals as well as societies remain open to the possibility that their estab-lished, ordinary patterns of living, including their institutionalized means of "producing order," might well have to undergo radical, even violent, change.

As Grosz suggests, not only does such a project undercut reductive binaries, it also undercuts a fixed sense of identity and thereby holds out the promise of new identities that resist the oppressive structures of the past and the present that seek to constrain them. To realize this promise, she suggests, is to embrace the openness that flows from the contingency of the future:

> An openness to futurity is a challenge facing all of the arts, sciences, and hu-manities; the degree of openness is an index of one's political alignments and orientations, of the readiness to transform. Unless we put into question archi-tectural and cultural identities—the identities of men and women, of different races and classes, and of different religious, sexual, and political affiliations, as well as the identities of cities, urban regions, buildings, and houses—this openness to the future, the promise of time unfolding through innovation rather than prediction, is muted rather than welcomed. (Grosz 2001: 91)

Ironically, the refusal to be open has historically produced more oppressive and longer-lasting violence than the refusal of closure, the refusal to inhabit the space of the "in-between." However, to remain open to the future does not mean that one fails to commit oneself to a definite path of action. Rather, I suggest, following Merleau-Ponty, that it involves seizing upon and taking responsibility for that "incarnate principle that brings a style of being wherever there is a fragment of being" (Merleau-Ponty 1968: 139). And this requires that human beings recognize, with Irigaray, that "the flesh of each one is not substitutable for the other," that one must always be attentive to the unique and changing demands that arise out of the stylized differentiations of incarnate existence (Irigaray 1993: 167). Thus, to maintain openness through the affirmation (rather than the denial) of difference does not mean embracing an "anything goes" perspective, but rather necessitates the acknowledgement of limit as the very condition of possibility. For, as Merleau-Ponty observes in *Nature: Course Notes from the Collège de France*, "Matter means that at any given moment, not everything is possible" (Merleau-Ponty 2003: 69).

When Merleau-Ponty is brought into a conversation with his future interlocutors, including contemporary phenomenologists and feminist theorists whose interests and commitments are not only different but also often at odds with his own, new spaces of possibility emerge, and new limitations must continually be confronted. Just as Odysseus's wife, Penelope, refused to stop weaving the fabric that, once finished, was supposed to define her identity once and for all as the wife of one of her unwanted suitors, the aim of the weavings enacted in this particular text is to produce new openings, new spaces for change, movement, and growth that can be taken up and woven afresh by others. For it is evident that expanding the possibilities for stylizing urban flesh requires new ways of understanding the dynamic relationship between bodies and cities. This in turn will involve new ways of living and loving, not to mention new ways of thinking about and doing philosophy.

Indeed, as Judith Butler forcefully argues in the final pages of *Undoing Gender*, in a chapter aptly entitled "Can the 'Other' of Philosophy Speak?" (a title that mimes, in Irigarayan fashion, Gayatri Spivak's classic postcolonial essay, "Can the Subaltern Speak?"), "with respect to the humanities, [philosophy] has been for the most part a loner, territorial, protective, increasingly hermetic" (Butler 2004: 246). I agree with Butler that the attempt by some philosophers to "protect" and "defend" the allegedly purely philosophical domain from "interlopers" who are not formally trained in its rigorous historical traditions is doomed to failure, since all these attempts achieve is an artificial isolation of philosophy from the rest of the humanities (not to mention the social sciences and sciences) that leads to the impoverishment of philosophy itself, since it is left out of the very exciting interdisciplinary conversations currently taking place within and among these other disciplines. As Butler notes, "In some ways, the most culturally important discussions of philosophy are taking place by scholars who have always worked outside the institutional walls of philosophy" (Butler 2004: 247). Recognizing that it is the alleged "purity" of philosophy that is at stake, she advocates that we abandon this notion altogether, for, as history has repeatedly shown, the arbiters of the standards of purity have tended to view themselves as self-legislating authorities who fail to interrogate the adequacy of the law that legitimizes their own work and existence and de-legitimizes that of others. Moreover, she maintains that "as philosophy has lost its purity, it has accordingly gained its vitality throughout the humanities" (Butler 2004: 247). By bringing non-philosophers into dialogue with philosophers, and by taking up topics that have been largely avoided by traditional philosophy (such as the ways in which severe oppression compromises the very concept of choice that is at the heart of ethical notions of freedom and autonomy), I seek to contribute to this crucial project of revitalization.

In the final paragraph of his *Phenomenology of Perception*, Merleau-Ponty observes that "[w]hether it is a question of things or of historical situations, philosophy has no other function than to teach us to see them clearly once more, and it is true to say that it comes into being by destroying itself as separate philosophy" (Merleau-Ponty 1962: 456). What I am arguing here, following Merleau-Ponty, Butler, and so many others, is that "to see clearly" is not synonymous with a Cartesian vision of "clear and distinct knowledge" that is accessed through strict adherence to a "pure" methodology that is indifferent to the infinitely varied ways in which those who exercise it meaningfully inhabit the world of their concern. To "see clearly" the complex ties that bind one individual to another and to the world that they share involves seeing that no one discipline can possibly hope to address all the mysteries that constitute human existence, or, for that matter, raise all the important questions that need to be asked and re-asked. As Alcoff observes in *Visible Identities*, "When truth is defined as that which can be seen, there develops an uncanny interdependence between that which is true and that which is hidden" (Alcoff 2006: 7). Moving beyond a preoccupation with what is clearly visible means delving into those murky, "hidden" areas against which the visible is defined as such, namely the invisible horizons that provide the contexts of significance against which the visible unfolds. To pursue this project, as the authors I have been discussing all emphasize, means giving up the false ideal of "purity" in favor of the far messier terrain that describes the reality in which human beings actually live, including its multiple, essentially indeterminate, horizons that contribute directly to the everlasting, always elusive, yet infinitely rewarding pursuit of what Alcoff, wielding the philosopher's ultimate weapon, properly calls "truth."

PART 5

Constraining Horizons

9
Death and the Other: Rethinking Authenticity

Death is a possibility of being that Da-sein always has to take upon itself. With death, Da-sein stands before itself in its ownmost potentiality-of-being. In this possibility, Da-sein is concerned about its being-in-the-world absolutely. Its death is the possibility of no-longer-being-able-to-be-there. When Da-sein is imminent to itself as this possibility, it is *completely* thrown back upon its ownmost potentiality-of-being. Thus imminent to it-self, all relations to other Da-sein are dissolved in it. This nonrelational ownmost potentiality is at the same time the most extreme one. As a poten-tiality of being, Da-sein is unable to bypass the possibility of death.
—Heidegger 1996: 232

Whether I was accepting my possible demise or denying it, I wanted very much to talk about it. I wanted to be keenly aware of what was happening to me, what death might mean, how it would feel. I didn't want to be cheated out of the experience because the subject was taboo. Of course, it was nearly impossible to discuss such an unknowable subject in any ratio-nal way. But I demanded that my family and friends engage me on this matter. And I'm happy to report that, to the last one, they have risen to the occasion.
—Hainer 1990: 29

To Share or Not to Share? Intersubjective Challenges to the "Mineness" of Death

Death, in many ways, seems like the horizon of all horizons; its universal appli-
cability not only to human beings but to all living beings is incontestable. Heidegger emphasizes in the passage above the essentially individuating dimension
of each being's death, for each individual being in the world has its own manner
of existing, and the transition from life to death fundamentally alters the way in
which that being exists as it moves from being animate to being inanimate.
This, in turn, guarantees that no two experiences of death will be identical, and
this becomes especially salient for human beings, who alone, Heidegger argues,
are able to recognize, reflect upon, and ask questions about the fact of their impending death. Only human beings, Heidegger asserts, experience what he
calls a "being-toward death," a way of existing in the world that reflects an ongoing awareness that one could die at any time. Of course, Heidegger is quick to
argue that the fact that human beings have the capacity to raise questions concerning the meaning of death in their lives doesn't mean that everyone exercises
this capacity; even if they do exercise it to some extent, he suggests that this is
most often done in an inauthentic fashion.

The classically inauthentic response to one's being-toward-death, in Heidegger's view, is the attempt to in any way share this radically individualizing
experience with others—the very path taken by USA Today reporter Cathy
Hainer in her published diaries chronicling her daily experience with stage-four
breast cancer. So the question becomes, or more precisely the questions become, what is an authentic manner of experiencing one's being-toward-death
for Heidegger, and why does his account preclude Cathy Hainer's very public
way of dealing with her own impending death from cancer as an authentic response to her being-toward-death? And, most importantly, is Heidegger's description of the essentially solitary quality of an authentic being-toward-death
convincing?

In his famous analysis of the existential phenomenon of being-toward-
death in *Being and Time*, he emphasizes again and again that the radical "mineness" of death renders me incapable of authentically communicating anything
about my own experience of its "indefinite certainty." Hainer, by contrast, suggests that one is "cheated out of the experience" of being-toward-death if one is
unable to talk about it with others. The contrast between Heidegger's claim that
death is Dasein's "ownmost *nonrelational* possibility" that "dissolves" its relations to all other human beings and Hainer's "demand" that others can and
must become actively engaged in the experience of her impending death could
not be more profound.[1] What is at stake here is precisely the status of "the
Other," or more specifically, human relations with others, in the pursuit of what

Heidegger terms "authenticity," or what others might call, despite his own protestations that this latter is not a normative notion, a meaningful ethical life.[2]

Cathy Hainer was not a philosopher like Martin Heidegger. She did not, to my knowledge, ever study phenomenology, but was a journalist for many years with the international newspaper *USA Today*. Hainer shared her own experience of "being-toward-death" not only with family and friends but also with thousands of *USA Today* readers as she publicly chronicled her battle with breast cancer for eighteen months before she died in December of 1999. I have chosen to focus on her very public response to her ultimately fatal diagnosis of stage-four breast cancer precisely because sharing one's feelings about this diagnosis with thousands of anonymous readers seems so directly opposed to an authentic experience of death on Heidegger's account. However, I will argue, against Heidegger, that sharing one's feelings about one's own death with others need not be an inauthentic response to death, and that in Hainer's case at least, the desire to share the experience with others was not intended either to (1) take away the "mineness" of her death or (2) mitigate Hainer's own anxiety concerning her being-toward-death.

One of the most important lessons that feminism has taught is not to seek wisdom only through established channels. That is, just as feminists and other critical theorists have sought to recover the lost wisdom of those whose voices were never heard while they were alive because they lacked the proper gender, proper race, proper sexuality, proper class, and proper education to have their knowledge recognized and affirmed, so too, I believe, must people continue to question false boundaries that artificially divide different forms of inquiry, including those that separate formal philosophies from more informal (but no less rigorous) discussions of the very meaning of human existence. Indeed, Hainer's poignant descriptions of her own being-toward-death will help me to demonstrate that (1) Heidegger ends up offering a very reductive view of the myriad motivations people might have for sharing their feelings concerning their anticipation of their own death with others and (2) he far too hastily embraces the solitariness of the Kierkegaardian knight of faith as the model for authentic existence, an individual such as Abraham, who is unable to share his experience of faith with any other individuals, including, in the latter's case, even his closest relations, namely, his wife and son. One should not be too surprised then, that, as with Kierkegaard's Abraham, silence turns out to be the only example of authentic discourse in *Being and Time*.[3]

Despite the criticisms of phenomenology that have been raised over the years by feminists and others who argue that its descriptions of lived experience are very limited insofar as they are utterly dependent on the perspective of the one who is providing them, I would argue that phenomenology is uniquely suited to the feminist political project of recognizing the legitimacy of the experiences of those people, such as Cathy Hainer, who lack the formal credentials to be recognized as "experts" in the interpretation of those experiences. Before I can make this case, let me acknowledge the force of the accusations against phenomenology as it has traditionally and officially been practiced.

The Power of Phenomenological Descriptions

Not only have phenomenological descriptions been viewed as suspect because of their alleged subjectivism, but they are also condemned because of the phenomenologist's presumed sleight of hand in presenting his (invariably, and significantly, it is a man's) own experience as the experience of all.[4] Paraphrasing Irigaray's objections to Merleau-Ponty's phenomenology in particular, Grosz succinctly articulates Irigaray's central concern as follows:

> [For Merleau-Ponty] The world remains isomorphic with the subject, existing in a complementary relation of reversibility. The perceiving, seeing, touching subject remains a subject with a proprietorial relation to the visible, the tactile: he stands over and above while remaining also within his world, recognizing the object and the (sexed) other as versions or inversions of himself, reverse three-dimensional "mirrors," posing all the dangers of mirror identifications. (Grosz 1994: 107)

While Merleau-Ponty's anti-Cartesian understanding of the "body-subject" as being of the same "flesh" as the world it inhabits would seem to make him less guilty of subjectivism than other phenomenologists, such as Husserl or Sartre, who base the uniqueness of the subject on the unique intentional activity of each human consciousness, the implication is that if Merleau-Ponty is guilty as charged, then all other phenomenologists and phenomenology itself are also discredited. The force and persuasiveness of this often-invoked criticism of phenomenology has led to something of an impasse for myself and other contemporary feminist phenomenologists. Not only are most, if not all, feminist phenomenologists eager to divorce themselves from the unsavory reputation of being "subjectivists," but one's own commitment to phenomenology must also be defended constantly through the much-repeated protestation that one does not intend to falsely universalize one's own experience by portraying it as the experience of all.

There are many ways, however, to rebut the claim that phenomenology is inescapably subjectivist, and therefore that its descriptions are applicable only to the individual who is promulgating them. One such strategy, and the one that I will pursue here, involves relaxing the relatively stringent criteria that determine who is and is not a philosopher, who is and is not a phenomenologist, by recognizing the prevalence and power of phenomenological descriptions of ordinary experience that are proffered in what may seem to be the most unlikely of places, such as the pages of USA Today, a media realm that seems to be an archetypical example of what Heidegger saw as the inauthentic domain of "the they." To be open, in advance, to the possibility that an authentic description of "being-toward-death" can come from an allegedly inauthentic venue is to acknowledge that there is no one privileged site or mode of being that alone can reveal the most meaningful aspects of human experience.

I will begin, then, by setting forth an antinomy between two views of being-toward-death, one offered by a professional philosopher in the course of a classic work of the twentieth century, Being and Time, the other offered by a professional journalist in the course of a series of newspaper articles that detailed her terminal illness with cancer. How, one might ask, can Hainer's personal testimony of the importance of sharing her experience with others possibly challenge the authority and veracity of Heidegger's proclamation that death dissolves my relations with all others by forcing me to confront on my own my "ownmost nonrelational possibility"? Doesn't her very attempt to share her experience, especially to share it in such an anonymous public forum as the media, condemn her from the outset to inauthenticity? Doesn't the radical "mineness" of death, a quality that I agree with Heidegger is one of its most crucial features, preclude the possibility of communicating anything about it to anyone else except insofar as we seek to avoid the anxiety of acknowledging that it is not only others but myself who is dying? To address this last question I will turn yet again beyond phenomenology proper, this time to the fictional account provided by Leo Tolstoy's Ivan Ilych, in order to illuminate what I take to be a crucial series of phenomenological insights regarding what is at stake in this terrible recognition of the "mineness" of one's own being-toward-death.

The Inauthenticity of "the They"

The syllogism he had learned from Kiesewetter's logic—"Caius is a man, men are mortal, therefore Caius is mortal"—had always seemed to him correct as applied to Caius, but by no means to himself. That man Caius represented man in the abstract, and so the reasoning was perfectly sound; but he was not Caius, not an abstract man; he had always been a creature quite, quite distinct from all the others. (Tolstoy 1981: 93)

In the transition from the true premise that all human beings are mortal to its necessary and equally true conclusion that as a human being "I, too, will die," Ivan Ilych experiences the tremendous anxiety of having his relations to all other Dasein undone. As he goes on to observe, "Caius really was mortal, and it was only right that he should die, but for him, Vanya, Ivan Ilych, with all his thoughts and feelings, it was something else again. And it simply was not possible that he should have to die. That would be too terrible" (Tolstoy 1981: 93–94). Indeed, Ivan Ilych's continual wavering between an authentic awareness that his death is imminent and cannot be avoided and an inauthentic denial that this could really be true for him offers an incredibly strong example of the power of the they, as described by Heidegger, to "tranquillize" individuals about their own (and others') deaths. As one who has lived his own life by conforming to the they's understanding of what is "pleasant and proper," Ivan cannot find any resources within the they to confront the unpleasantness and impropriety of his illness and impending death. Indeed, "[h]e saw that the awesome, terrifying act of his dying had been degraded by those about him to the level of a chance unpleasantness, a bit of unseemly behavior (they reacted to him as they would to a man who emitted a foul odor on entering a drawing room); that it had been degraded by that very 'propriety' to which he had devoted his entire life" (Tolstoy 1981: 103).

Over time, with great difficulty and much suffering, Ivan comes to recognize that while his inability to resume his position as an active participant in the public domain of everyday life sets him apart from others, it also provides him with a unique and hitherto unlooked for opportunity to interrogate his own existence on its own terms, apart from the dictates of the they. In his solitary meditations on his own being-toward-death, Ivan Ilych affirms Heidegger's assertion that

> [d]eath is the *ownmost* possibility of Da-sein. Being toward it discloses to Da-sein its *ownmost* potentiality-of-being in which it is concerned about the being of Da-sein absolutely. Here the fact can become evident to Da-sein that in the eminent possibility of itself it is torn away from the they, that is, anticipation can always already have torn itself away from the they. The understanding of this "ability," however, first reveals its factical lostness in the everydayness of the they-self. (Heidegger 1996: 243)

As a result of his previous "lostness in the everydayness of the they-self," Ivan Ilych finds himself poorly equipped to confront the limitations of the knowledge provided him by the they head-on. "[W]hy should I have to die, and die in agony?" he asks. " 'Something must be wrong. Perhaps I did not live as I should have,' it suddenly occurred to him. 'But how could that be when I did everything one is supposed to?' he replied and *immediately dismissed the one solution to the whole enigma of life and death, considering it utterly impossible*" (Tolstoy 1981: 120, my emphasis). In this pivotal passage in the text, Tolstoy shifts swiftly and almost imperceptibly from a first-person account to the narrator's observation that in Ivan Ilych's rejection of the idea that he may have lived inappropriately even though he faithfully followed the dictates of the they on how to live appropriately, he at the same time "dismissed the one solution to the whole enigma of life and death." Paradoxically, Tolstoy reverts to the voice of the anonymous narrator to convey a truth about the protagonist's own experience that is, at the time, no more than a nightmarish possibility to the protagonist himself, a possibility that he hastily repudiates, namely, that the socially acceptable life he has hitherto led has been inauthentic precisely because it is society (and not Ivan Ilych) who has dictated the very terms through which that life has been given meaning and value.

Can There Be Authentic Relations to Others?

Although Ivan Ilych seems like a perfect example of Heidegger's call to throw off the shackles of the they when confronting one's own being-toward-death precisely because the they, with its constant and myriad forms of tranquillization about death can never provide one with the resources to deal with it on a personal, immediate level, Tolstoy also challenges Heidegger's picture of Dasein resolutely facing its death cut off from all others in his description of the final moments of the title character's life. As he acknowledges without flinching that the entire way in which he has lived his life, that is, in accordance with social convention, has been the wrong way to live, Ivan Ilych suddenly is freed from his former resentment (and even feelings of hatred) toward his wife and all those others who are still able to live life in accordance with the they and for whom his pain and suffering has been an unseemly and irritating burden to bear. Even while recognizing that his wife, his daughter, his former colleagues, and the doctors will resume their habitual activities without giving his death more than a passing thought, he also recognizes that his suffering has tortured them and that he must forgive them for not also confronting the inadequacy of the they, which has served them so well: "And suddenly it became clear to him that what had been oppressing him and would not leave him suddenly was vanishing all at once—from two sides, ten sides, all sides. He felt sorry for them, he had to do something to keep from hurting them. To deliver them and himself from this suffering. 'How good and how simple!' he thought" (Tolstoy 1981: 133).

Despite the fact that Ivan Ilych is too weak to communicate these feelings of love and regret to his family, Tolstoy depicts him as at peace because "He who needed to understand would understand" (Tolstoy 1981: 133). In his sudden discovery of God's presence (a presence that has not manifested itself until this point), Ivan Ilych is able to forgive himself and forgive others for their previously inauthentic relations by presumably entering into an authentic relationship with God. Unlike Tolstoy, however, Heidegger does not hold out the hope that God will provide an authentic alternative to the inauthenticity of the they. For Heidegger, one cannot appeal to any transcendent being to give one peace in reckoning with one's own being-in-the-world without also condemning oneself to inauthenticity yet again precisely because God is, by definition, not of this world.

Camus describes this appeal to the religious in order to escape the absurdity of an existence that lacks any source of external justification as a primary example of "the spirit of nostalgia" (Camus 1983: 42), and he excoriates it even more vigorously than Heidegger, who simply identifies it as a common strategy employed by the they to diminish Dasein's anxiety toward death.[5] Despite the power of Heidegger's and Camus's respective rejections of any appeal to God to alleviate one's suffering in confronting one's being-toward-death, and despite the artificiality in which God suddenly appears to "save" Ivan Ilych from the they at the end of Tolstoy's story, one may still question whether Heidegger and Camus have not reacted too hastily in seeing any reaching out to others (or to God) as attempts to mediate that which cannot be mediated, namely a personal confrontation with one's own mortality.

In *The Stranger*, Camus's Meursault, on the eve of his death by the guillotine, rejects and even mocks Ivan Ilych's divine vision of the possibility for human love and forgiveness in the very presence of the priest who comes, against Meursault's will, to administer the last rites:

> Actually, I was sure of myself, sure about everything, far surer than he; sure of my present life and of the death that was coming. That, no doubt, was all I had; but at least that certainty was something I could get my teeth into—just as it had got its teeth into me. I'd been right, I was still right, I was always right. I'd passed my life in a certain way, and I might have passed it in a different way, if I'd felt like it. I'd acted thus, and I hadn't acted otherwise; I hadn't done x, whereas I had done y or z. And what did that mean? That, all the time, I'd been waiting for this present moment, for that dawn, tomorrow's or another day's, which was to justify me. Nothing, nothing had the least importance, and I knew quite well why. He, too, knew why. From the dark horizon of my future, a sort of slow, persistent breeze had been blowing toward me, all my life long, from the years that were to come. And on its way that breeze had leveled out all the ideas that people tried to foist on me in the equally unreal years I then was living through. What difference could they make to me, the deaths of others, or a mother's love, or his God; or the way a man decides to live, the fate he thinks he chooses, since one and the same fate was bound to "choose" not only me but thousands of millions of privileged people who, like him, called themselves my brothers. (Camus 1954: 151–152)

Camus goes one step further than Heidegger, in fact, by rejecting the very possibility of authenticity insofar as it connotes the possibility of giving meaning to one's existence (even on one's own terms). For Camus, human existence has no meaning at all; it is simply absurd. Or, one might say, the meaning of human existence *is* its absurdity. Camus acknowledges the human demand for meaning and justification but also proclaims that it will never be met.

Caring for Others and Being Cared For: Understanding Authenticity Relationally

How might the following entry from Hainer's journal be squared with Camus's bleak vision?

> And I can't help imagining what my own obituary will say: "Cathy Hainer graduated from college and went to work for a newspaper." Will I be disappointed that it doesn't describe me as "Pulitzer Prize winner and author of best-selling novels"? A little. But I hope I'm more concerned with my legacy than my obituary. Will people remember me fondly? Have I brought a smile to anyone's face, helped anyone out of a difficult time? Have I made someone laugh when they were down, done anything for the common good of mankind? (Hainer 1999: 34)

Whereas the "deaths of others, or a mother's love or his God" or even the love of his girlfriend Marie are of no concern to Camus's Meursault, Hainer worries about how she will be remembered. She is not concerned with recognition of her professional accomplishments but with the effects, both small and large, that she hopes to have had on the lives of others. As Hainer anticipates her death, contemplating the transformation of its indefinite certainty to a definite one, she receives her greatest pleasures from the affection and love she exchanges with her family and friends:

> Saturday mornings can be a hectic time at my house, but a few weekends ago we actually were able to lounge late in bed. David [her fiancé] was dozing peacefully on one side of me, and Maggie, my adorable new dachshund puppy, was curled up in the crook of my other arm. For me, that was nirvana. I feel a little sheepish having such ungrandiose dreams, but my friend Anne says that's the sign of a life well lived. I hope she's right. (Hainer 1999: 30)

It is clear that the peace and happiness Hainer feels with loved ones by her side does not eviscerate the anxiety she experiences knowing that her cancer and bodily discomfort will get much worse and that it will end up killing her. She does not evade this realization in the journal, but she does share the intimacy of this personal journey with family, friends, and millions of strangers. From a Heideggerian perspective, as his previously cited claims about being-toward-death make clear, the radical individualization of death separates me from all others, undoing my relationship with other Dasein and presumably with animals such as Hainer's dog, Maggie. To attempt to share the experience, he suggests, is a form of inauthentic flight that distorts its very essence as mine. It is important to note that in the example above, Hainer is sharing her experience silently, through the warmth of her body as it embraces the warmth of David's and Maggie's bodies. Here, there is an intercorporeal exchange taking place, simply through the communication between bodies. Would Heidegger view this nonverbal exchange as inauthentic as well? And, why should words render a relationship inauthentic to begin with?

In the following passage, Heidegger reiterates but then seems to retreat from the strong claim that Dasein can no longer have any relations at all with others when it is authentically confronting its ownmost possibility, namely, death:

> The nonrelational character of death understood in anticipation individualizes Da-sein down to itself. This individualizing is a way in which the "there" is disclosed for existence. *It reveals the fact that any being-together-with what is taken care of and any being-with the others fails when one's ownmost potentiality-of-being is at stake.* Da-sein can *authentically* be *itself* only when it makes that possible of its own accord. But if taking care of things and being concerned fail us, this does not, however, mean at all that these modes of Da-sein have been cut off from its authentic being a self. As essential structures of the constitution of Da-sein they also belong to the condition of the possibility of existence in general. Da-sein is authentically itself only if it projects itself, *as* being-together with things taken care of and concernful being-with, . . . primarily upon its ownmost potentiality-of-being, rather than upon the possibility of the they-self. Anticipation of its nonrelational possibility forces the being that anticipates into the possibility of taking over its ownmost being of its own accord. (Heidegger 1996: 243, my emphasis)

One might understand Dasein's failure to "take care" of things when confronting authentically its being-toward-death as a failure to express its previous level of concern for its everyday projects, just as Ivan Ilych failed to take the same pleasure in playing cards, working, and decorating his house that he had before his serious illness. However, when Heidegger says that there is also a failure to be concerned more generally, this suggests that Dasein no longer experiences the same sense of care for its own existence. The question becomes, is the failure to be concerned a failure in one's very ability to care? But care constitutes the very structure of Dasein's being for Heidegger, so if its ability to care is at stake, then Dasein's own being as Da-sein, that is, its own "being-there," is also at stake. Perhaps for this very reason, Heidegger goes on to suggest that even though there is a failure to take care of things and a failure of concern when one confronts one's impending death authentically, these "modes of Da-sein" haven't been cut off completely since they are the very "condition of the possibility of existence in general."

As existential structures, then, taking care of things and being concerned are still part of the very make-up as Dasein and so they remain structures of human being-in-the-world, Heidegger implies, even as they suffer failure. But the question I am interested in here is about not the formal persistence of these existential structures but their content or lack thereof. For if the structures remain, but are empty, then how much can they really be contributing to the meaningfulness of my existence? Is there any ontic content that can be given to these structures and to the relationships that flow (or fail to flow) from them without falling into inauthenticity? What, precisely, is the status of Dasein's concrete, everyday relations with others and with the world of its concern, relations that Heidegger has claimed are dissolved when Dasein confronts its *ownmost* potentiality that cannot be outstripped?

In the quote above, Heidegger attempts to negotiate this tension by distinguishing between grounding these relationships upon the they-self, an inauthentic move, versus "the possibility of taking over its ownmost being of its own accord." On a generous reading, one might say that Dasein is able to live its relationships authentically in its being-toward-death so long as it grasps these relations on its own terms rather than society's. Fair enough. But what about the terms of the other, terms that are not reducible to my own but that also play a key role in my relations with that other? There seems to be no room for any other perspective here.

Defending Heidegger against the charge that an authentic life can be lived only solipsistically, Tina Chanter asserts that "Dasein's self-understanding is structured by its tendency to derive its meaning from its meaningful relations with the world" (Chanter 2001: 80). If this is so, she suggests, then relations with others can and should play a valuable role in Dasein's authentic relationship to its own being-toward-death, especially since others are included in that being as it is ontically lived. The problem, both she and I agree, is that Heidegger's own account seems to preclude this possibility because of his failure to distinguish the inauthentic public domain of the they sufficiently from an authentic way of being-with-others in the form of a community. While Heidegger does emphasize the importance of social and political traditions in establishing Dasein's own historicity, he also laments Dasein's tendency to become *ensnared* in those traditions, depriving itself of its own voice and perspective:

> Da-sein not only has the inclination to be entangled in the world in which it is and to interpret itself in terms of that world by its reflected light; at the same time Da-sein is also entangled in a tradition which it more or less explicitly grasps. This tradition deprives Da-sein of its own leadership in questioning and choosing. This is especially true of *that* understanding (and its possible development) which is rooted in the most proper being of Da-sein—the ontological understanding. (Heidegger 1996: 18–19)

Pulling Dasein away from its "proper" ontological understanding of its being, Heidegger suggests, is not only tradition but our own they-self. "In being-toward-death" he tells us, "Da-sein is related to *itself* as an eminent potentiality-of-being. But the self of everydayness is the they which is constituted in public interpretedness which expresses itself in idle talk. Thus, idle talk must make manifest in what way everyday Da-sein interprets its being-toward-death" (Heidegger 1996: 233–234). How is one to distinguish between the inauthentic they-self and an authentic self on this account? Ultimately, Heidegger see-saws back and forth on whether or not human beings' relations to others and to the world of their concern are necessary casualties along the path of authenticity. What is clear is that he can give no content to such relations and that his own views must cause us to view loving descriptions of those relations, such as those provided by Hainer, with suspicion.

Alterity and Responsivity

Chanter turns to Levinas for a more satisfactory account of the essential role played by the other in a human being's being-toward-death. Indeed, for Levinas, Death is the Other, pure alterity, violent and beyond comprehension. "The violence of death" he claims,

> threatens as a tyranny, as though proceeding from a foreign will. The order of necessity that is carried out in death is not like an implacable law of determinism governing a totality, but is rather like the alienation of my will by the Other. It is, of course, not a question of inserting death into a primitive (or developed) religious system that would explain it; but it is a question of showing, behind the threat it brings against the will, its reference to an interpersonal order whose signification it does not annihilate. (Levinas 1969: 234)

Death, on Levinas's account, cannot take a person away from the other but leads straight toward the other; death, he suggests, is a most special instance of the ineradicable transcendence of the other in relationship to me.

But Hainer's descriptions of her relations with others in the months before her death focus not on the radical alterity of the other(s) but on the intimate ways in which she and they are able to *traverse* the distance between them, enriching their respective lives in the process. The fact that her personal narrative of this process also had an impact on millions of people she never met makes it extremely problematic for both Heidegger and Levinas. Undoubtedly, Hainer had a *relationship* with her readers, one that she nurtured in the final months of her life in full awareness of the power of her narrative to trigger a personal response from them. Such a relationship seems to typify the very meaning of the they-self on Heidegger's account; after all, what could be a more effective use of public interpretedness than the media? However, what I am arguing here is that

Hainer's clear-eyed phenomenological description of her being-toward-death provides evidence of the limitations of Heidegger's account not only of being-toward-death and the role of the they, but also of authenticity itself.

In the New York Times publication Portraits: 9/11/01: The Collected "Portraits of Grief," a volume collecting the brief biographical sketches that were published in the New York Times on a regular basis during the year after 9/11/01 (and on a less regular basis after that as a few more victims' body parts were exhumed and identified), family members and friends provided interviewers with brief descriptions of the life of a particular individual who had died that day. These "profiles of grief," as I have previously discussed, tended to emphasize the mundane aspects of each individual's existence, including where these people lived and how they got to work each day, the names of their partners, children, and pets, the food they best liked to eat, the places they most liked to travel, and the things in life they valued most.[6] One of the reasons the accounts have been so moving, I maintain, is because in the very mundanity of the life being described, something unique about each life is simultaneously communicated. The paradoxical ability to reveal the unique in the typical and familiar, I argue, is precisely what must be done justice to if one is to make sense of the relationship between death and the other. Rather than encountering an ineffable alterity on the one hand or the inauthenticity of the they-self on the other, Hainer's narrative and these profiles offer, I believe, more compelling alternatives, alternatives that both challenge and reconfigure the very notions of subjectivity and alterity, death and authenticity.

Another alternative to solipsistic conceptions of subjectivity is provided by Kelly Oliver in her discussions of witnessing. According to Oliver, "addressability and response-ability are the conditions for subjectivity. The subject is the result of a response to an address from another and the possibility of addressing itself to another. This notion of subjectivity begins to go beyond the categories of subject, other, and object that work within scenarios of dominance and subordination" (Oliver 2000: 41). Despite the promise of such a relational account of subjectivity, Oliver ends up embracing a Levinasian vision of a human being's relationships with others, insofar as the other is depicted as being beyond an individual's comprehension:

> To recognize others requires acknowledging that their experiences are real even though they may be incomprehensible to us; this means we must recognize that not everything that is real is recognizable to us. Acknowledging the realness of another's life is not judging its worth [Taylor], or conferring respecting [sic], or understanding or recognizing it, but responding in a way that affirms response-ability or addressabiliy. We are obligated to respond to what is beyond our comprehension, beyond recognition. Ethics is possible only beyond recognition. (Oliver 2000: 41–42)

While it is certainly true that I cannot be said to comprehend the other in his or her entirety without vanquishing that very otherness, and while it is clear that cognitive comprehension of the other would give us only a very partial view of who that other really is, I would argue that an *existential* comprehension of the other *as* other is possible and that it can be made even more meaningful precisely when an individual comes face to face with her own mortality.

Authenticity Reconsidered

In opposition to what I take to be a false dichotomy between the absolute alterity of the other on the one hand, and the complete knowability of the other on the other hand, my point is that one does not need to embrace the incomprehensibility of the other in order to do justice to the other's alterity. Although I agree that my comprehension of the other will always exceed the capacity of conventional discourse to represent it, I am also maintaining that it is conventional discourse that continually points us toward it. Thus, conventional discourse, as I have endeavored to demonstrate through the examples of Cathy Hainer's journals and Tolstoy's story of Ivan Ilych, *can*, contra Heidegger, lead toward authentic experiences of oneself in relation to the other and to one's own death, experiences that *can* and indeed *must* be expressed and communicated through the language of the they.[7] Moreover, these experiences, even when enacted through discourse, inevitably possess, as Merleau-Ponty has shown, a corporeal and, more precisely, intercorporeal dimension. That is, the response-ability and addressability discussed by Oliver always involves one's body as it is engaged in "corporeal dialogue" with the bodies of others.[8] These intercorporeal exchanges between bodies issue, I argue, from what I have elsewhere called a series of "bodily imperatives" that demand them.[9] Certainly a person can meet these bodily imperatives, including the imperative of impending death itself, authentically or inauthentically; however, authenticity properly understood within a non-solipsistic, intersubjective ontology could never be a function of the ability to separate oneself from the ties that bind one to others, ties that persist, albeit in altered forms, in death as in life.

10

Challenging Choices

The question of choice and related concerns about free will that have preoccupied philosophers for centuries are no more resolved today than they were in St. Augustine's medieval times. So much ink has been spilled, primarily (and almost exclusively!) by professional philosophers, who have sought to prove either that human beings have choices and therefore free will or, equally strongly, that they do not and are therefore determined. Of course, there are many others who have strenuously argued for a "middle of the road" or compatibilist position, claiming that human beings are both free and determined at one and the same time. While I will not be engaging the vast literature on this subject, most of which comes out of the field of moral philosophy and is dominated by the analytic tradition, I am interested in exploring some of the presuppositions that underlie the very notion of choice. In a phenomenological spirit, I will pursue this inquiry without seeking to make prescriptive claims; rather, my intention is to examine descriptively assumptions about human agency, its possibilities, and its limits that almost always seem to be at work when a question of choice is raised concerning a particular human (or more frequently inhuman) action.

There is a deliberate ambiguity in my title, and both of its possible meanings address directly the issues I will be discussing. On the one hand, the term "challenging choices" most commonly refers to the necessity of making difficult decisions, where choosing a particular course of action is fraught either because another choice appears equally compelling or because the choice I am making poses challenges that cannot fully be foreseen in advance and over which I have little control. A less common reading of "challenging choices," and one that I will be exploring at some length, has to do with the challenges the very notion of choice poses to an understanding of the motivations that lead people to act in ways that are often deemed to be socially and morally unacceptable. What does it mean to make a choice? What are some of the challenges human beings face in attempting to make choices in and about their lives? Does the very notion of choice sometimes do more harm than good when it is used to evaluate the underlying forces that may drive an individual to act in one way rather than another? And if this is so, then what are the implications of this challenge to the ethical hegemony of choice for the moral tradition and, equally importantly, for an understanding of the extraordinary circumstances that can come to define a particular individual's "ordinary" experience?

A Philosophical Tale of Seduction

Most of the time, I tend to be an optimist, searching for possibilities when others see limitations, hoping for the best to come out of what look like fairly bad situations. Perhaps this is one of the reasons I've found Merleau-Ponty's philosophy so appealing. While Sartre was my first introduction to continental philosophy as an undergraduate, I became an immediate "convert" when I was later introduced to the work of Merleau-Ponty. Despite the difficulties I encountered when first reading *Being and Nothingness* and *Phenomenology of Perception* as an undergraduate majoring in philosophy, I welcomed the challenges both philosophers posed to my own uncritical assumptions about the meaning of human experience. Sartre's negative descriptions of human beings' continuous attempts to justify their actions to themselves and to others in his famous chapter on "Bad Faith" certainly resonated with my own experience, and, like my own students today who encounter this work for the first time, I was seduced by the power associated with being able to identify bad faith in others who, for one reason or another, chose to abdicate their freedom and corresponding responsibility for their situation. Of course, it was (and still is!) more painful to identify the ways in which one's own actions are undertaken in bad faith, but this task, too, I took up with proper philosophical seriousness. It was hard not to agree with Sartre's harsh assessment that most human beings live in bad faith most of the time, looking to blame others or their situation for the unpleasant, and usually unanticipated, consequences that issue from their own actions.

One year later, as I struggled as a senior to navigate the equally dense pages of Merleau-Ponty's *Phenomenology of Perception*, which was published a mere two years after *Being and Nothingness* and constituted a direct challenge to it, I was seduced yet again, this time by Merleau-Ponty's critique of the disembodied Cartesian subject that he claimed underlay Sartre's entire existential ontology and that led, in Merleau-Ponty's eyes, to Sartre's unsatisfactory accounts of both human embodiment and intersubjective experience. Merleau-Ponty's own body-subject, in contrast to Sartre's being-for-itself, seemed to be so much more happily mired in the world of its concern, the former being defined by its possibility of engaging the world and others within the world in new and different ways that were not dominated by the specter of bad faith. I was also (and continue to be) captivated by Merleau-Ponty's invocation of the Husserlian concept of the horizon and, more specifically, the notion that there are not one but rather multiple horizons that collectively help to constitute the meaning of any given experience in all of their splendid indeterminacy. Indeed, this very indeterminacy, an openness that guarantees what Derrida later called the "undecidability" of meaning, while serving as the bane of most analytic philosophers' existence insofar as it poses an impossible challenge to the Cartesian goal of attaining complete knowledge or truth concerning a particular phenomenon, I found to be an accurate and refreshing description of the reality of ordinary human experience. At the same time, it was undeniable that this indeterminacy I was so happily embracing also created its own challenges for making definitive and coherent philosophical claims about human experience.

When, years later, I was introduced to Beauvoir's equally voluminous work, *The Second Sex*, which was published four years after *Phenomenology of Perception* and six years after *Being and Nothingness*, and shortly thereafter to her much shorter 1948 volume, *The Ethics of Ambiguity*, published just one year before *The Second Sex*, texts that responded in turn both to Sartre and to Merleau-Ponty, I was seduced yet again, a seduction that continues to this day and whose effects are reflected in so much of what I write. This time, the seduction was not due to the expansive sense of possibility I feel when reading Merleau-Ponty, nor to the dreadful but nonetheless intoxicating power of being the source of freedom and responsibility I experience when reading Sartre, but rather, to Beauvoir's straightforward but nonetheless complex understanding of the incredible daily challenges human beings face in making sense of themselves and of others in a world that is shot through with conflict, suffering, injustice, and oppression, but also with love, beauty, adventure, and delight.

Beauvoir, in many ways, seems to incorporate the best aspects of both Sartre's and Merleau-Ponty's philosophies, while at the same time avoiding at least some of the serious criticisms that continue to be leveled against their respective thought. Of course, this does not mean that Beauvoir's work is immune to criticisms of its own; indeed, I myself have raised some in both current and previous work. However, her simultaneous affirmations of freedom, responsibility, embodiment, and human relationships, along with her recognition that all of these phenomena are experienced through the lenses of gender, race, and class, provided a new model for philosophy that I still do not believe has been utilized to its full potential.

While I remain a strong proponent of the phenomenological and herme-neutic view that the multiple horizons an individual brings to bear on her expe-riences open up new interpretative possibilities within that experience, it is also abundantly evident that the multiple and often incompatible demands of the different situations in which human beings find themselves on a daily basis are not always reconcilable. When such conflicts emerge, maintaining an openness to the different possible interpretations that stem from the multiple horizons that are potentially operative in any given experience becomes extremely diffi-cult, if not impossible. Indeed, as I will be arguing, racist, sexist, and classist behaviors are often directly connected to a refusal to be open to different hori-zons that would yield different (i.e., non-oppressive) interpretations of one's en-counters with others. In such cases, the possibilities for alternative interpretations are closed down in advance, as a result of a refusal to be open to what Ricoeur calls the different *configurations* of meaning that can be derived from one and the same situation.[1]

In her recent work, Alcoff takes up this same issue by addressing at some length the constitutive role played by the horizon in the formation of identity. In her words, "identities operate as horizons from which certain aspects or lay-ers of reality can be made visible" (Alcoff 2006: 43). More specifically, Alcoff asserts that

> [i]n stratified societies, differently identified individuals do not always have the same access to points of view or perceptual planes of observation. Two indi-viduals may participate in the same event but have perceptual access to differ-ent aspects of that event. Social identity is relevant to epistemic judgment, then, not because identity determines judgment but because identity can in some instances yield access to perceptual facts that themselves may be rele-vant to the formulation of various knowledge claims or theoretical analyses. As [Satya] Mohanty and others have also argued, social location can be corre-lated with certain highly specific forms of blindness as well as of lucidity. (Alcoff 2006: 43)

As Alcoff emphasizes, different identities and/or horizons reflect different social locations and yield different perceptions and/or experiences. While I have been stressing the importance of actively recognizing and affirming the multiple hori-zons that collectively constitute the background context against which individual experiences unfold as a viable strategy for combating the tendency to arbitrarily close down the meaning-making process, thereby leading to rigid interpretations of other people and/or specific events, it is also important to acknowledge, with Beauvoir and Alcoff, that in cases of severe oppression it may well be impossible for individuals to step out of the narrow horizons that constrain their daily lives. I will now turn to two concrete examples of the reality of oppression and the ways in which it can force a rethinking of the notion of choice that is implicitly, if not explicitly, invoked when someone is urged to "move on" from an oppressive experience and to step "outside" of that experience so that "the true situation" can be seen from a new, allegedly unbiased perspective.[2] Moreover, since the very notion of choice is presupposed in virtually every ethical theory (for if one doesn't *choose* to be ethical, how can one be blamed for failing to make ethical choices?), exploring the limitations of the notion of choice in cases of severe oppression leads directly to an exploration of the ethical challenges posed by too strong an emphasis on the capacity to expand one's horizons when this is simply not an option for many people in the world today.

Destructive "Choices"

One summer morning in June 2001, Andrea Pia Yates, a Texan mother of five, drowned all of her children in the bathtub one by one. Severe postpartum depression, early press reports speculated, was a primary motivating factor in her actions since she had been under psychiatric care and had been taking antidepressant medication for this very condition following the birth of both her fourth and fifth children. After the murders took place, her husband defended her in the press, calling her a loving mother and denying that she would willingly have harmed their children. Indeed, despite accusations from Andrea Yates's family after her March 2002 trial that her husband's controlling behavior helped to "push her over the edge," he continued to be supportive of her (at least in the public media) from the day of their children's deaths through her trial and subsequent conviction, and in the face of the overturning of her conviction by the First Court of Appeals in Houston in January 2005.[3]

In Morrison's novel *Beloved*, the main character, Sethe, also attempts to kill her three children, but she succeeds with only one, her baby daughter. Morrison depicts Sethe as an enigmatic but nonetheless intelligible, and even sympathetic, figure. Readers of her story are led to believe that Sethe was a loving mother who murders her daughter (and attempts to murder her sons) in the conviction that death is preferable to being condemned to a life of slavery. Although she is never tried or imprisoned, Sethe's actions dramatically affect herself as well as her surviving family members, ultimately leading to the breakdown of her relationship with her two sons.

Andrea Yates and Sethe can be starkly contrasted with one another in terms of race, class, historical time period, age, and their personal histories, but they are bound by the horrifying nature of their respective acts.[4] Both women, it could be argued, seem to have been moved by forces beyond their control, forces that presented the murder of their children as their best or even only viable option.[5] Adopting such an interpretation, one could maintain (as many critics have) that Sethe, experiencing her family's situation as hopeless, murdered her daughter so that her daughter would not have to experience life as a slave. Despite the initial Texas jury's rejection of Andrea Yates's plea of not guilty by virtue of insanity, one might nonetheless plausibly conjecture that it was a state of psychosis brought on by severe postpartum depression that led her to violently terminate her children's lives.[6]

Both cases, despite the crucial differences already noted above (and despite the fact that one example is fictitious and one is not), may be more similar than not from this perspective, because for each woman, due to her oppressive situation, the horizons that gave significance to her actions seem to have been narrowed to the particular place and time in which she found herself at the moment she acted.[7] More precisely, what each woman seems to have lacked at the moment she was acting was an awareness of the broader context for her actions, a context that may have provided her with alternative ways of construing her situation as well as possible responses to it. Indeed, it is this broader context, a context that includes strong social taboos against the murder of children, especially one's own children, that outsiders usually appeal to in judging both women's actions.

In what follows, I will argue that one can best understand the tragic deaths of these children at the hands of their mothers as failures of relation rather than as failures of choice. The oppression experienced by the mothers themselves (for Sethe, through her fugitive existence as a runaway slave, and for Andrea Yates, through her severe postpartum depression), make it difficult to understand their actions through a traditional rational framework that blames the individual for failing to utilize her rational capacities before acting. Even an existential framework is problematic, for although the latter draws attention to the broader situation that provides the context for the individual's actions, it too emphasizes the individual's responsibility for her choices, and grounds this responsibility in an ontological notion of freedom that is itself challenged by both of these cases.

Oppressive Constraints and Narrowed Horizons

As I have stressed by emphasizing the crucial but often invisible role played by the horizon in situating the meaning of particular experiences, considerations of context are absolutely crucial to any investigation into how a particular individual acts within a given situation, much less a traumatic situation.[8] Despite Beauvoir's own emphasis on freedom and individual choice throughout her work, an emphasis that aligns her very closely with Sartre, she also, unlike the early Sartre of *Being and Nothingness*, anticipates the difficulties that arise when one attempts to make sense of different people's actions in the face of oppressive circumstances.[9] The task of understanding the experience of oppression, she claims, is a problem "complicated in practice by the fact that today oppression has more than one aspect" (Beauvoir 1976: 89). Not only may there be more than one source of oppression, but the forms that the oppression itself may take can vary tremendously and may include both psychical and physical abuse. In what follows, I will offer a critical analysis of Beauvoir's own remarks on oppression in various texts, including *Pyrrhus et Cinéas*, *The Ethics of Ambiguity*, *America Day by Day*, and *The Second Sex*. Through an examination of Beauvoir's discussions of oppressed individuals, I will show (1) why the experience of oppression poses a severe challenge to traditional ethical theories that presuppose the existence of a rational, autonomous moral agent and (2) how Beauvoir sets the stage for an alternative conception of morality that, unlike her earlier existential ethics presented in *The Ethics of Ambiguity*, or Sartre's existential ethics grounded in the choices made by a single individual in response to the facticity of her situation, is not grounded in freedom.

To return to my previous examples, those who acknowledged that Andrea Yates was most likely suffering from acute postpartum depression but who still held her accountable for her actions tended to blame her for not seeking more aggressive treatment for her mental condition.[10] But to seek such treatment presupposes that one recognizes that one is, in fact, depressed, and it is precisely this broader perspective on her situation that seemed to be unavailable to Andrea Yates at the time she was drowning her children.[11]

By contrast, as noted earlier, Sethe's violent stabbing of her children has largely been viewed by Morrison's readers as less blameworthy even if no less horrific. This is due not only to the fact that *Beloved* is a fictional narrative and that the costs of identifying with Sethe are therefore not so high but also to a recognition that Sethe's own oppression as a slave and her desire that her children not live a life of slavery is a rational, maternal desire even if her means of achieving this desire appear to be unacceptably extreme. Moreover, since the institution of slavery cannot be rationally justified, Sethe's seemingly irrational actions can themselves be seen as being the effect of an unjust social institution, and thus she may not seem personally to blame for what she did. However, in the case of Andrea Yates, a middle-class housewife with a seemingly loving and supportive spouse, a nice home, and a family, there doesn't appear to be any direct source of institutional oppression one can appeal to in order to make sense of her actions.[12] Clearly, one may blame the depression itself, as her supporters have done, but here too, many people who grant that she may have been severely depressed still faulted her for not availing herself of the medical care to which she had access to help combat it.

Ultimately, regardless of how one views each woman, the enclosed space of the shed depicted by Morrison and the equally enclosed space of the Yateses' bathroom (vividly described in the media coverage of her trial) present images of physical containment that are unable to contain the events that occurred within. This is true not only for those who vicariously experience these events by reading of them, but also for the women themselves. In *Beloved*, the legacy of her actions haunts Sethe for the rest of her life, a haunting that is materialized in the sudden appearance of the title character, Beloved, whom Sethe takes to be the literal (re)incarnation of her murdered daughter. And one can only presume that the trial and imprisonment of Andrea Yates, her vilification in the media, her isolation from friends and family, and most of all, her change in status from a mother of five to not being a mother at all cannot help but transform her relationship to her actions in the bathtub that morning in June.

If one accepts that both Sethe's and Andrea Yates's actions seemed to have been radically restricted to the immediacy of the "here and now," the question becomes, how might one understand such a reduction of one's entire life-world and, accordingly, of one's actions to a particular place and time?[13] Elaine Scarry, in her award-winning book *The Body in Pain*, provides poignant phenomenological descriptions of just this type of experience. Specifically, she offers the testimony of torture victims who claimed that when they were in the throes of extreme pain inflicted by their oppressor, the only reality that they experienced was the pain itself. In her words, "torture consists of acts that magnify the way in which pain destroys a person's world, self, and voice." A bit later she adds,

> To acknowledge the radical subjectivity of pain is to acknowledge the simple and absolute incompatibility of pain and the world. The survival of each depends on its separation from the other. To bring them together, to bring pain into the world by objectifying it in language, is to destroy one of them: either . . . the pain is objectified, articulated, brought into the world in such a way that the pain itself is diminished and destroyed; or alternatively, as in torture and parallel forms of sadism, the pain is at once objectified and falsified, articulated but made to refer to something else and in the process, the world, or some dramatized surrogate of the world, is destroyed. (Scarry 1985: 50–51)

Although Sethe and Andrea Yates were not physically tortured, and despite the differences in their respective situations, I am claiming that both women suffered from severe cases of psychological oppression that were no less real in their corporeal effects. I also argue that Beauvoir's analysis of oppression provides a framework for rendering these women's actions intelligible as responses to situations over which they felt they had no control. To say that their actions can be rendered intelligible does not, of course, sanction them. What it does do is restore the humanity of these alleged "monsters" by enabling these women to be recognized as moral agents operating outside the realm of choice and possibility that so many people take for granted in their daily lives.

Starting from Sigmund Freud's insistence that the abnormal is not radically distinct from the normal case but can shed light on the latter since both form part of a single continuum of behavior, I would like to examine the broader contexts of significance that helped to define Sethe's and Andrea Yates's respective situations, contexts that were present but presumably not efficacious for the women themselves. Merleau-Ponty's discussion in the *Phenomenology of Perception* of Schneider, a World War I shrapnel victim, is instructive here. He argues that although Schneider's brain damage causes a reduction of his world to a very concrete horizon of significance that is limited to the here and now, rendering him incapable of formulating abstract plans that extend beyond his current situation, Schneider's existence must not be seen as incomplete or impoverished, because he experiences his world as a coherent whole; that is, Schneider doesn't perceive his world as lacking in any way. The lack, if you will, is applied to Schneider's experience from the outside, by "normal" subjects who view his world and his subjectivity to be defective. According to Merleau-Ponty, for Schneider just as for these "normal" subjects, "[e]xistence has no fortuitous attributes, no content which does not contribute towards giving it its form" (Merleau-Ponty 1962: 169).

Interestingly, both Beauvoir and Sartre also describe individuals who, like Schneider, are unable to depart from fixed ways of understanding their situation. The individuals they describe, however, are this way not because of a particular disability, as in Schneider's case, or because of a specific experience of oppression, as in the two mothers' or the torture victims' cases, but rather because they choose to ascribe a necessary meaning to their situation, one that precludes alternative interpretations and yields comfort and security in the process. In *Being and Nothingness*, Sartre claims that such an individual exists in bad faith, failing to recognize that the value she gives to her existence is self-created, not eternal. One example he gives of this is the sincere person who identifies herself with a certain essential nature and attempts to coincide with that nature at all times, a project that can be summed up in the statement "I am who I am." If this project is realizable, Sartre maintains, "[i]f man is who he is, bad faith is forever impossible and candor ceases to be his ideal and becomes instead his being." "But," he quickly asks, "is man what he is?" (Sartre 1956: 101).

Beauvoir provides an even earlier example of such an individual who attempts to "be herself" at all times, namely Françoise, the main character in her 1943 novel, *L'Invitée* [*She Came to Stay*].[14] While Françoise eschews any belief in a God-given nature, she exhibits the extreme arrogance of assuming that her perspective on her situation, including her relationship with her lover and intellectual partner, Pierre, represents the truth of that situation for both herself and others. In the course of the novel, Françoise discovers that her self-assured attempt to avoid bad faith by seeing the world on her own terms is precisely what produces it.

For both Sartre and Beauvoir, the answer to the question of whether one can ever be who one is, is a resounding "no!" And in *The Second Sex*, Beauvoir complicates matters further by showing that the essence women are often urged to coincide with to fulfill their so-called feminine destiny is inherently impossible to achieve because it is full of contradictions.[15] While Sartre focuses on the bad faith of the sincere individual who presumes to be able to "be who he is," Beauvoir turns the reader's attention beyond the individual to a powerful societal bad faith that pressures women to seek to realize an impossible ideal. For Beauvoir, "a fundamental ambiguity marks the feminine being," an ambiguity that cannot be eliminated by identifying with a fixed essence. And, she adds, "[t]he fact is that she would be quite embarrassed to decide *what* she *is*; but this is not because the hidden truth is too vague to be discerned: it is because in this domain there is no truth. An existent *is* nothing other than what he does; the possible does not extend beyond the real, essence does not precede existence: in pure subjectivity, the human being *is not anything*" (Beauvoir 1989: 257).

In *The Ethics of Ambiguity*, Beauvoir claims that the individual who nonetheless identifies with a given essence has succumbed to "the spirit of seriousness," and she, like Sartre, finds him culpable for his abdication of personal responsibility for his situation. The serious man, she tells us, "forces himself to submerge his freedom in the content which the latter accepts from society. He loses himself in the object in order to annihilate his subjectivity" (Beauvoir 1976: 45). Beauvoir invokes Hegel, Kierkegaard, and Nietzsche as philosophers who also "railed at the deceitful stupidity of the serious man and his universe." Sartre's *Being and Nothingness*, she asserts,

> is in large part a description of the serious man and his universe. The serious man gets rid of his freedom by claiming to subordinate it to values which would be unconditioned. He imagines that the accession to these values likewise permanently confers value upon himself. Shielded with "rights," he fulfills himself as a *being* who is escaping from the stress of existence. The serious is not defined by the nature of the ends pursued. A frivolous lady of fashion can have this mentality of the serious as well as an engineer. There is the serious from the moment that freedom denies itself to the advantage of ends which one claims are absolute. (Beauvoir 1976: 46)

As Beauvoir deftly weaves her condemnation of the serious individual into Sartre's, it is easy to forget the crucial differences between their respective positions. Not only does Beauvoir emphasize the major role that society plays in inculcating the spirit of seriousness in the individual, an acknowledgement that Sartre does not fully make until years later in the *Critique of Dialectical Reason*, but she also explicitly invokes the experience of oppression as one that can vitiate the ambiguity of existence by disallowing the individual the opportunity to give more than one meaning to her situation.[16] In both *The Ethics of Ambiguity* and *The Second Sex* in particular, Beauvoir suggests that severe oppression can lead an individual to view her possibilities in life as predetermined, and, against the Sartrean position outlined above, she claims that one must not judge such a person to be in bad faith.[17] In contrast, she tells us, to those who choose a serious existence in bad faith, artificially limiting the significance of their actions and denying their freedom to act otherwise in the process, there are also those who "live in the universe of the serious in all honesty, for example, those who are denied all instruments of escape, those who are enslaved or who are mystified" (Beauvoir 1976: 47–48). In the passage that follows, Beauvoir asserts that "to the extent that it exists, their freedom remains available, it is not denied. They can, in their situation of ignorant and powerless individuals, know the truth of existence and raise themselves to a properly moral life" (Beauvoir 1976: 48).

What is striking about this passage is that Beauvoir does not distinguish between the dishonest serious individual and the honest one on the basis of the former possessing but denying her freedom and the latter failing to possess this freedom altogether. For it would seem quite plausible to argue that the serious individual who is guilty of bad faith attempts to deny her freedom (to create value) in order to endow her values with an absolute justification that comes from without, while the severely oppressed lack freedom altogether and therefore cannot be understood as proper moral agents. However, attractive as such an explanation might be, it runs the risk, as Beauvoir well seems to realize, of further dehumanizing the oppressed insofar as freedom, and the concomitant capacity for a moral existence, for both Beauvoir and Sartre, is precisely what distinguishes human beings from all other types of beings. Accordingly, Beauvoir maintains not only that the severely oppressed may still have a measure of freedom, but in addition that they can "know the truth of existence and raise themselves to a properly moral life." But what type of freedom do they possess, and what kind of moral life do they have? Beauvoir, having taken her readers to the precipice of a breach with an existentialist ethics grounded in freedom, goes no further. And yet, by throwing down the gauntlet, she forces her readers to follow through the implications of her claims.

Compromised Freedom and the Possibility of Ethics

For both Beauvoir and Sartre, freedom is not an objective phenomenon but a subjective experience whose effects are realized through concrete actions capable of transforming one's situation. Hence, it will not suffice to look at a situation from the outside in order to determine whether the agents within that situation have acted freely. However, while both Beauvoir's and Sartre's early work strongly suggests that the exercise of freedom is purely an individual affair, incapable of being affected by others or by the situation itself, Beauvoir, as Kruks, Bergoffen, and others have pointed out, also acknowledges very early on that both others and the situation can place real constraints on human freedom.[18] In *Pyrrhus et Cinéas*, for instance, Beauvoir claims that "my action is for others only in fact that which they make of it." "How then," she asks, "can I know in advance what I do?" (Beauvoir 1944: 51, my translation).[19] As Bergoffen observes, Beauvoir's "focus in *Pyrrhus et Cinéas* is on the ways in which we are alien to each other. Here she is interested in analyzing the implications of this alienation for the ethics of the project. She takes up a twofold task: one, to create an ethic that respects the other's strangeness; and two, to prevent the idea of the other's strangeness from sliding into the idea of our necessary estrangement (the look)" (Bergoffen 1997: 50). Beauvoir fulfills this task, Bergoffen claims, by arguing that my projects must incorporate the projects of others. Since I have to confront the alterity of the other from one moment to the next in my existence, I cannot ignore the presence of others but must act in concert with them. In Bergoffen's words:

> Because there is no givenness, no God, no temporal continuity, no human essence to ground or guarantee the fulfillment of my vision, I cannot pursue my project without at the same time appealing to others to recognize the value of my actions and to preserve their meaning. As Beauvoir sees it, in embarking on my project I also take on the task of creating a public to whom I can appeal. This public is essential to my project. It is through the project that I am linked to/with others and it is through these others that I, as my project, am linked to the future. (Bergoffen 1997: 52)

The case of the severely oppressed individual, however, seems to contest the positive implications of this depiction of myself and others. Is the severely oppressed individual even in a position to create a public to whom she can appeal? And if "this public is essential to my project," the inability to create such a public means that the ethical project itself, and therefore the individual's very future, is endangered from the outset. Before developing this point further, it is important to remember, as noted previously, that oppression may take many different forms and have a variety of effects in the life of an individual and/or community. As the earlier examples of Andrea Yates and Sethe amply illustrate, even when two seemingly loving mothers undertake a similar destructive action, namely murdering their children, the oppressive forces that may have influenced that action can be quite diverse.

Kruks, following Beauvoir, distinguishes between less severe cases of oppression, in which the individual may too willingly claim the mantle of victim in order to discharge herself of responsibility for changing her situation, and more severe cases, in which one cannot hold the individual culpable for failing to pursue alternatives. She eloquently sums up Beauvoir's position as follows:

Some of the oppressed are complicitous in their oppression and, in bad faith, evade the revolt that alone could open the way to freedom for them. But others simply do not have that choice. Their situation has so penetrated even their ontological freedom, so modified it, that not even the commencement of a transcendent project is possible. The very withdrawal of consciousness which, for Sartre, is the origin of transcendence and which enables freedom to choose its way of taking up its situation (for example, whether or not to give in to the torturer) has ceased to be possible. (Kruks 1990: 97)

In this passage, Kruks applauds Beauvoir's recognition that the situation can actively limit one's freedom, a view that she claims is in keeping with a Marxist acknowledgment of the power of the situation to shape not merely one's material reality but also an individual's very subjectivity.

While it is impossible from the outside to determine how oppressed a given individual actually is, and whether or not one considers controversial figures such as Andrea Yates and Sethe to be examples of severely oppressed individuals, ample evidence for the existence of severely oppressed people is readily available throughout the world. And it is precisely the actions undertaken by these latter individuals that Beauvoir wants to do justice to by acknowledging that they are not morally culpable for failing to recognize, much less seeking to liberate themselves from, the source of their oppression. For such individuals, she maintains, the possibility of liberation must come from without. In her words:

There are cases where the slave does not know his servitude and where it is necessary to bring the seed of his liberation to him from the outside: his submission is not enough to justify the tyranny which is imposed on him. The slave is submissive when one has succeeded in mystifying him in such a way that his situation does not seem to him to be imposed by men, but to be immediately given by nature, by the gods, by the powers against whom revolt has no meaning; thus, he does not accept his condition through a resignation of his freedom since he can not even dream of any other; and in his relationships with his friends, for example, he can live as a free and moral man within this world where his ignorance has enclosed him. (Beauvoir 1976: 85)

In this passage, Beauvoir seems to equivocate on the issue whether or not a severely oppressed individual has freedom. On the one hand, she states that such a person cannot be said to have resigned his freedom because he does not feel that he has chosen this situation to begin with; rather, his situation appears natural, and he is not even capable of imagining any alternatives to it. Thus, not only freedom but also the power of imagination seem to be radically compromised. On the other hand, Beauvoir emphatically maintains that such a person can still live as "a free and moral man within this world where his ignorance has enclosed him." But what kind of freedom and what kind of morality is this? Certainly, it does not seem to be the genuine moral freedom in which I will the disclosure of the world that Beauvoir discusses at length in *The Ethics of Ambiguity*. Neither does it seem to resemble the absolute, unconditioned freedom that Sartre champions as the exclusive birthright of the for-itself in *Being and Nothingness*.

Rather than deny the plausibility of Beauvoir's claim that the severely oppressed individual can be considered as free and moral within the confines of her situation, I argue that she is unable to do justice to her own insight precisely because it challenges the entire existential ethics that both she and Sartre are committed to, an ethics that is built on the foundation of an original, ontological freedom. And yet, despite the difficulties they introduce for her position, Beauvoir returns to these challenges to the very notion of choice again and again.

In both *The Ethics of Ambiguity* and *The Second Sex*, Beauvoir not only discusses the constraints that the oppressed must contend with on a daily basis but also argues that the role of oppressor itself limits the possibilities of one who is in a situation of power over others but wishes not to oppress. For, she maintains, "[a] colonial administrator has no possibility of acting rightly toward the natives, nor a general towards his soldiers; the only solution is to be neither colonist nor military chief" (Beauvoir 1989: 723). Unlike the severely oppressed individual, then, the colonist or military chief can refuse to continue on in his position.

And yet, despite her more general argument in *The Second Sex* that women have historically occupied a more immanent position in society, and men the more transcendent one, with more choices available to the latter than to the former, she goes on to argue that even though the colonialist or military chief may choose a different path, his options are still limited because "a man could not prevent himself from being a man." "So," she concludes, "there he is, culpable in spite of himself and laboring under the effects of a fault he did not himself commit; and here she is, victim and shrew in spite of herself" (Beauvoir 1989: 723). "A well-disposed man," she maintains, "will be more tortured by the situation than the woman herself: in a sense it is always better to be on the side of the vanquished" (Beauvoir 1989: 724).

Why is this so? The simple answer, I think, is power. To have power and yet at the same time to experience oneself as powerless is more devastating than to lack a power one never had to begin with. Once again, Beauvoir seems to be departing radically from her own as well as Sartre's emphasis on the inalienable freedom of the for-itself because the situation of both men and women within a patriarchal society is presented as *inherently* constraining for both genders. In such situations, she maintains, "it is useless to apportion blame and excuses: justice can never be done in the midst of injustice" (Beauvoir 1989: 723).

What are the ethical implications of these claims? To argue, at this point, that one could still achieve genuine freedom by willing oneself free, by willing oneself to be a disclosure of the world, as Beauvoir does in the early pages of *The Ethics of Ambiguity*, seems inadequate. For what is disclosed is a world that limits the very movement of freedom itself. Addressing this problem in the context of anti-black racism, Lewis Gordon, in *Existentia Africana*, introduces a distinction between "choices" and "options" in order to preserve the primacy of freedom in the face of oppressive situations that seem to preclude its being exercised. "A condition of one's freedom" he states,

> [i]s that one is able to choose. Yet, choosing and having options are not identical: choices may work in accordance with options, but one may choose what is not a live option. The choice, then, turns back on the chooser and lives in the world of negation. There the choice at best determines something about the chooser, though it fails to transform the material conditions imposed on the chooser. Theories that fail to make the distinction between choice and option carry the danger of using gods as the model for human choice. For gods or for that matter, God, there is no schism between choice and option, so whatever such a being chooses *is*, absolutely, what *will be*. (Gordon 2000: 76–77)

In an oppressive situation, Gordon maintains, an individual still has choices but lacks the options necessary to enable those choices to be realized. In his words: "Where there are many options, choices can be made without imploding upon those who make them. If a set of options is considered necessary for social well-being in a society, then trouble begins when and where such options are not available to all members of the society" (Gordon 2000: 86).

Useful as I find this distinction to be, I'm not convinced that it succeeds in capturing what is at stake in the examples with which I began this chapter. In the case of Sethe, one would have to understand her actions as stemming from a choice that reflected a lack of options. That is, one could claim that she chose to kill her children because she felt that the other option available, namely, a life of slavery, was worse than death itself and hence no option at all. And although from the outside Morrison's readers may perceive Sethe to have had more options, the point is that presumably *she* did not perceive this to be the case. As a result, the reader may feel compassion for her terrible choice and lament her inability to recognize that other options were available. But such an interpretation seems patronizing. While it may encourage individuals, as Gordon surely intends it to do, to fight to increase the options available to the oppressed so that their choices do not become self-negating but can find fulfillment in a liberatory praxis, it also can promote a sense of superiority on the part of those who stand outside this situation because they are able to perceive options that the individual in question cannot. Beauvoir herself, I believe, would not support such a view since her existential ethics is grounded in the individual's own lived experience and not in the perspective of others.

The shortcomings of Gordon's analysis are revealed even more strongly, I would contend, in the case of Andrea Yates. For it is difficult to maintain that she *chose* to drown her five children even if one is willing to grant that she may have perceived this to be her only option. The lucidity of consciousness, so championed by Sartre and Camus as requisite for freedom, seems difficult to locate in the indirect, fragmentary accounts proffered by the media of Yates's feelings as she killed her children one after the other (and I'm not sure one can claim that this lucidity is present in Sethe's case either, despite the deliberateness of both women's actions).

Once again, it is relatively easy from the outside to see other options. Unlike in Sethe's case, where most would blame the institution of slavery itself for limiting Sethe's horizons, with Andrea Yates the source of the blame is less clear. Some may blame her doctors or her husband for not recognizing the severity of her depression; as noted earlier, many blame Yates herself for not realizing that she was in need of help. Beauvoir undoubtedly would have called attention to the oppressive institution of motherhood that sets up maternity as the quintessential source of personal fulfillment for women. The multiple factors that potentially contributed to this tragedy, I argue, are precisely what point to the complexity of this woman's experience, a complexity that defies a simple distinction between choices and options.

Instead of trying to salvage the primacy of choice for ethics in order to preserve the freedom and humanity of the self who chooses, as Gordon valiantly does, perhaps it is time to rethink the existentialist emphasis on choice as the very mark of the human. For once one acknowledges, with Gordon, that if individuals lack options their choices turn out to be self-negating, in danger of destroying the very self that chooses, then one also must ask, why should choice be the mark of ethical privilege? With Beauvoir and Gordon, I would maintain that even the severely oppressed individual can lead a moral life, but I think that this can occur in the absence of both options and choices. Elsewhere, I've argued that such a person can manifest a simple "will to endure" in the face of what others may regard as an unlivable situation.[20] This "will to endure," however, does not seem to me to fall under the category of choice as Beauvoir and Sartre have used the term. It does not presuppose a clear conscious awareness of one's situation. One simply "does what one must" to preserve one's existence at all costs.

At this point one may legitimately ask, "If choice and freedom are not central to the ethical existence of the severely oppressed, what is?" Here, I believe, one can take as a point of departure a fundamental insight from the feminist ethics of care, namely, that it is the ability to enter into relations with others that precedes choice and provides the necessary grounding for an ethical life. Focusing on relations with others, rather than choices, allows one to see moral failures as failures of *relation* rather than merely failures of the individual in question (though this is not to deny that there are also personal failures for which an individual alone is primarily responsible). Moreover, rather than promoting an "us versus them" mentality, in which one can blame an individual for failing to make the right choices, or even blame a society for failing to provide that individual with more options, everyone is implicated in an ethics of relation, for there are no omniscient, transcendental observers standing in judgment on the individual and her situation. As I have argued in *Body Images: Embodiment as Intercorporeality*, the *bodily imperatives* that issue forth from the oppressed are addressed not only to her immediate others, but to all other human beings as well, transforming each of the latter from observer into participant in the process.[21] And it is precisely insofar as these others may have new perspectives to offer on her situation that they are well positioned to respond to her call.

Indeed, in the closing pages of *The Second Sex*, Beauvoir asserts that changed perspectives offer the best hope of improving the immanent situation of women. "Woman," she asserts, "is the victim of no mysterious fatality; the peculiarities that identify her as specifically a woman get their importance from the significance placed upon them. They can be surmounted, in the future, when they are regarded in new perspectives" (Beauvoir 1989: 727). As Beauvoir well recognizes, individuals face challenges to their choices (and for those who are severely oppressed, it is the very notion of choice itself that is challenged) from one moment to the next insofar as they must, in the face of an inherently ambiguous, constraining situation, commit themselves to a particular course of action, an action that helps to define the situation as such and that always implicates others and their needs and desires in the process. Rather than view the existence of others and the unique demands of any given situation as threats to one's own freedom, it is important to recognize that it is precisely because an individual's actions always take place in an intersubjective context that one is able to create new, shared horizons that have the potential to "bring the seed of liberation" to those who are oppressed, thereby enabling the collective achievement of a more liberatory future.

Inspired by Beauvoir's own preoccupation with how to do justice to the reality of oppression, I argue that it is time to challenge choice itself as the distinctive quality that makes people human. Indeed, disability theorists and activists have also been engaged in this battle for quite a while now, insofar as those who are severely mentally and even physically disabled have been consistently dehumanized because of their inability to make basic choices about their daily lives. To challenge choice, one must challenge the hegemony that the discourse of freedom and choice has enjoyed not only in existentialist ethics but also in deontological and consequentialist views. This means not rejecting the importance of freedom and choice (or even existentialism) in the pursuit of an ethical existence, but rather recognizing that freedom and choice are best understood not as *preconditions* for morality but as *goals* to strive for. The starting point for this process, I claim, must be a re-evaluation of the importance of preserving and enriching one's relations with others, a possibility that presupposes not a self-aware, autonomous consciousness, but no more and no less than one's own *intercorporeality.*

As intercorporeal beings, human bodies are always already linked in inextricable ways to other bodies, both animate and inanimate. A relational ethics that affirms these bodily ties must acknowledge the obligations they generate, obligations that are often not chosen.[22] And yet, to move away from the notion of choice as constitutive for existential ethics is not to reject existential ethics altogether, because the relational ethics I am sketching out here springs directly from the concrete situation human beings share with both human and non-human others. However, its emphasis is not, as it is for Sartre, and at times for Beauvoir, on human beings' consciousness as the sole ground of agency, freedom, and choice, but on embodied beings with intertwined pasts, presents, and futures.

Beauvoir poignantly invokes these intercorporeal connections in her visceral reaction to the oppressive Jim Crow laws that she experienced firsthand when she took a bus tour of several southern states on her first trip to the United States in 1947: "And throughout the day the great tragedy of the South pursues us like an obsession. Even the traveler confined to a bus and waiting rooms cannot escape it. From the time we entered Texas, everywhere we go there's the smell of hatred in the air—the arrogant hatred of whites, the silent hatred of blacks" (Beauvoir 1999: 233). Beauvoir inhales and exhales the smell of hatred, her body registering the difference between the "arrogant hatred of whites, the silent hatred of blacks." Through this process, and through the unearned privilege she receives as a white woman, she comes to feel complicit with the racism that is all around her. Unable to maintain the isolated stance of "foreigner," Beauvoir assumes the failure of American democracy as her own failure to overcome the physical, social, and institutional boundaries that separate the black oppressed from their white oppressors. Even after she and her white female companion, "N.," help a pregnant black woman who has fainted repeatedly while sitting in the crowded rear seat of their segregated Greyhound bus, Beauvoir experiences the strength of the barriers that divide them: "She thanks us, but she seems worried and goes away quickly without accepting further aid: she feels guilty in the eyes of the whites, and she's afraid. This is only a small incident, but it helps me understand why, when we're traveling through the overcrowded black districts, the placid Greyhound gets such hostile looks" (Beauvoir 1999: 233).[23]

Through Beauvoir's eyes, we see how even the Greyhound bus becomes complicit in the perpetuation of oppression. The vehicle's own massive presence is a tangible daily reminder of the intractability of racism, and for the overheated bodies pressed into the bench at the rear who face the whites in front sitting comfortably in rows of two, oppression is materialized from all sides at once. While it is the very intercorporeality of human experience that enables oppression to be intensified, I would also argue that it is this same intercorporeality that provides the grounds for its eradication. For in the face of challenging choices and even in the face of situations in which freedom does not seem to be present and the very notion of choice appears to be meaningless, what defines the humanity and moral status of those who are oppressed is the same thing that defines every person's humanity and moral status, namely, their concrete relations with others.

It is crucial to realize that the failures of relationship experienced by Sethe and Andrea Yates respectively are not reducible to their relations with any one individual or even a set of individuals. Rather, both cases poignantly reveal that one's relations to others always unfold within a broader context that includes one's relations with the institutions that define the very terms of social existence (e.g., motherhood, slavery, the medical establishment, etc.).[24] When these relations with others are irretrievably damaged, as was the case for both Sethe and Andrea Yates, one must always look not only within but also outside the relationships to the larger social situation in which those relationships are embedded to assess why, where, and how they have broken down. Cases of extreme oppression are rarely attributable to a specific relationship alone, but require, for their eradication, a transformation in the very conditions, and therefore the very horizons, that render a situation intelligible (or unintelligible) as such.

Through the new relationship Sethe builds with Beloved, whom she accepts as her long-lost daughter, she is able to begin to work through the horrific demons of her past, though Beloved's own phantasmatic status raises questions about how successful this relationship itself will be in opening up a new future.[25] In the case of Andrea Yates, who, in contrast to Sethe, moved from the (relative) freedom of white bourgeois motherhood into solitary confinement for twenty-three hours a day in a small cell in a state penitentiary, the legal institution that overturned the validity of her first trial, which found her guilty, holds out more hope for a positive change in her situation than any relationships she may have managed to form and/or restore as a maximum-security prisoner. In both of these cases, despite their significant differences, the language of freedom and choice seems woefully inadequate to address these shattered lives and the communal efforts that will need to be made to rebuild them.

If one affirms, along with care theorists, that choice and freedom are themselves grounded on the human capacity to sustain loving relationships with others, one will also recognize that the work that has to be done to repair the fabric of those relationships is itself moral labor. Beauvoir's texts are instructive here, for she stresses again and again that the freedom and choices of the self have no meaning without reference to the freedom and choices of others, that is, without reference to the shared situation that marks human being-in-the-world. Rather than deny the importance of freedom and choice in human lives, then, I argue that if one's fellow human beings lack the conditions necessary to make informed choices and exercise genuine freedom, one's failure to relate to them as moral subjects impoverishes us all.

11

Mothers/Intellectuals: Alterities of a Dual Identity

Thinking through Identity

Multiple identities, especially identities that are usually thought to be oppositional to one another, such as "mother/intellectual," can produce confusion and
anxiety not only for those who witness their co-existence in another person's life
but also for those who embody them. Whereas I would argue that virtually every
person has more than one identity (e.g., including gendered, racialized, class,
family, and religious identities), it is evident that some identities co-exist more
peacefully within one and the same individual than others. Indeed, when identities reinforce one another, such as a masculine identity and an athletic identity, for instance, there is often very little tension between them since fulfilling
the expectations for one also can serve to fulfill the demands of the other (e.g.,
being a successful, competitive male athlete).

According to Alcoff, who offers a full-length study of the multiple identities
that collectively provide self-definition as well as establish the ground for one's
identification by others, "[i]dentities must resonate with and unify lived experience, and they must provide a meaning that has some purchase, however partial, on the subject's own daily reality" (Alcoff 2006: 42). If it is indeed the case

that identities help to make sense of and unify lived experience, as Alcoff maintains, it might seem that the best way to accomplish this would be if an individual's identities were themselves unified. Indeed, one's proper name serves symbolically to unify an individual's identity, and, as Althusser and Butler respectively maintain, it facilitates a person's interpellation as a singular individual.[1] Both Althusser and Butler emphasize, however, that while it is through interpellation that one becomes a subject in her own right, at the same time, it is also through being interpellated by others that one is subjected to those others. The process of subjectivation, as it is discussed not only by Althusser and Butler but also by Foucault, is thus both enabling and disabling: enabling insofar as it grants an individual social recognition, disabling because one ultimately lacks control over the forms that recognition will take since it issues from others and not from oneself.[2]

To the extent that a person's identities are constituted out of multiple facets of that individual's own experience and include multiple encounters with (the experiences of) others, it is inevitable that an individual's identities themselves will express that very multiplicity, even when they appear to be unified and coherent. Alcoff, appealing to Teresa De Lauretis's work, reinforces this view of identity as incorporating not only the desires of a particular individual but also the responses to that individual by others when she claims that "[t]he fluid historical context in which we negotiate our identities is a context in which we are both subjects of and subjected to social construction" (Alcoff 2006: 146). If one views a person's multiple identities as involving a constant negotiation between an individual's view of herself and the perspectives others have of her, or between what Alcoff refers to as subjective lived experience on the one hand and one's social identity on the other, it is evident that even the most rigidly defined identity is never fixed in stone but can always be transformed.[3]

There are countless historical examples of such transformations in both individual and group identity. For instance, as Michel Foucault emphasizes in *Discipline and Punish*, a single illicit action may forever after brand an individual with the identity of criminal, an all-encompassing identity that has the power to fundamentally alter how that individual views herself and how she is viewed by others. And, as Gordon, Fanon, and many other critical race theorists have argued, the very appearance of a black man in an antiblack world is capable of generating a phobic response that becomes part and parcel of his identity in a racist state, placing "ontological limits" on his own subjectivation.[4]

Given the sheer complexity of the issues that must be addressed when one seriously raises questions about identity and its influence on oneself and on others, it can be tempting to avoid discussions of identity altogether. What mitigates this tendency is the fact that questions of identity arise continuously in daily life even though often they are not explicated as such. Alcoff emphasizes that questions of identity are part and parcel of mundane experience: "[I]dentities" she claims, "are constituted by social contextual conditions of interaction in specific cultures at particular historical periods, and thus their nature, effects, and the problems that need to be addressed in regard to them will be largely local" (Alcoff 2066: 9). The different ways even people in the same culture embody the identity "mother" is a perfect example of this point.

For instance, it is evident that the identity of "mother" varies widely within and across cultures and time periods, as well as in different religious, social, and political contexts. Even if to be a mother, at the most minimal level, means to be a pubescent or post-pubescent female and to have and/or raise a child, this "bare" meaning is never all that is implied in a given society's or a given individual's respective understandings of this particular identity. Moreover, even this minimal definition is problematic because it is possible for a male-to-female transsexual to be a mother even though she isn't born female, and so this biologically based definition excludes some people who might identity themselves and/or be identified by others as mothers. The meaning of being a mother is never just a matter of a "bare" definition in any case, since how any given individual understands the term is clearly influenced by the experience of being (or failing to be) mothered, having close (or distant) relations with mothers, social understandings of what it means to be a mother, and/or being a mother oneself. Religious conceptions of what mothers are or should be also play a role, as do the legal and political rights that mothers have or lack within a given society.[5] Especially influential has been the role of men, the non-mothers who are excluded by the very definition of motherhood from being mothers themselves and yet who, as the historically dominant sex, have largely been responsible for determining the daily expectations placed on mothers in particular societies.[6]

It is arguable that the identity of "intellectual" has perhaps not changed as much as "mother" within and across cultures, because the former is closely associated with the activities of thinking, speaking, and writing (with thinking being the most privileged in determining that one is an intellectual, and the latter two activities being seen as discursive expressions of one's thought), and therefore encompasses a narrower range of behaviors than is associated with someone who is identified as a mother. However, at the same time, it is also readily evident that the issue of *who* is qualified to be an intellectual has been contested for centuries. In virtually every culture that recognizes the identity "intellectual," certain people have been viewed as incapable of being identified as intellectuals because of their allegedly inferior race, sex, or lack of formal education (which was often a result of being the "wrong" race or sex to obtain it!). And, to turn to a primary issue that I will be concerned with here, it has also been the case that certain identities, such as mother, have oftentimes been seen as so comprehensive that they seem to rule out the ability to simultaneously possess another identity, such as intellectual.

Since it is clear that there may be contexts in which I ascribe a particular identity to myself that others do not ascribe to me (or vice versa), one must reckon in any discussion of identity with a traditional philosophical concern, namely, with how to resolve the self/other binary according to which there is a fundamental separation between my view of myself and the view the other has of me.[7] Within this dualistic framework, identity is seen as encompassing both a "subjective" perspective that reflects and expresses my own view of myself and, at the same time, the perspective of the other (or others), which is typically regarded as totally distinct from my own. Working within such a binary model, the central issue then becomes, how are these dual (and often competing) perspectives reconcilable into a coherent identity that is lived by and associated with a concrete individual?

Merleau-Ponty raises this type of concern in relation to Sartre's ontological distinction between the experience of being-for-itself (*être pour-soi*) and the experience of being-for-others (*être pour-les-autres*). Merleau-Ponty attempts to move beyond this oppositional framework by positing a chiasmatic relationship between the perspective one has of oneself and the perspective the other has of one. To call the relationship between my own perspective and the perspective of the other chiasmatic means that it is a reversible relationship that allows one to experience the perspective of the other toward oneself (even without having full access to it), even as the other can do the same, all the while preserving the differences between the two perspectives. In the essay *Eye and Mind*, he suggests that human beings chiasmatically encounter inanimate as well as animate others. On his account, individuals reckon with the perspective of others all the time, even if these latter can never be known with Cartesian clarity and distinctness. Insofar as a person can enter into chiasmatic relationships with non-conscious entities, it should be evident that a chiasmatic relationship does not, for Merleau-Ponty, presuppose that one or both entities must be aware of that relationship in order for it to exist. In his most famous example of a mundane chiasmatic encounter, which I have previously discussed, namely, one hand touching the other, one doesn't have to be *aware* that one hand is touching the other in order to have the experience. Awareness does, undeniably, affect and transform the experience (of touching and being touched) and therefore alters its meaning, but it does not create the experience in the first place *nor* is it required to make the special reflexivity that is operative within the experience significant in one's life.

Merleau-Ponty opposes the self/other binary, then, because he maintains that even *before* the recognition of the unique perspective of the other occurs, one is always already acting within an intersubjective context and so is already affected by the perspective of the other, whether or not one is aware that this is occurring. This is why he proclaims that

> what is given . . . is the taking up of each subjectivity by itself, and of subjec-
> tivities by each other *in the generality of a single nature, the cohesion of an in-*
> *tersubjective life and a world.* . . . True reflection presents me to myself not as
> idle and inaccessible subjectivity, but as identical with my presence in the
> world and to others, as I am now realizing it: I am all that I see, I am an inter-
> subjective field, not despite my body and historical situation, but, on the con-
> trary, by being this body and this situation, and through them, all the rest.
> (Merleau-Ponty 1962: 452)

Irigaray, though accusing Merleau-Ponty of ultimately privileging subjectivity (and male subjectivity at that) over intersubjectivity, agrees with his claim
above that subjectivity is grounded within a fundamentally intersubjective experience. The experience of the look, as Sartre describes it in *Being and Nothing-*
ness, and of the master's need and demand for recognition by the slave, for
Hegel, highlight the moments one is forced to *acknowledge* the radical alterity
of the other, but they fail, Irigaray argues, to acknowledge properly the significance of more primordial contacts with the other, most particularly, the encounters that begin even before human beings are born, as their bodies grow within
the bodies of their mothers.

Through a compelling historical analysis of the rationalist philosophical
tradition, Alcoff reinforces Irigaray's critique, demonstrating that the inherently
intersubjective features of identity have most often been seen as a threat to a human being's status as an autonomous moral agent. Within this tradition, with
relatively few exceptions, the roles of others and of society, history, politics, and so
on in the formation of a given identity have often been downplayed. More specifically, these latter have frequently been seen as collectively determining the
"accidental" features of particular identities, not the essential ones. And, Alcoff
contends, within these accounts the most essential aspect of identity turns out to
be general and universal, namely the capacity for rationality itself.

A major problem with such an ahistorical approach to identity is that there
are countless individuals (all of whom possess their own distinctive identities)
whose disabilities, sex, and/or race have precluded them from being seen as having the capacity for rationality in the first place.[8] Not surprisingly, with regard to
the self/other binary that frames these discussions, the emphasis is overwhelmingly placed on the autonomous self's ability to express its own identity through
its willed choices. And, as I and many feminist ethicists and disability theorists
have argued, those individuals who are viewed as unable to do this often have
their very humanity placed in question.

According to a rationalist Cartesian view, then, the perspective of the other is not granted the same legitimacy as one's own perspective, and, even within the phenomenological and existential tradition, as Heidegger illustrates in his condemnation of the perspective of "the they" in *Being and Time*, the choice to give weight to the view of the other regarding oneself can even be regarded as potentially inauthentic.[9] Thus, existentialists as well as rationalists have placed the primary weight upon the self in determining its own identity even while recognizing that to be human means, to use Sartre's language, to be not only a being-for-itself but also a being-for-others.[10]

In his essay "Identity: Cultural, Transcultural, and Multicultural," Peter Caws reinforces this position, maintaining that "[t]here is a sense—the existentialists were good at dramatizing it, but I think they were also right—in which I am alone in the world and have to forge my identity in isolation" (Caws 1994: 379). From this perspective, identity is an individual project, and Caws distinguishes it from an identification, which can be imposed on one by others. This occurs, for instance, when one is identified as a citizen of a particular country (e.g., a Spaniard or a Turk). Caws claims that children are born into a "first" or "native" culture that is "imposed from without." It is a culture, he continues, that they belong to but that they have not "made their own" (Caws 1994: 371). For Caws and other existentialist thinkers, identity is something one largely fashions oneself, working from the "raw" (and not so raw) materials provided by the surrounding world, including all the people, places, and things an individual comes in contact with on a daily basis. In Caws's words: "Identity, psychologically as well as logically, is a *reflexive* relation, a relation of myself to myself, but it can be a mediated relation: I relate to myself through my interaction with others *and with the world*" (Caws 1994: 379).[11] Ultimately, for both him and Sartre, identity is something one individually *chooses*; however, it also must be distinguished from the mundane choices a person makes from moment to moment throughout her life. For Sartre as well as for Beauvoir, the choice of an identity should be understood as an *existential* choice that unifies my less momentous choices such as which outfit to wear in the morning, what to eat for lunch, and whom to spend time with.[12]

In contrast to the strong individualist emphasis in the existentialist tradition, Marxists maintain that others play the crucial role in determining an individual's identity, and they understand this identity to be primarily a function of one's social class. Even when one emerges from the "false consciousness" of believing one's class status to be natural and inevitable, one does so not by affirming one's individuality but by recognizing that one is a member of a socially constructed, subjugated (or dominating) economic group. In short, one attains *class consciousness*.

While the recognition that others play a central role in the formation of one's identity is a compelling feature of a Marxist position, on the other hand, this view also runs the danger of making it seem as if the individual has virtually no agency in determining her identity. Moreover, it is not only Marxists who are subject to this critique. In her book *Volatile Bodies*, Grosz calls positions that emphasize the role of society in determining the identity of the individual "outside in" perspectives, and she argues that Nietzsche, Foucault, Deleuze, and Guattari all subscribe to this model, in which the individual's identity is primarily constructed not by herself but by the society in which she lives.[13] Bourdieu's discussions of the power of the habitus to shape individual's desires, hopes, fears, and beliefs in accordance with the standards of taste operative for their social class is a perfect example of this view. It should not be surprising that just as the Cartesian emphasis on the autonomous self has been critiqued for its "subjectivism," so too have serious objections been made concerning Bourdieu's reduction of individual taste to the taste that has been indexed for that individual's social class.[14]

Rather than embracing one side of the self/other binary or the other, Alcoff attributes equally primary roles both to the self and to the other in the constitution of identity. Like Merleau-Ponty, she views subjectivity and intersubjectivity as inseparable from one another; as discussed earlier, both philosophers maintain that individuals always emerge as subjects in and through their interactions with others. And, as I have suggested, insofar as these interactions are multiple, it follows that a person's identities themselves are multiple. Moreover, as I argued previously, even if an individual has a dominant identity, for instance as a mother, the meaning of being a mother is never fixed in her life but changes over time and in different situations in accordance with her own experiences of mothering and/or being mothered as well as with the way society as a whole and other individuals respond to (or fail to respond to) her as a mother. While society may promulgate specific standards for motherhood, it is clear that even the woman most devoted to these standards will inevitably end up embodying them in her own way. This is why Alcoff declares that "social identities are relational, contextual, *and* fundamental to the self" (Alcoff 2006: 90).

Up to now, I have focused more generally on the complexity of the issues that must be addressed when one seeks to make claims about the meaning of particular identities. As I have shown, there are a variety of conflicting perspectives regarding how much weight to give to the self and how much weight to attribute to the other (including society at large) in the construction of an individual's identity. With regard to the dual identity "mother/intellectual" that is the focus of this particular discussion, it is evident that both terms have long social and political histories that must be reckoned with. Since I cannot do justice to all of the possible issues that can be raised with regard to the changing meanings of both mothers and intellectuals over time, I would like instead to focus in depth on a particular set of concerns, namely, how these dual identities seem to be very inclusive insofar as they provide an individual with access to two different worlds (with their differing horizons) simultaneously, and yet, the demands placed upon one by both motherhood and intellectual life respectively are frequently so all-encompassing that it is virtually impossible to live these identities in a unified, coherent manner throughout one's life. Rather than abandoning this (or another) set of multiple identities as an impossible project, being both a mother and an intellectual is, I would argue, an excellent example of the limits of privileging a unified identity as a goal one should be striving for to live a meaningful life.[15]

The Inclusive Exclusivity of the Both/And

When I first began to ponder seriously the meaning of the hybrid term "mother/intellectual," my thoughts moved from a consideration of its significance in my own life to a more sustained reflection concerning the way in which this very expression, and the dual existence implied by it, is simultaneously inclusive and exclusive. The expression is inclusive because it encompasses two identities that have traditionally been seen as oppositional. That is, the inclusivity of the term is directly a function of the way in which it brings together two identities customarily conceived to be mutually exclusive, even antagonistic to one another. The opposition between mothers and intellectuals respectively has been due not only to the different spheres with which they are associated, namely, the world of the home for mothers and the "world of ideas" for intellectuals, but also to the totalizing quality of these two identities. I call them totalizing because each has typically been seen as completely defining the individual who is associated with motherhood, on the one hand, or intellectual life, on the other hand. While striving to overcome the tensions between these two roles is an important and ongoing project for many of the women who share them, I argue that it is impossible to integrate fully these two respective identities into a single, harmonious whole.[16] Further, I maintain that the attempt to be inclusive by coordinating the respective demands of motherhood and intellectual life will never eliminate the specter of exclusivity but, in fact, will produce new forms of exclusivity between those who live the life of a "mother/intellectual" and those who do not.

Before turning to consider what is at stake in the attempt to integrate the practice of mothering with an intellectual life, more needs to be said about why these two identities have most frequently been seen as exclusive of one another. Let's start with the intellectual. Ever since Socrates' famous injunction to "know thyself," the pursuit of wisdom has been viewed, at least in democratic societies, as intrinsically rewarding and therefore as self-justifying.[17] Moreover, those who devote their life to this endeavor tend to be defined by their commitment to it. What this has meant, historically speaking, is that the intellectual's "extra-curricular activities" including her past, present home life, likes and dislikes, friendships, and daily routines, are typically seen as irrelevant, except insofar as they offer the promise of enabling us to better understand the individual's intellectual development.

Martin Heidegger, in his "Letter on Humanism," provides a wonderful example of the unsettling effects of being forced to recognize that the intellectual can also have a home life. He describes a group of travelers who come to visit the famous pre-Socratic philosopher Heraclitus in his home, hoping to catch him in the act of thinking great thoughts. Instead, they find him humbly warming his hands by a fire. Taken aback, they prepare to leave. Before they can go, however, Heraclitus urges them to enter his domestic domain. Challenging the very dichotomy between the life of the home and the life of the intellect, he tells them, "Here too the Gods come to presence" (Heidegger 1993b: 257).[18]

Not unlike the situation of the intellectual, a mother's prior life before she became a mother, her current non-mothering activities, and future non-maternal aspirations are most often deemed to be superfluous except insofar as they provide insight into the kind of mother she has turned out to be.[19] If one discovers that a particular mother also engages in intellectual activities, these are usually seen as providing her with another identity completely separate from her identity as a mother. That is, she is seen as someone who possesses dual identities, identities that are independent of one another. The fact that historically men have been associated almost exclusively with the role of intellectual and women almost exclusively with the role of mother creates additional difficulties for the woman who seeks to live as both an intellectual and a mother. To think these two identities together, as my title "Mothers/Intellectuals" seeks to do, requires that one buck a long tradition by challenging both the exhaustiveness of these two identities and the contradictory associations that present them as incompatible.

One of the appealing aspects of the inclusivity invoked by the expression "mothers/intellectuals" is that the use of the plural implies the presence of a community of women who are both mothers and intellectuals, rather than a single, exceptional figure who is somehow able to be a mother *and* an intellectual. On the other hand, the very attempt to be inclusive by acknowledging that there is, in fact, a community of women who are both mothers and intellectuals at the same time performs an exclusion. Not only are women (and men) who are neither mothers nor intellectuals placed outside this special group, but so are non-intellectual mothers and women who are intellectuals but not mothers. Additional problems surface when one acknowledges the instability of all of these groupings. For, as I will go on to show, the more one reflects on these various groups in relation to one another, the more artificial the distinctions between them seem to be.

As Patrice Di Quinzio has compellingly argued, there is no way to talk about the practice of mothering without having to contend with the ideological effects of the institution of motherhood that underlies it. Similarly, there is no way to talk about what it means to live an intellectual life without having to address the dominant ideologies that help to establish the parameters within which such a life unfolds and attains significance. For instance, it is impossible to discuss the maternal and intellectual domains seriously without acknowledging how the former is thoroughly feminized and the latter masculinized. This means that anyone who engages in the activities of mothering (whether male or female) has to reckon with their traditional feminine connotations and that anyone who participates in intellectual activities at the same time assumes (problematically or unproblematically) their masculine associations. Moreover, these specific gendered expectations play out differently in different cultures, and so one must be attuned to how the very notions of the "feminine" mother and the "masculine" intellectual have changed not only over time but also cross-culturally. Age, race, ethnicity, and social class must also be taken into account since gender never operates in isolation from them. For instance, while fourteen-year-olds can be mothers, they are rarely seen as intellectuals. There is an assumption that a longer period of maturation is involved in the process of becoming an intellectual than the nine months of pregnancy that is still the most common way of becoming a mother. Moreover, while mothers are readily acknowledged to come from all races, intellectuals have historically been seen as emanating from a dominant, white, male, ruling class. The very existence of women of color who are both mothers and intellectuals challenges several of these presuppositions at once and intensifies the constant struggle to negotiate disparate identities.

Critically examining the processes of inclusion and exclusion that are produced in and through the tensions between these two identities as they come to be embodied within one and the same person enables one to see why the adoption of an inclusive identity such as mother/intellectual inevitably seems to lead to practices of exclusion even if these latter are unintentional. And, although I will conclude with some personal reflections on the challenges of living as a mother/intellectual in a both/and rather than an either/or fashion, for the majority of this discussion I will be problematizing these categories themselves.

Motivated by an inclusive impulse, I initially titled this chapter "Mothers/Intellectuals: Both/And, Either/Or, or Neither/Nor." This title reflected my desire to recognize the different options for women today vis-à-vis the very question of being a mother and/or an intellectual. My goal was to acknowledge the various, equally authentic ways in which a woman can live: (1) simultaneously as a mother and an intellectual (a both/and); (2) as a mother who is not an intellectual (an either/or); (3) as an intellectual who is not a mother (another either/or); and (4) as a woman (or a man for that matter) who does not fit into either category (a neither/nor). With these basic categories in hand, my original project was to articulate some of the points of tension as well as the points of commonality that emerge within and across these groups. However, as I increasingly realized when I thought more about these issues, such a project, laudable as it might be, presupposed that the categories themselves are self-evident and unproblematic.

As a phenomenologist, I have been trained to describe lived experience without relying on presuppositions regarding that experience. And while I agree with phenomenology's critics that it is impossible to eliminate, in advance, all of the presuppositions that one may bring to a given experience (indeed, one is often unaware of what these presuppositions even are!), nonetheless I have found the attempt to be aware of one's presuppositions and to minimize their influence to be a useful goal to strive for in one's work. To view mothers and intellectuals as clear-cut identities itself seems to me to be just such a presupposition, one that is reinforced by the Bourdieusian habitus that characterizes contemporary life in a Western capitalist society. So, before one can even begin to explore the tensions that exist between women who seem to share both, one, or neither of these identities, one must first address the problems associated with the terms themselves.

As I hope to demonstrate in what follows, as soon as one starts to think carefully about these identities and the various ways in which one can be seen as belonging or failing to belong to them, the meanings of the both/and, either/or, and neither/nor categories respectively become quite complex, ultimately deconstructing of their own accord. For instance, with respect to the first category, the both/and (mothers/intellectuals), what about mothers who don't consider themselves to be intellectuals but are considered to be such by others? Or, perhaps more commonly, what about mothers who view themselves as intellectuals but who aren't viewed this way by anyone else? This latter situation occurs most frequently in the case of those mothers who do not have the educational background, formal credentials, or professional affiliation that publicly confers this title upon them. For those who lack a formal relationship with a college or university or who do not participate in intellectual discussions in an official workplace or at professional conferences, maintaining one's intellectual credentials may be difficult indeed. For example, the presentation of an earlier version of this chapter at a philosophy conference and the presence of the audience serve as visible guarantors of both my own and my audience's respective intellectuality, thereby legitimizing any claims they or I might make regarding being an intellectual.[20] But it is also evident that very few people have the interest or the opportunity to express their intellectual inclinations in such a structured way.[21]

Regarding the attempt to live the both/and, that is, to live an inclusive existence, Søren Kierkegaard's *Either/Or* (1843) suggests quite clearly that the ethical individual should not strive to "have one's cake and eat it too."[22] For Kierkegaard, attempting to "have it all" is a sign of a purely aesthetic existence, such as that lived by the fictitious "A" depicted in his text. To live on a moral plane, Kierkegaard maintains, one must confront the Either/Or by choosing the ethical over the aesthetic, which in turn involves another series of Either/Ors, including choosing the community over the individual, the public over the private, infinitude over finitude, and duty over pleasure. Kierkegaard well recognizes the sacrifices involved in these choices but argues nonetheless that the ethical life *demands* them and that one will be rewarded amply for any hardships one experiences along the way. And hardships there will be. For, as he frequently observes in his writings, one cannot choose to exist on the moral plane and expect that choice to hold firm over a lifetime. Instead, in true existentialist fashion, Kierkegaard claims that the Either/Or, and more specifically the absolute nature of the choice between them, must be affirmed again and again throughout one's life. As Judge William, Kierkegaard's exemplar of the ethical, states, "The original choice is forever present in every succeeding choice" (Kierkegaard 1987: Part 2, 219).

But what is the nature of this choice? One cannot read Kierkegaard for long before one begins to question the absolute nature of the Either/Or he has depicted. For, one soon learns, the path not chosen not only remains as a constant temptation, but also is somehow incorporated in the choices one makes. For instance, the ethical individual can still enjoy what had heretofore been purely aesthetic pleasures, but now, the reader is led to believe, she does so in a different way. That is, she can enjoy a good walk, a warm meal, or a fine play, but she has learned not to view such activities as ends in themselves as the aesthetic individual might; rather she can appreciate them as meaningful, pleasurable aspects of her existence that contribute toward, but are never sufficient to procure, her well-being. And, Kierkegaard implies, so long as she continues to affirm the value of the community over her private interests, especially when these conflict, such an individual need not be seen as choosing a path of renunciation in her daily life.[23]

While Kierkegaard may seem to be a very unlikely point of reference for a discussion of mothers/intellectuals, I can't think of anyone who has done a better job of revealing the complexities of the Either/Or and, more specifically, the ways in which what may look like absolute choices always seem to incorporate the very things they are excluding. Ironically, although Kierkegaard saw his own work as being in direct opposition to the dominant Hegelianism of his time, something very much like an Hegelian *Aufhebung* seems to be operative in the ethical (and later in the religious) individual's relationship to the aesthetic existence that she has allegedly left behind. This is because, rather than having the choice of the ethical absolutely exclude the choice of the aesthetic, the former finds a place for the enjoyment of the aesthetic aspects of existence that it seems to renounce. Heidegger's story of Heraclitus enjoying the domesticity of the hearth reinforces this message, one that I believe has a direct bearing on either/ or understandings of the relationship between mothers and intellectuals.

Returning to a consideration of the category mother, it is clear, as noted earlier, that there are many ways to *be* one, and many ways *not* to be one, not all of which are universally acknowledged. Is a woman who gives her child up for adoption and never has any other children a mother? Should a woman who is raped and becomes pregnant (as happened all too often in the late twentieth century in Rwanda, Bosnia, and Afghanistan and as continues to occur all over the world on a regular basis, especially now that rape with the goal of impregnation has increasingly been sanctioned by commanding officers as an effective war strategy), or should any woman who becomes pregnant against her will, be considered a mother even when she does not want to be a mother and has a very conflicted relationship with the child to whom she gives birth?[24] Is a gestational or surrogate mother who carries a child to term in order to turn that child over to others a mother? Is a woman who never has any children of her own (whether naturally or through adoption) but who helps to raise other people's children a mother?

Examples of women in this latter category include those whom Patricia Hill Collins identifies as "othermothers," women who may or may not be biologically related to a child and who take partial or sometimes even full responsibility for caring for that child. Citing Rosalie Troester's work, Collins notes that "othermothers—women who assist bloodmothers by sharing mothering responsibilities—traditionally have been central to the institution of Black motherhood" (Collins 2000: 119). However, this role, as well as the joys and responsibilities that go along with it, is often not recognized in the United States outside of African American communities because the dominant white society's ideological commitment to the primacy of the traditional nuclear family above all other domestic arrangements privileges first biological mothers, then adoptive mothers, and in cases where neither is present, legal guardians (including foster mothers). As a result, an othermother who may consider herself to be a mother and who may be considered to be a mother by members of her own community may fail to be viewed as a mother outside of that community.

Collins views this conflict between communities regarding the othermother's status as indicative of a broader conflict between two worldviews, what she terms the Afrocentric perspective and the Eurocentric perspective respectively.

Interestingly, she refers to the former as a both/and perspective and the latter as an either/or perspective. Unlike Kierkegaard, who seems to valorize the either/or even as he complicates the relationship between the two alternatives, Collins stresses the limitations of either/or dichotomous thinking and presents the more inclusive both/and perspective as a compelling foundation for black feminist thought. And, although it is possible to criticize Collins's own account for (1) falling prey to the limitations of either/or dichotomies by setting these perspectives in such sharp opposition to one another and by clearly valorizing the Afrocentric perspective over the Eurocentric one (thereby replicating the hierarchization that she claims marks the Eurocentric worldview), and (2) problematically collapsing many different cultures and traditions in both Africa and Europe into two hegemonic perspectives, her account of the clashes produced by competing worldviews that individuals and communities must contend with on a daily basis is extremely compelling. For, it is evident that there *are* crucial differences between how communities see themselves and how they are seen by others. These differences may in turn lead to major social, political, and, as Fanon has so poignantly shown, psychic conflicts that can leave permanent scars on both the individuals and the communities in question.

On the psychical level, Fanon argues that the project of making sense of one's existence in the face of a double standard (i.e., the negative judgment of the Other and the more positive judgment that arises out of one's own community) can lead to neurosis. However, given the reality of the conflict between the two competing perspectives, he also believes that it is very difficult, if not impossible, to avoid these tensions altogether. In response to these conflicts, Fanon maintains that the individual (and the community) must strive to move beyond identificatory labels. In his words: "In order to terminate this neurotic situation in which I am compelled to choose an unhealthy, conflictual solution, fed on fantasies, hostile, inhuman in short, I have only one solution: to rise above this absurd drama that others have staged round me, to reject the two terms that are equally unacceptable, and, through one human being, to reach out for the universal" (Fanon 1967: 197).

Although Fanon's appeal to universal humanity as the way out of the conflict between the judgment of the self or community and the judgment of the other may be attractive, it is also a very dangerous proposition. For not only can one raise questions about the viability of ignoring the social, political, and psychic conflicts that are produced through the clash between competing perspectives, but Fanon's appeal to a universal humanity that transcends race, gender, class, ability, and ethnicity appears to be both naïve and politically suspect. While Fanon claims to be addressing the universal situation of colonized black men and women, who must always contend with their subordination by the white colonizer, it is clear, as several Fanon scholars have observed, that his own work focuses particularly upon the situation of the colonized black male, leaving the specific experiences of black women out of the picture almost altogether. And since his account is proffered as a comprehensive description of the racial oppression inflicted by the French colonizer upon the colonized Antilleans, it is difficult to raise the question of gender difference, much less to have it addressed within the parameters of his analysis. This puts the sympathetic reader in a difficult position, for however much one may want to agree with the general points Fanon is making about the psychic tolls of racism, one also has to resist the tendency to accept uncritically his description of the colonized black male's embodiment as characterizing the experience of both sexes.

Collins's work, because of its explicit focus on black women, is particularly helpful in addressing the impact of gender difference in the experience of racial oppression. Her claim that black women must continually contend with a set of "controlling images" that seek to define and contain them supports Fanon's discussion of the power of the Other to set the terms according to which one is summarily judged and found deficient. However, Collins also acknowledges that there are not one but several controlling images that are applied to black women (e.g., the mammy, the matriarch, the welfare mother, the Jezebel, and the super-strong black mother), and this opens up the possibility that there may well be different controlling images applicable to the experience of black men. Like Fanon, Collins calls upon black women to resist the oppressive judgment of the Other; however, her response to this judgment is not to seize upon one's universal humanity, but rather to embrace the healing power of self-definition. "Black women's lives," she tells us,

> are a series of negotiations that aim to reconcile the contradictions separating our own internally defined images of self as African-American women with our objectification as the Other. The struggle of living two lives, one for "them and one for ourselves" (Gwaltney 1980, 240) creates a peculiar tension to construct independent self-definitions within a context where Black womanhood remains routinely derogated. (Collins 2000: 99–100)

Fanon's and Collins's respective solutions to the oppressive judgments of the other seem at first glance to be directly opposed to one another. Collins advocates that Black women "extract the definition of [their] true self" from their experiences of racism, sexism, and classism, "re-articulating" their lives on their own terms, while Fanon advocates that one free oneself from the particulars of one's own experience altogether to embrace one's universal humanity. However, what is common to both accounts is the hope that one can somehow transcend the controlling images that structure how one is viewed by the other, by refusing to let them influence the meaning of one's existence. And while I am not as optimistic as either Fanon or Collins that a person (or even a larger group) can eventually get beyond the negative judgments of the oppressor, both of their accounts are extremely helpful in elucidating the unlivability of the dilemma that individuals nonetheless live from one moment to the next in their daily lives.

The conflict between competing perspectives discussed respectively by Fanon and Collins helps one to see why the very question of who, exactly, is a mother or who, exactly, is an intellectual cannot be addressed without confronting the tensions between how an individual may view herself and how she is viewed by others. What complicates this process of identification further is a point I emphasized earlier, namely, that mothers and intellectuals have historically been seen as at odds with one another, that is, as oppositional identities. This means that those who seek to embrace the "both/and" by simultaneously identifying as mothers *and* as intellectuals already are subverting the established parameters for these two identities. One way of minimizing the tensions between them is what I would call the "compartmental approach," namely, to view (and live) them as two self-contained identities that one can alternate between depending upon one's situation. However, even if one is relatively successful at doing this, there will always be occasions when one's identity as a mother intrudes upon one's identity as an intellectual, forcing the individual to shift her priorities suddenly and radically. Far from a rare occurrence, it takes no more than the interruption of a sick child when one is in the midst of intellectual labor for these conflicts to emerge.

Ideological Tensions

In *The Impossibility of Motherhood: Feminism, Individualism, and the Problem of Mothering*, Di Quinzio offers a critical account of the effects of competing ideologies regarding the practice of mothering as codified in the institution of motherhood. Specifically, Di Quinzio examines the conflicts as well as the points of resonance between what she refers to as "essential motherhood," a reigning ideology that conflates women, femininity, and maternity and views the latter as a woman's natural destiny, and the ideology of individualism that has been effectively deployed by the feminist movement to argue that each woman possesses an embodied subjectivity and agency that is unique to her alone and that gives her equal standing with all other women as well as all men. Although these ideologies often seem to be in opposition to one another insofar as individualism emphasizes that each person must be viewed as an autonomous moral agent and essential motherhood emphasizes that women are first and foremost mothers (read caretakers of children), these ideologies also, as Di Quinzio carefully shows, reinforce and depend upon one another. In the case of othermothers, for instance, essential motherhood and individualism can work hand in hand to maintain that (1) each child can only have one mother and

(2) if one isn't a natural or legal mother, one is not a mother. More generally, both ideologies work against my earlier claim that one and the same person can possess multiple identities, a point I will return to shortly.

Before turning to the challenges of a both/and existence insofar as it seems to support multiple identities, I want to trouble the either/or categories of mothers who are not intellectuals and intellectuals who are not mothers further. While the case of othermothers offers a compelling example of women who may view themselves and be viewed by their communities as mothers even while having no children of their own, there are also women who may actively refuse to be identified as mothers but nonetheless find this label thrust upon them. For instance, how is one to view older women who mentor younger women and who may be regarded by the latter as mothers even when they do not view themselves in this way? Simone de Beauvoir, the often acclaimed "mother of feminism," comes to mind in this regard. For no one has delivered a more contested critical analysis of the mother than Beauvoir and, at the same time, so frequently had that moniker applied to her own influence as a feminist on generations of younger women. So, while Beauvoir might initially seem to be a paradigm exemplar of the second either/or category, namely an intellectual woman who is not a mother, some arguments could also be made for placing her in the both/and category. And, for those who might wince at placing "symbolic mothers" into this grouping, Beauvoir's adoption of Sylvie Le Bon de Beauvoir as her legal daughter later on in her life weakens even the literalist's defense of Beauvoir as an intellectual non-mother.

Feminist theorists Adrienne Rich, Sara Ruddick, and Eva Feder Kittay emphasize that each human being has had the experience of being mothered (regardless of who has performed the labor of mothering). Radically different as these experiences may be, there are also certain commonalities that link them, in particular the experience of being completely dependent early on in one's life on the care of others. Many women who would be viewed by the literalist as non-mothers may find themselves, by either choice or necessity, performing the labors of mothering if one understands the latter as involving caring for dependent beings. These mothering activities can encompass diverse dependents such as a small kitten that one may have to feed by hand, an elderly parent with Alzheimer's who may need to be fed, bathed, and diapered, or even a garden that requires daily watering, weeding, and pruning.

In addition, as Rich observes, to recognize that each human being is "of women born" also makes it difficult to differentiate absolutely between those who have the experience of being mothers and those who do not. For, as previously noted, the very experience of being mothered (and this may run the entire gamut between love and abuse), leaves its own constitutive effects upon the psyche and can directly influence the ways in which one identifies or dis-identifies with the activity of mothering as well as the broader institution of motherhood. If, as Di Quinzio argues, it is impossible to separate the activity of mothering from its institutionalization, then one must also be attuned to the structuring role this latter plays in individual as well as societal judgments regarding the quality and status of mothers. Against individualist accounts of maternal practices that would define these practices as specific acts performed by specific caregivers in specific situations, she insists that these practices themselves never take place in a vacuum, but achieve significance against the background of dominant (and frequently competing) ideologies of motherhood.

The ideology of essential motherhood, as Di Quinzio points out, proclaims that the very definition of a woman is inextricably tied to her capacity to be a mother. The deleterious effects of this ideology are readily seen in the case of infertile women, who may view or have others view their inability to get pregnant as a challenge to their femininity. Or for those women who actively choose not to have children, their refusal to reproduce is often construed through the ideology of essential motherhood as a refusal to *be* a woman. Di Quinzio suggests that tempting as it may be to think that one can resist the influence of the ideologies of individualism and essential motherhood upon one's own self-definition, it is not possible to do so. Following Gayatri Spivak, she argues that "[i]n the context of the hegemony of individualism and essential motherhood, it is impossible to refuse the terms of these ideological formations entirely, but it is possible to resist them to one extent or another" (Di Quinzio 1999: 28). Given that one can't transcend these ideologies and their corresponding contradictions altogether, the form such resistance can take, according to Di Quinzio, is an affirmation of a "paradoxical politics of mothering." It is a politics that, in her words,

> accepts the impossibility of motherhood and the impossibility of individualist subjectivity and that does not require for its foundation a univocal, coherent, and exhaustive position on mothering [but which] might instead make possible multiple and overlapping positions of resistance to individualism and essential motherhood, and might show how to achieve or constitute the possibility of movement among such positions. (Di Quinzio 1999: 248)

Although my own analysis of the problems associated with identifying who, exactly, is a mother or who, exactly, is an intellectual supports a politics of resistance to these hegemonic labels, what I have been concerned with here is the necessary preliminary work of destabilizing the terms themselves. Such an endeavor, I believe, is already an act of resistance to the constraining effects of these identities not only upon those who seem to neatly fit one or both categories, but also upon those neither/nors who are excluded from them altogether. Moreover, it is important to acknowledge that, historically speaking, the intellectual has more readily been granted an authoritative, powerful voice in society than the mother, and so the two identities have not been equal in social, political, and symbolic value.[25]

Ruddick attempts to counter the traditional devaluation of the mother's thought processes (which are usually seen as limited to a narrow domestic context) by affirming the active intellectual labor performed by mothers on a daily basis. Through her analysis of the complexities of maternal thinking, a thinking that continually must negotiate and develop practical solutions to the contradictory demands of one's children, oneself, and one's society without ever hoping to resolve these contradictions altogether, Ruddick offers us one way of deconstructing an either/or understanding of mothers and intellectuals. I agree with Ruddick that it is crucial that the practice of mothering more generally and individual mothers in particular receive the respect, dignity, and value from society that they deserve. However, while she seeks to accomplish this by pointing out the ways in which mothers are themselves engaging in serious intellectual activity, it is also important to recognize that the intellectual life brings with it its own pressures and insecurities that can be incredibly constricting, and in extreme cases debilitating.

Since the both/and category might seem, at face value, to avoid the difficulties associated with the either/or dichotomy, and since the both/and category is the one with which I am most often identified, let me turn to a more concrete examination of it. At various points in this discussion I have suggested that the inclusivity seemingly promised by living one's life both as a mother and as an intellectual may turn out to be a false illusion insofar as one may find oneself living these dual identities not in a cohesive, integrated fashion but by compartmentalizing one's existence into distinct, and surprisingly separate, spheres. Moreover, as Lorde, Alcoff, and many other feminist and cultural theorists have asserted, no individual ever possesses simply one or even two identities. Lorde's description of herself as "a forty-nine year old Black, lesbian, feminist socialist mother of two, including one boy, and a member of an inter-racial couple" points toward the complex, multiple identities that a particular individual can live from one moment to the next (Lorde 1990: 281). Though Lorde herself does not describe the relationship among these various identities in depth, it is evident that even when someone is most solidly anchored in one of them, the other identities continually intrude, sometimes in negative ways but also in positive ones.

Let me illustrate the constant challenge of living the both/and life of a mother/intellectual in an integrated, harmonious fashion through the following example. One Saturday in late September several years ago, no sooner did I get two grant proposals sent off via express mail to meet October 1st deadlines then I had to rush off to the first of several soccer games (in accordance with my responsibilities as a "soccer mom"). As I settled into my chair besides the other parents, patting myself on the back for succeeding in fulfilling my dual responsibilities as an intellectual and a mother, my enjoyment of the game was interrupted by having to rush to take one of my five-year-old twins to a secluded spot to "do a poop." Immediately, I became consumed by the challenge of finding a way to clean him, clean myself, and dispose of the evidence without detection.

As I resolved the problem more or less satisfactorily, I settled back into my seat, only to be beset by anxieties about how I was going to finish a paper I had to deliver at a conference later that week when I still had to rush back and forth between six more games over two days (including one an hour away in Baltimore), bring snacks for one of the teams, attend back-to-school day at Sunday school for my fourth grader and my sixth grader, and help to get my three younger kids with signed cards and wrapped presents to two different birthday parties. At this point, it was hard to see the both/and existence as desirable. In fact, the kids' multiple activities have continued unabated for years now, and trying to fulfill both my maternal and my intellectual responsibilities simultaneously often seems out-and-out crazy. While people often tell me they don't know how I "do it all," it is also clear that most are also wondering why I or anyone would willingly pay the price that "doing it all" involves. My usual answer is that one can't stop to think about it because (1) there is no time and (2) if one thought about it one would realize the whole enterprise is insane and one wouldn't be able to muster the resources needed to do it.

Rather than present only a negative picture however, it is also important to provide at least one positive example of how one's life as a mother and an intellectual can also be brought together, even if only for a relatively short period of time. In the summer of 2001, in the midst of chaperoning my oldest son's soccer team in Spain, I found myself at an amusement park running from ride to ride with four boys and one other parent, a father who had spent his entire career planning military strategy for the U.S. Air Force and who continues to serve as a consultant for the Pentagon. While waiting on one of the interminable lines for one of the attractions, he and I entered into a long discussion of Kierkegaard's ethics. From a comparison between the knight of faith and the ethical individual, we moved on to Heidegger's view of death. Then, after finishing this ride and waiting for another one, we talked seriously about the commitment to monogamy in marriage. And, if my memory serves me correctly, we concluded a few hours later with a discussion of the difficulty of negotiating the tensions between raising kids to take care of their problems on their own and knowing when to intervene on their behalf. Our conversation, though intense, was hardly uninterrupted. Keeping one eye on the boys as we talked, we continually had to exhort them to stop complaining about how long the line was, to stop unfavorably comparing the rides at this Spanish amusement park to bigger and better rides they had enjoyed in the United States, and, most of all, to settle down and stop horsing around.

Intertwining maternal and intellectual labors can be incredibly rewarding, but it is also exhausting, and one rarely succeeds in genuinely integrating the two. As such times, Virginia Woolf's appeal for a "room of one's own" to engage in reflection seems incredibly appealing even if one would only plan to use the room of one's own to take a nap! On the other hand, to the extent that one can seize upon spontaneous opportunities to make what might seem like disparate identities intersect with one another, one can help to break down the barriers that separate them and, in so doing, can enrich the meaning of one's life. It is important to realize, however, that the more one takes on with the goal of being as inclusive as possible, the more one inevitably excludes others who do not share one's multiple concerns. At such moments, one must remember that each person lives their own both/ands, and though one can gain an extraordinary amount in the process, there are also opportunities that are lost along the way.

By thinking about the inclusions and exclusions that are simultaneously performed by mothers who are intellectuals, one can see that although one of these identities may be more salient than the other in a particular context, both identities can themselves be displaced in turn. In the post-9/11 climate that has dominated early twenty-first century U.S. politics, including both domestic and foreign policy, U.S. citizens are frequently urged to overlook their differences and to embrace their common identity as patriotic Americans.[26] Yet here, too, the attempt at inclusiveness generates its own exclusions, exclusions that are all the more dangerous precisely because they are violently performed and, at the same time, disavowed insofar as they run counter to the spirit of inclusivity.[27] This shows that the very call to be inclusive, precisely when it is manifested as a plea to overcome difference, must always be examined critically. And if it is impossible to eliminate exclusion through appeals to inclusivity, then this means that human beings must face the limits not only of the either/or but also of the both/and categories.

If the identities mother and intellectual both have their own priorities, their own horizons of significance that frequently conflict with one another, as I have suggested, it is also important to remember, as Alcoff observes, that "[h]orizons are open-ended, in constant motion, and aspects of our horizon are inevitably group-related or shared among members of a social identity" (Alcoff 2006: 102). This means that no social identity is ever completely severed from other identities that a person (or a group) may possess. As a result, very few people will ever achieve the kind of unity and coherence in their identities that a Cartesian values. And, I have implied, this would not even be desirable; to the extent that such a goal requires the denial of some of one's identities in order to affirm others, it can even be pathological. Moreover, I have argued that the compartmental approach that would advocate separating one's identities and their respective concerns into different spheres of one's life is also ultimately doomed to failure even though it might be an effective strategy for brief periods of time. This is because the bridges between human beings' various identities (both one's own and those of others) are always already there, generated through the ongoing project of making sense of one's life as an embodied human being in an inter-subjective world of mutual concern.

Individually and collectively, human beings must work harder, then, to develop new interpretive horizons that will allow for greater recognition of, as well as more satisfactory responses to, the conflicting demands generated by the co-existence of various and sometimes incompatible identities both within and across individuals.[28] This will in turn involve acknowledging that these identities, their respective horizons, and, most importantly, the conflicts they inevitably produce are not accidental by-products of the self but fundamentally constitutive of who that self was, who that self is, and who that self can become.

Notes

Introduction

1. Moreover, these memories, traditions, experiences, and expectations include those of others as well as one's own; that is, as I will argue throughout this book, they are not restricted to the individual alone but reflect a broader intersubjective, historical reality.

2. Lesbian separatists, for instance, have often invoked this tension between themselves and heterosexist society, maintaining that the solution is to reject the latter and live independently in a self-defined fashion. Monique Wittig has been one of the most eloquent proponents of this view, famously arguing that "it would be incorrect to say that lesbians associate, make love, live with women, for 'woman' has meaning only in heterosexual systems of thought and heterosexual economic systems. Lesbians are not women" (Wittig 1992: 32). Desirable as it might be to repudiate the grounds of one's own repudiation by society, it is nonetheless difficult to understand how lesbians are able to escape "heterosexual systems of thought and heterosexual economic systems" since these latter form the horizons within and against which they articulate their lives. And it is precisely because these horizons are historical phenomena (rather than natural kinds) that are differentially constituted across cultures that they are not as fixed as they might seem; for this reason they are always capable of being transformed even if this latter is usually accomplished only one small step at a time.

3. Alcoff stresses that "[i]dentities are relational both in the sense that their ramifications in one's life are context dependent and that the identity designations themselves are context dependent" (Alcoff 2006: 91). And in *Body Images: Embodiment as Intercorporeality*, I examine how this relational aspect of identities plays out at the level of our body images, which "are themselves always characterized by a series of intercorporeal exchanges that break down the boundaries both between the body images of one individual, and the body images of that individual and other individuals" (Weiss 1999: 86). Audre Lorde was an early advocate of the view that identity is always plural rather than singular, and her famous description of her own multiple identities in "Age, Race, Class, and Sex: Women Redefining Difference" is a wonderful example of how these identities all combine to constitute a single individual (Lorde 1990: 281).

4. It is important to acknowledge that the drama of self vs. other is not central to all philosophical traditions. For instance, many Eastern religions and philosophies reject this dichotomy altogether; to the extent that self and other are even distinguished, they are often depicted as indissolubly linked. Indeed, Buddhism identifies a clinging to the self and its desires as the very obstacle that must be overcome to achieve spiritual enlightenment. In addition, Michel Foucault argues that the focus on the self as a unique entity separated from others by its own interests, desires, ambitions, etc., is a historical phenomenon that did not exist in ancient times but is instead a product of a specific, modern (Western) epistemic tradition (Foucault 1988).

5. Martin Buber is a notable exception in this regard. In *I and Thou* he suggests that the most authentic human experiences necessarily involve the mutual acknowledgement of oneself and another (whether this other is human or even nonhuman).

1. Context and Perspective

1. I am grateful to Daniel Susser for bringing the "frame problem" in cognitive science to my attention through his discussion of it in "Challenging the Binary: Toward an Ecological Theory of Intentionality," his 2007 senior philosophy honors thesis at The George Washington University.

2. Husserl's distinction between an object's inner and outer horizon, which I will be discussing subsequently, further complicates the task of determining with precision the influence horizons have upon one's individual experiences; indeed, this distinction itself makes a discussion of how horizons structure what counts as ordinary experience all the more urgent.

3. It is Husserl who first adopts Franz Brentano's "intentionality thesis" to describe the very essence of consciousness itself, arguing that to be conscious is to be conscious of some specific object or other. Consciousness, for Husserl, is not a substance but rather pure intentional activity (noesis) directed toward an intentional object (noema). For Husserl, these two terms are interdependent: there can be no noesis without a corresponding noema and vice versa. However, it is Merleau-Ponty who extends the intentionality thesis beyond consciousness to the body itself, viewing the body and not consciousness as the locus of human intentionality. Of course, consciousness is viewed as part of the body in this account; however, the point is that intentionality cannot be restricted to the activity of the mind since it is also expressed in the very movements of the body, whether or not one is conscious of these latter. Although Husserl's own account of intentionality can be understood in terms of the relationship between figure and ground, it is Merleau-Ponty who explicitly makes the connection between Gestalt

insights concerning the fundamental interdependence of figure and ground and how bodily intentionality is structured. Taking up the notion of the horizon as it is introduced by Husserl, Merleau-Ponty is able to further an understanding of it in Gestaltist terms to show how contexts and perspectives are formed. For this reason, I concentrate on Merleau-Ponty's insights in what follows, though many of these insights receive their earliest elaboration in Husserl's work, especially in the two volumes of his *Ideas Pertaining to a Pure Phenomenology and to a Phenomenological Philosophy*.

4. See Silverman's *Male Subjectivity at the Margins,* Irigaray's *Speculum of the Other Woman,* and Beauvoir's *The Second Sex* for their respective critiques of the uncritical tendency to posit a universal, one-size-fits-all perspective that is actually derived from a decidedly masculinist experience. This is a perfect example, in fact, of how a sexist horizon of significance sets the parameters for a particular perspective that masquerades as the (gender-blind) perspective of any possible viewer.

5. Nonetheless, Mead would acknowledge that some perspectives might be more viable than others, and he would understand viability in functional terms; that is, the more viable perspective would be one that allowed the organism to interact more effectively with its environment.

6. It should be noted that in cases of psychosis, a patient's perspective is often grounded more in a (phantasmatic) past or future than in the present, but that, for this very reason, the patient's perspective is viewed as dysfunctional.

7. In her book *In a Different Voice* Carol Gilligan argues that a failure to assess adequately the contexts within which women's perspectives to moral issues have developed has led to theories of morality that place very little emphasis on context at all, but rather treat moral judgments as depending strictly upon such abstract concepts as justice and fairness that are supposed to be independent of contextual concerns.

If Gilligan is correct in her observation that women tend to rely more heavily than men on contextual features of the situation before making moral decisions, then it is especially important that the relationship between context and perspective be examined since this might provide a basis for discussing gender differences in perspective.

8. However, when there are conflicts among these contextual levels then it may be impossible to experience them in a unified fashion. Indeed, it is precisely when one acknowledges the contextual influences provided by race, gender, class, ability, and sexual differences, for instance, that one can see how problematic it is to presume that different contextual levels can and do function together as "unarticulated wholes" in everyday experience. Alcoff's discussion in *Visible Identities* of the perceptual and psychic conflicts that are common to "mixed race" individuals because of the tensions among contexts that they bring to bear in their experience and that are applied to them by others is a perfect example of the dangers of assuming (and privileging) unified experience as a norm.

9. This is not to say that the figure-ground structure is merely a spatial phenomenon, but rather that the figure-ground structure is directly tied to a *particular* spatial situation in a way that a context is not.

10. The relationship between gesture and perspective becomes especially complex at the level of symbolic gesture, where the gesture itself becomes "invisible" insofar as it serves as a kind of "window" through which a perspective can be revealed.

11. Even if a specific gesture is perceived to be extremely idiosyncratic, when the gesture is later recalled it is through a particular perspective—usually one heavily influenced by the events that followed.

12. Even a perspective resists precise definition since it evolves out of a series of gestures that are not always contiguous in time and space. Moreover, people more frequently attempt to communicate their perspective on a given issue, problem, or experience through their gestures rather than by reference to the broader context out of which their perspective has emerged. On the other hand, when disagreements or misunderstandings arise, context may indeed become the center of both individual and group attention.

13. In fact, it is Sartre who provides a comprehensive account of the notion of situation as an existential "structure," in 1943 in *Being and Nothingness*, and who assesses the implications of "situation" for human freedom and responsibility. Two years later, Merleau-Ponty addresses the role of the situation in making human freedom meaningful in the final chapter on freedom in *Phenomenology of Perception*. An extended examination of the notion of situation as it is taken up in different ways by Sartre, Beauvoir, and Merleau-Ponty can be found in Sonia Kruks's *Situation and Human Existence*. Sara Heinämaa's *Toward a Phenomenology of Sexual Difference* is another excellent resource if one is trying to tease out the lines of influence from Husserl to Beauvoir and Merleau-Ponty, especially with regard to their respective conceptions of the lived body that is at the center of each and every situation as well as the contexts and perspectives that emerge in and through those situations. Moreover, Heinämaa's attention to how sexuality and gender differences help to define the meaning of the lived body provides a much-needed corrective to Husserl's and Merleau-Ponty's accounts in particular.

14. It must be noted that the figure-ground structure also operates at several levels in giving meaning to perceptual experience. When I read the letter, the squiggles on the page are perceived as letters, letters merge into words, words form sentences, which take their place in paragraphs; the paragraphs are organized to form the letter as a whole, and the letter itself becomes the ground for the situations it describes. Once a person has learned how to read fluently, this whole process takes place immediately, and, unless one has trouble reading a particular word or letter, readers do not tend to isolate out any of the constituent factors that culminate in their own response to what they are reading.

15. Following Beauvoir, however, I want to acknowledge that in the case of severe, sustained oppression, it may become virtually impossible for an individual to develop a new perspective on herself, on others, and on her situation. Beauvoir describes such individuals as "beings whose life slips by in an infantile world because, having been kept in a state of servitude and ignorance, they have no means of breaking the ceiling which is stretched over their heads" (Beauvoir 1976: 37). In such extreme circumstances, Beauvoir declares, it is up to others to provide the external motivation that will lead the oppressed person to see that there are alternative ways of viewing and responding to her situation. However, it is also clear that presenting an individual with other people's perspectives on her situation is not sufficient to transform how the individual herself views it. For these outside perspectives, in turn, must be recognized as viable by the individual in order for her to develop new perspectives that challenge (rather than tacitly accept) the very terms of that situation. I would argue that what other people can collectively offer the oppressed individual is a broader context for interpreting salient features of her current situation, one that is informed directly by their different perspectives on it.

2. Ambiguity, Absurdity, and Reversibility

1. Descartes seeks the elimination of indeterminacy by strictly employing the Cartesian method, which involves refusing to make rational decisions until one has

clear and distinct knowledge concerning a given object, event, or idea. His confidence that his method can be applied to all sorts of different experiences and used by any rational being reveals his strong aversion to leaving a stone unturned in the effort to eradicate conceptual as well as perceptual indeterminacy.

2. Derrida's notion of "the trace," which structures the "field of the entity" (*Of Grammatology* 1974: 47), and Bataille's discussion of laughter as a way of attaining the "peripheral regions of existence" (*Visions of Excess* 1985: 176) are just two voices in this discourse that force us to consider the dissimulations we individually and collectively engage in to avoid recognizing the indeterminate residue that both escapes and underlies our practical and theoretical activity.

3. "Eidetic" is a technical term in Husserl's work that refers to an essential description of a particular phenomenon under investigation. To perform an eidetic inquiry is to look at how things appear and to uncover those features without which something could not appear the way that it does. The "natural attitude" is a Husserlian concept that describes what I call our "default" way of grasping the world of our concern. Paradoxically, the natural attitude is not natural, but rather archetypically a matter of convention that becomes naturalized over time. In Heidegger's *Being and Time,* which is dedicated to his teacher Edmund Husserl, Husserl's natural attitude is transformed into the world of "the they," an anonymous public comprised of anyone and no one that dictates social norms, mores, attitudes, and behaviors. While Heidegger claims that those who uncritically accept the dictates of the they as their own are living inauthentically, Husserl's view of the natural attitude is much more neutral. The natural attitude is not a site of either inauthenticity or authenticity for Husserl but a way of relating to our situation without thematizing the situation as such. In Husserl's work, to adopt the natural attitude is not something for which one should be condemned, even though he argues that it must be suspended if one is to do phenomenology. Indeed, it is inevitable that even the phenomenologist takes up and returns to the natural attitude throughout her daily life because it would be tedious and exhausting (not to mention annoying to others!) to try to thematize all aspects of one's situation at every moment one is living it.

4. Ultimately there are three such horizons: the internal horizon, which is tied to the possible perceptions available through any one thing; the external horizon, which consists of the perceptual field in which that thing is situated; and the world horizon, which in turn situates the perceptual field.

5. Although Husserl and other phenomenologists tend to distinguish phenomena from things fairly sharply, claiming that things are experienced every day within the world, whereas phenomena are encountered only when one performs the phenomenological epoché by bracketing one's ordinary presuppositions about the familiar things one is encountering, and seeing them as if they are unfamiliar, I am using the terms interchangeably here since the point I am making about the essential indeterminacy of experience applies at the level of phenomena no less than at the level of things. However, it is important to acknowledge that while things are ordinarily understood to be material entities located in specific places and times, phenomena can include nonmaterial entities such as ideas, imaginings, memories, etc., and hence are not restricted to the material world. This means, moreover, that perception is not the only or even the best way to access them.

6. In a sense, Descartes also acknowledges this in the *Discourse on Method.* However, he places the primary blame for this indeterminacy on memory, which is limited in its ability to keep a large number of ideas clearly and distinctly before our view.

7. See Weiss (2004), introduction to Beauvoir's 1946 "Introduction to an Ethics of

Ambiguity," and Weiss (2002), "Freedom, Oppression, and the Possibilities of Ethics in Beauvoir's Work," for more detailed discussions of the ethical implications of the multiple ambiguities that constitute human existence for Beauvoir.

8. A famous example of such a dilemma comes from "Existentialism Is a Humanism," when Sartre discusses the need for a young man to decide whether to fight for his country or to stay home and care for his mother. A decision must be made, and it requires choosing one of the two alternatives. The situation is ambiguous because both courses of action can be ethically defended, and yet they are incompatible. One and only one of the alternatives *must* be chosen, and this requires fulfilling some responsibilities at the expense of others. The ethical challenge, Sartre declares, is not for the young man (or for us) to proclaim that one alternative is right and one is wrong, but to decide, *individually*, which course of action is right for oneself, at that time, in that situation. And, once decided upon, Sartre suggests, one's commitment should be to that choice, *even while* one acknowledges the validity of the option not chosen.

3. Reading/Writing between the Lines

1. Rosemarie Garland Thomson makes an analogous point in *Extraordinary Bodies: Figuring Physical Disability in American Culture and Literature*, in reference to disability, namely, that American fiction has tended to reinforce the stigmatization of disability by presenting able-bodiedness as the sine qua non that invisibly but nonetheless extremely powerfully defines its characters' well-being (or lack thereof).

2. In a sense, to refer to this text as "Søren Kierkegaard's *Fear and Trembling*," as I have done, is to beg one of the primary questions I am raising about too closely identifying authors with texts. I refer to the text in this way in order to offer a preliminary context that will itself be problematized in the discussion that follows.

3. It is not only this particular epigraph that requires that the reader move beyond the text; the very notion of the epigraph, as such, through its incorporation of other texts, indicates that the relevance of the text that follows extends beyond the confines of the text itself.

4. Alternative interpretations of this parable are readily available. In the interpretation handed down to me, the father and son represent the forces of good who succeed in vanquishing the forces of evil, represented by the ministers. In other versions, the father and son are depicted less honorably and succeed in preventing a coup that was initiated to get rid of a corrupt ruling family. On both readings, however, the messenger does not understand the message he is conveying, which is the crucial point for Kierkegaard.

5. Both Morrison in *Playing in the Dark* and Luce Irigaray in *Speculum of the Other Woman* reveal how problematic such "faithful" readings can be insofar as they so often function (on both conscious and unconscious levels) to reinforce the hegemony of white male privilege. Indeed, both authors can be understood as engaging in deliberately "unfaithful readings" that expose the hidden and sometimes not so hidden presumptions that are embedded within literary as well as philosophical texts and that limit, in oppressive ways, the imaginations and therefore the realities of both writers and readers.

6. Not only the midwife but also the mother seems to vanish in the focus on the newly born child. Her glory historically has resided in her maternity, that is, in the outcome of her production. By contrast, the paternal authority, who plays only a small (and not so laborious) role in the production of the child, and who consequently maintains a

more indirect relation to his "offspring," is the one who has been more successful in establishing his independence from and power over both mother and child.

7. I don't believe Sartre tried very hard to discourage such a reading. Why is it, we might ask in a Freudian vein, that these sons never seem content in their role as heir, but must establish their authority once and for all as king of the throne? It is striking, in following this line of thought, that neither Kierkegaard nor Sartre ever were actually fathers of "real" sons or daughters. The absence of their own "flesh and blood" seems to make their symbolic role as fathers all the greater since it can't be diminished in any way by the misbehavior or disloyalty of their offspring.

8. For Sartre this moral commitment is political through and through; for Kierkegaard, the moral commitment binds one to the ethical sphere of existence and is religious in nature.

9. See "Sartre on Language and Politics (with Reference to Particularity)" in Busch (1999).

10. Whereas in the phenomenon of the look described in *Being and Nothingness*, both the one looking and the one looked-at tend to be temporally and spatially contiguous, the model of reading and writing presented in *What Is Literature?* presupposes a time lapse between the act of writing and the act of reading as well as a spatial dislocation between the writer and reader. Sartre never discusses this important difference between looking/being looked-at and reading/writing, but an exploration of this difference is crucial to an understanding of how freedom and responsibility play out in these respective situations.

11. If the mother and daughter are denied, in this phallocentric economy, the possibility of performing their own reading and writing, then the (gendered) status of this particular reading/writing is inevitably called into question as well. This latter is a point Irigaray does not take up in "Sorcerer Love: A Reading of Plato, *Symposium*, 'Diotima's Speech,'" but its rich implications are pursued throughout her work.

12. Barthes's *The Pleasure of the Text* lyrically invokes the affective, intersubjective, and intertextual dimensions of what he identifies as "texts of pleasure" as well as "texts of bliss" (*jouissance*). In his words, the text of pleasure is "the text that contents, fills, grants euphoria; the text that comes from culture and does not break with it, is linked to a *comfortable* practice of reading," and the text of bliss is "the text that imposes a state of loss, the text that discomforts (perhaps to the point of a certain boredom), unsettles the reader's historical, cultural, psychological assumptions, the consistency of his tastes, values, memories, brings to a crisis his relation with language" (Barthes 1975: 14). Though Barthes's emphasis is upon the response of the reader and not the writer, it is clear, as Sullivan argues, that, "For Barthes . . . reading and writing are inextricable from the fleshly" (N. Sullivan 2001: 151).

13. See Richard Howard's "A Note on the Text," p. viii, from Barthes's *The Pleasure of the Text*.

14. We should also include the desire of what Barthes calls the "mother tongue" to generate an extension of its own body (via the text) as an integral component of this process. (See Barthes 1975: 37.)

15. The contrast between the sacrifice of the father (and mother) to "save" the son (the writing) and Kierkegaard's discussion of the sacrifice of Isaac to "save" Abraham (specifically to affirm his faith in God) is striking, and deserves further discussion. Invoking the privilege of the author, I'll defer it for another place and time.

16. Although Keenan emphasizes how language undermines subjectivity in this

text, this quotation itself substantializes the subjective horizon in the form of an "it" that linguistically, at least, appears to be coherent and self-identical, thereby illustrating Kierkegaard's paradoxical claim that one drives out the devils only by utilizing the power of the devil itself.

17. Comparatively few writers are fortunate (or unfortunate) enough to have their work published, much less formally reviewed. If these comments about reading and writing are extended to non-written exchanges, to oral communications or even non-linguistic, gestural interactions, it is possible to see similar reversals occurring. George Herbert Mead referred to this latter type of dialogue as a "conversation of gestures," an expression that conveys perfectly the reciprocity that I am claiming is essential for co-responsibility.

4. The Body as a Narrative Horizon

1. While it is beyond the scope of this investigation to address the ethical implications of the narrative structure of corporeal experience, I hope to provide a grounding for just such a discussion. I should also note that there are important differences between the claim that bodies are discursively constructed, on the one hand, and that bodies constitute narrative horizons, on the other hand. I am grateful to one of the anonymous reviewers for the reminder that while narratives are a kind of discourse, not all discourses are narrative in structure. I am especially interested in the narrative effects produced by the body's multiple sites of discursive construction because these narrative effects are both politically and ethically efficacious. Clearly there are many non-narrative effects of embodiment that play important roles in everyday experience; however, they are not my central concern here.

2. As will soon become clear, I am using the term "configure" in a Ricoeurian sense to indicate the way in which specific experiences each possess their own unique structure. Louis Althusser might argue that these seemingly idiosyncratic "constellations of meaning" themselves reflect the influence of particular ideological state apparatuses (such as the family, political, legal and religious systems, etc.) and their accompanying discourses (Althusser 2001). It would be fascinating to do an in-depth comparative study of the varying roles played by Foucault's disciplinary regimes, Bourdieu's habitus, and Althusser's ideological state apparatuses insofar as they all function as material horizons within which individuals produce configurations of meaning.

3. Gertrude Stein's 1914 collection of poems, *Tender Buttons*, offers an excellent example of the malleability of language. By displacing ordinary words from their ordinary contexts she is able to generate new meanings that, at the same time, never lose their traditional referents. This makes the reading of the poems a playful exercise for those who revel in the elasticity of expression, and a frustrating experience for those who seek univocal and stable meanings. As Lisa Ruddick and other Stein critics have argued, Stein's experimental strategy does not preclude the ability to raise serious issues within her work, including an ongoing challenge to reductive interpretations of everyday domestic experience within patriarchy.

4. Beauvoir understands this quest in a much more expansive way than MacIntyre. For Beauvoir (although she does not use the language of a quest), it involves more than a desire for intelligible narratives. She develops the ontological dimensions of this existential project and shows how they exceed the limits of intelligibility. Indeed, there is a lack of intelligibility in the existential project itself, as this latter is depicted by

both Beauvoir and Sartre. To "coincide with oneself," to reconcile one's transcendence (as a free subjectivity directed toward the future) with one's immanence (as an embodied individual with a specific past) can never be accomplished once and for all, Beauvoir suggests; however, she also observes that "without failure, no ethics" (Beauvoir 1976: 10). She argues that by accepting the failure of the "quest" to coincide with myself, I can "win," ethically speaking, for I embrace both my transcendence and my immanence, with all of the tension that persists between them.

Like MacIntyre, Camus implies that the desire for intelligible (Camus would define them as rational) narratives is "hard-wired" into human nature. However, like Beauvoir, Camus suggests that this pervasive desire tells us only part of the story. The world, with its essential irrationality, Camus maintains, thwarts the effort to generate intelligible narratives at every turn. While MacIntyre worries about these threats to narrative intelligibility (e.g., as in his Kafka critique), seeing them as threats to the intelligibility of the self that is constructed through them, Beauvoir and Camus see the subject as defined by her reactions to these threats whenever and wherever they emerge. Indeed, the acceptance of his human "fate," which consists in the need to ceaselessly take up the project of existence in the face of ongoing obstacles, is precisely what identifies Sisyphus, for Camus, as the absurd hero.

Threats to narrative intelligibility, from the existentialist perspective, are part and parcel of ordinary experience, and, I argue, they play their own role in the development of the self. Rather than view them as obstacles to enlightenment that one must seek to vanquish, a Cartesian strategy that has dominated the rationalist philosophical tradition (with which MacIntyre is himself closely associated), the existentialists argue that one must find ways, individually and collectively, to reckon with the failure to make the world and one's own existence within it intelligible within conventional rationalist terms.

5. It is important to note, however, that the transformation of exceptional bodies into "normal" bodies can be very costly when their flexible adaptation to their new designation consolidates rather than subverts hegemonic demands for compliant bodies. I am indebted to Robert McRuer's *Crip Theory: Cultural Signs of Queerness and Disability* for his trenchant critique of the desire as well as the demand for normalization, and the way it reinforces neo-liberal capitalist ideologies.

5. Can an Old Dog Learn New Tricks?

1. I am very grateful to Wendy Burns-Ardolino, Howard Hastings, and J. Z. Long for their published responses to an earlier version of this chapter that I presented at George Mason University. Burns-Ardolino foregrounds the strong gendered association of habitual multi-tasking with women rather than men and argues that women are expected to interrupt their habitual routines more readily than men in order to attend to the demands of significant others. Hastings emphasizes the close connections between Bourdieu's understanding of the habitus and Marx's historical materialism, and suggests that Bourdieu's materialist view of the habitus provides an opportunity to rethink the traditional antimony between freedom and determinism. He also argues that recognizing "the material situation of subjects and bodies means discussion of the freedom of individuals or groups cannot meaningfully go forward without recognizing that the division of labor in class societies is also a division of control over value collectively produced by that labor, a division of society into dominating and dominated groups"

(Hastings 2003). Long turns to Deleuze's and Guattari's work to explicate the process by "which thoughts, habits, perceptions, and affects are embodied in supra-molecular intensities that we have come to know as 'individuals'" (Long 2003). All three authors have deepened my own understanding of the power of habitual horizons to reinforce gender and class divisions as well as the possibility of developing habitual resistances to these oppressive structures.

2. Habit, I suggest, is as important as time and memory for Proust, and it serves as one of the most pervasive leitmotifs in his work. While I do not have time to develop this argument here, I also maintain that Proust's ambivalence toward habit seems to flow from his recognition that habit is a primary means through which time and memory are registered corporeally. If this is so, then we need to turn to the phenomenon of habit, in all of its ambivalence, in order to understand more concretely how time and memory function in everyday life.

3. I say "adults" here because children are often prone to lose their interest in the previous project if they are distracted from it. Indeed, one of the frequently heralded signs of adulthood is an ability to "stay on task" in the face of appealing alternatives. Today, it seems, the emphasis has switched from being able to "stay on task" to being able to "multi-task." While the former involves being able to retain one's concentration on a single activity and to follow it through from beginning to end, an individual who is able to focus on only one project at a time and who cannot spread her interest and attention across several different activities simultaneously can also be seen as limited.

4. See Hubert L. Dreyfus and Stuart E. Dreyfus, "The Challenge of Merleau-Ponty's Phenomenology of Embodiment for Cognitive Science" for a more in-depth account of Merleau-Ponty's notion of the intentional arc. Dreyfus and Dreyfus argue that the functioning of neural networks as they have been observed and described by cognitive scientists provides empirical support for the presence of an intentional arc. While it is beyond the scope of this inquiry to pursue this further, it would be interesting to explore the connections between James's view of the neural pathways that are responsible for the formation of specific habits and the activity of neural networks operating in the brain.

5. For Kant, volition is absolutely central to morality since one must will to do one's duty in order for an action to be considered moral. What is crucial for Kant, however, is not so much volition itself but rather the force that motivates the will. He asserts that both reason and the inclinations (emotions) have the power to propel the will to action, but, on his account, an act is moral only if reason alone is the determining ground for volition. In at least one sense, however, Kantian morality and Jamesian morality may not be so far apart after all, since morality for Kant hinges not on the presence or absence of volition but on the presence or absence of rational intent, which will in turn serve as the motivating force for volition. Indeed, Kant would very likely have been sympathetic to an exhortation to make an appeal to reason habitual in one's daily life, though James would have argued, in a Humean vein, that it is the emotions that must propel one to be influenced by reason in the first place.

6. In the months and even years following September 11, 2001, much media attention was devoted to showing how U.S. leaders *should* have anticipated the terrorist strikes. While this is certainly in keeping with the old adage that "hindsight is 20/20," it also reflects, I think, the tendency Bourdieu has articulated so well, namely, an effort to reconcile what may look like aberrant events or stray data into the familiar habitus that defines ordinary life within a given community (or, in this case, a nation). Even when

the acts in question are acts of atrocity, it seems to lessen the sense of collective cultural discomfort if they can somehow be reconciled with what is already known rather than being viewed as radically unprecedented and incapable of incorporation into the world of the familiar.

7. Both James and Bourdieu, however, embrace to some extent, the possibility for social change. David Hoy's essay "Critical Resistance: Foucault and Bourdieu" argues that individual political resistance to a given habitus is indeed compatible with Bourdieu's theoretical framework. And one need only look to James's work on multiple realities, freedom of will, and the latter's role in the formation of belief to see why, despite being a "bundle of habits," human beings have the potential on his account to draw on new experiences to create new associations that in turn can produce new meanings and new values. For both authors, nonetheless, it remains difficult to reconcile the self-perpetuating or conservative quality of habits or the habitus, respectively, with the spontaneity they nonetheless maintain is an essential component of everyday experience.

8. In "An Answer to the Question: 'What is Enlightenment?'" Kant distinguishes between the public and private use of reason and argues that the former rather than the latter must be the goal of the Enlightenment. Kant defines the Enlightenment itself as a movement out of "self-incurred immaturity" (Kant 1991: 54). According to Kant, while the Enlightenment requires freedom, it can also involve restrictions on freedom if the individual's interests come in conflict with those of the larger society. In his words: "The *public* use of man's reason must always be free, and it alone can bring about enlightenment among men; the *private use* of reason may quite often be very narrowly restricted, however, without undue hindrance to the progress of enlightenment (Kant 1991: 55). Kant's defense of freedom in the public domain (which he identifies as essential to the continued progress of enlightenment) even when it restricts freedom in the private domain is precisely the theoretical framework George W. Bush implicitly (and most likely unwittingly!) appealed to in order to justify the Patriot Act, which authorizes the denial of basic civil liberties, such as the right not to be incarcerated without being charged with a crime, to suspected terrorists. While, as many have argued, Kant seems to be articulating a very reactionary politics with potentially dangerous consequences on both a civil and individual level, what interests me here is his recognition that the single moral agent who is at the center of her own deontological ethics is not all that counts, and that the interests of the community always need to be reckoned with and addressed.

9. Recent Holocaust literature on the power of "witnessing" that which is incapable of being described in words is particularly relevant here. Kelly Oliver's and Giorgio Agamben's accounts of this process and application of it to contemporary social existence would be especially interesting to explore in relation to this discussion of habit.

10. Although I am using the term "community" in the singular here, I do not mean to imply that there is only one community (e.g., a single, global community), or that an individual can only belong to one community. Indeed, the majority of people, as Amartya Sen emphasizes in *Identity and Violence: The Illusion of Destiny*, are part of several different (and usually overlapping) communities simultaneously. Moreover, the significance of particular habits themselves clearly varies from one community to another, and this further complicates attempts to fix their meaning and influence once and for all.

11. Nietzsche can be read both as supporting James's more pessimistic view of the possibility of breaking with old habits in his discussion of the power exercised by the "herd" mentality in promoting social conformity (e.g., see his *Genealogy of Morals* for a

lucid explication of how this mentality promotes negative responses to alterity), and as supporting a more optimistic perspective on the possibility of casting off these sedimented ways of thinking and being through the practice of self-overcoming, which Diprose discusses at some length. Ladelle McWhorter provides an especially rich account of the transformative dimensions of the project of self-overcoming in *Bodies and Pleasures: Foucault and the Politics of Sexual Normalization*.

12. Fertilization and pregnancy provide obvious examples of how my body is from the start produced in and through the bodies of others; however, both Merleau-Ponty and Diprose emphasize that this process does not stop with birth but continues throughout an individual's life, extending to a person's ongoing interactions with non-human and even inanimate bodies as well as with other human beings.

6. Imagining the Horizon

1. Indeed, both Husserl and Merleau-Ponty suggest that rather than reveal the endpoint of vision, the presence of the horizon constitutes the very condition for visibility.

2. In an essay entitled "The Political Incompetence of Philosophy," Gadamer even argues that philosophers should not be expected to concern themselves with concrete social, political, or even ethical matters. This essay was written, it should be noted, as a defense of Heidegger's philosophy against the charge that Heidegger's affiliation with the Nazi party while he was a professor at Freiburg forces a critical reassessment of the alleged political neutrality of his work and thought.

3. Jeffrey Paris points toward some of the rich possibilities offered by Husserl's notion of the empathy horizon for a future liberatory praxis, in his 2001 essay, "Overcoming Our Empathy-Deficit: Phenomenological Reflections on the WTC-Event," available at http://pages.prodigy.net/gmoses/nvusa/paris1.htm, accessed October 29, 2007.

4. Some would argue that the incident began decades before that infamous day on March 3, 1991, given the long history of ill-treatment of blacks and other minorities by the Los Angeles Police Department and other law enforcement agencies. This history, moreover, is by no means restricted to Southern California but encompasses the entire United States of America. Thus there are both past and future dimensions to the Rodney King incident that defy any attempt to view it as an isolated, unique event.

5. To claim that the Rodney King incident has become part of the historical horizon that establishes a collective American racial consciousness in the early twenty-first century is in no way intended to imply that it functions in the same or even a similar matter for all Americans. Indeed, one of the key features of the horizon qua horizon is that its significance is not reducible to a conventional perspective or a fixed interpretation.

6. Wilhelm Dilthey's early-twentieth-century discussion of objectivity in the human sciences is instructive on this issue (see Dilthey 1976). Dilthey claims that there is no such thing as objectivity if it is conceived in terms of an aperspectival standpoint. He does maintain, however, that it is possible to evaluate a given perspective critically from the standpoint of another one. Thus, although human beings always occupy some perspective or other, they can nonetheless shift their perspectives and use a new perspective to assess a previous one. It is not uncommon, in fact, to hear someone say, "I used to view this type of situation like this, but now I see things differently." In the account I am providing here, this notion of seeing differently should be taken literally and not just figuratively. In her recent work, Alia Al-Saji (2007) addresses directly the question of

what "seeing-differently" entails, identifying it as a "critical-ethical vision" that is necessary to overcome racist and sexist patterns of seeing and responding to others.

7. As one respondent pointed out when I presented an early version of this paper at York University in Toronto, contemporary technology actually promotes such techniques and reinforces the notion that by slowing time down or stopping it altogether (as in the slow-paced "instant replay" that has become a familiar staple of sports events) human beings are being presented with a more accurate picture of what "really" happened. Although I would not dispute the usefulness of this technique in determining in a close race exactly *who* crossed the finish line first, I am arguing (with Crenshaw and Peller) that it presents a misleading view of what was happening in the beating of Rodney King by the Los Angeles policemen precisely because the beating itself and King's response to it was a continuous event rather than a series of discrete actions. How the beating terminated was not a central issue, but this is precisely what is at stake in the case of a question regarding who won (and thereby ended) a race. This is why the use of the "instant replay" (a term that connotes both that it takes an instant to get the replay and that the replay offers an instantaneous version of the events just witnessed) is appropriate in the latter case but totally inappropriate in the former.

8. See Helen Fielding's essay "White Logic and the Constancy of Color" for an extended critical discussion of how the alleged neutrality of whiteness functions both aesthetically and ethically in film. Jorella Andrews's "Vision, Violence, and the Other: A Merleau-Pontian Ethics" also provides an excellent discussion of how racist patterns of seeing become naturalized, doing violence to the racial Other in the process.

9. Those who would discount the significance of the color of the poster board need only consult with advertisers to learn how the latter use color and other subliminal cues to effect the nature and impact of a given message. Advertisers well know how crucial every detail of a given presentation is in supporting the overall effect of the narrative.

10. I am grateful to Bill Wilkerson for pointing out the significance of the whiteness of the poster board in supporting the defense team's strategy of "whitewashing" the racist framework in which both the crime and the trial itself unfolded.

11. To give just one example, the Rodney King verdict and the public outrage that resulted from it arguably played an important (even if unacknowledged) role in the subsequent acquittal of O. J. Simpson a few years later in his criminal trial for the murder of his wife Nicole Brown Simpson and her friend Ronald Goldman.

7. City Limits

I would like to thank Sam Brooke for reading the initial drafts of this essay and for making such helpful suggestions to improve it. Eduardo Mendieta's invitation to submit an earlier version of this chapter to the journal City provided the motivating force for this particular analysis. Aron Vinegar and participants in the May 2005 conference he organized through the Department of Architecture at The Ohio State University on "The Concept of the Horizon and the Limits of Representation" offered useful feedback on the first incarnation of "City Limits" and led me to think in more depth about the relationship between limit and horizon.

1. The sharply circumscribed horizon bounded by the building directly across from his bedroom window that Kafka's Gregor Samsa spent hours viewing more and more dimly as he was dying comes to mind here (Kafka 1996).

2. This is not to say that it is impossible to have experience without its being

organized in terms of a primary figure that is manifested over and against a ground; however, as John Dewey also maintains in *Art as Experience*, any experience qua experience possesses a particular structure that reflects both temporal and spatial organization. And, the figure-ground structure clearly operates both temporally and spatially since I can make an event in the past the focus of my attention (the figure), with the present and future and other past events serving as the background against which it appears, just as easily as I can focus on a particular aspect of my perceptual field, with the remainder of the field along with my memories, and expectations functioning as a ground. If experience lacks this structure, I would argue it also lacks the coherence that marks it as *an* experience in the first place. Indeed, since the persistence of the figure-ground structure gives stability to experience even as both the figures and grounds themselves are continuously changing, the absence of this structure can function as a sign that experience has become pathological. In chapter 4 of *Body Images: Embodiment as Intercorporeality*, I argued that when the figure and ground become too fixed and lose their fluidity, pathology also can emerge, so it is evident that the disintegration of a figure-ground structure is not the only way in which experience can become dysfunctional.

3. Toni Morrison's *The Bluest Eye* is an especially striking example of this, and the experiences of the entire Breedlove family powerfully illustrate how racism, classism, and sexism form the crucial ingredients in a terribly lethal potion that kills the dreams and thereby the futures of all those who drink it. To give a powerful, nonfictional example of this phenomenon, in his autobiographical narrative *Angela's Ashes*, Frank McCourt shows how poverty, discrimination, and degradation become part of the air one breathes, and yet he also reveals the power of literature itself to open up new horizons, new dreams, and new futures that are otherwise unavailable in one's daily life.

4. In his essay "The Social Formation of Racist Discourse," David Theo Goldberg calls this exclusionary logic the "principle of differential exclusion" and claims that it constitutes the "deep structure" of racist discourse, that is, the unifying feature that all forms of racist discourse have in common. While Goldberg maintains that this principle is the basic distinguishing feature of racist discourse in particular, I claim that a similar principle is operative in sexist and classist discourse as well. Moreover, I argue not only that this logic functions in relation to specific racist, sexist, and/or classist acts, but also that it is constitutive of the background context in which these actions unfold and against which they come to take on specific meaning.

5. I am thinking here of Luce Irigaray's famous proclamation, at the outset of *An Ethics of Sexual Difference*, that the question of sexual difference is perhaps "the issue of our age" (Irigaray 1993b: 5). In a way, I'm not so much disagreeing with Irigaray, but rather extending her subsequent claim that "sexual difference is probably the issue in our time which could be our 'salvation' if we thought it through" to encompass racial and class differences as well as differences of religion, age, ability, ethnicity, etc. This brings me more in line with the work of Audre Lorde and bell hooks, both of whom suggest that it is an inability to respect and appreciate difference more generally, rather than any one particular difference, that is a primary source of oppression.

6. I am grateful to one of the anonymous readers for pointing out the danger of "posing literature as a way of resolving or addressing class and other social differences that mark the occupants of the city" insofar as this runs the risk of unduly privileging literature over other possible strategies and can thereby reinforce a middle-class bias (for instance, one that associates a literary response with an educated or reflective response

to a given situation). I do not intend to privilege literature in this way even though I am arguing for the power of literary examples in revealing the oppressive qualities of urban life, especially for its more marginalized inhabitants. One of the reasons I believe literature is so powerful is because people are often more willing to recognize the everyday social and material practices that produce the abjection of the city's less fortunate residents in a fictional context than to confront the inequities that characterize urban life on their own. The hope, of course, is that rendering urban oppression visible in a literary context will lead not only to sustained reflection, but more importantly, to an active confrontation of and response to the various forms of marginalization and suffering that are readily visible in urban (as well as non-urban) experience.

7. In *White Women Race Matters: The Social Construction of Whiteness*, Frankenberg defines a racial social geography as follows: "*Racial* social geography, in short, refers to the racial and ethnic mapping of environments in physical and social terms and enables also the beginning of an understanding of the conceptual mappings of self and other" (Frankenberg 1993: 44). In what follows, I suggest that it is not merely conceptual mappings of self and other that are at stake but what I would call the *intercorporeal cartography* that provides individuals with a sense of their bodily place in the world in relation to one another. As I hope to show, it is the perceived limits as well as the possibilities attributed to the city that offer the indispensable context within which these relationships unfold.

8. Naylor's graphic depiction of the gang rape of Lorraine, a lesbian protagonist, in an alley off Brewster Place, provides one of the most indelible images of how both bodies and streets are inscribed within complex racial social geographies. The extreme violence of Lorraine's rape, provoked by nothing more than her quiet refusal to position herself within a heterosexual matrix, also reveals how these cartographies not only generate but actively enforce sexual as well as racial and class boundaries.

9. I am using the term "horizon" here in the Gestaltist sense of a background context or ground against which a figure can emerge. Just as what was once the figure can become (part of) the ground, what was once the ground can become the figure. What this transformation requires is nothing more or less than a change in perspective. While the Gestalt psychologists focused primarily on the ambiguous perceptual cues that are differentially resolved in one perspective or another (such as the famous duck/rabbit, old woman/young woman examples), I am especially interested in the cultural influences that can promote as well as inhibit a reversible relationship between figure and ground.

10. It would be interesting to examine the way the city functions as an imaginary horizon for both its residents and non-residents in relation to Benedict Anderson's view of the nation as an imaginary community. Indeed, for Anderson, every community is imaginary to the extent that the relations between its members rely upon projected identifications that presume a common experience even with people one has never met; this is precisely what produces the (often misbegotten) sense that it is "our" nation, "our" community, or, in this case, "our" city. This emphasis upon the nation, community, and city as shared possessions, however, obscures the different modes of access and acceptance that people enjoy (or fail to enjoy) with respect to them.

11. I am utilizing a Merleau-Pontian notion of the chiasm as a crossing or place in which difference is directly and dynamically encountered. For instance, Merleau-Ponty concentrates in *The Visible and the Invisible* on the chiasm that indissolubly links the visible and the tactile in a particular perceptual experience even as it preserves their sensory specificities. Here, I am focusing on the chiasmatic relationship between the

material conditions of urban experience and phantasmatic constructions, such as a racial social geography, that provide varying frameworks for interpreting that experience.

12. Eisenman's innovative, award-winning design has come with a cost, namely,
the closure of the building for two years for structural renovations because of leaks. One
might say that the original exhibit space blurred the borders between interior and exte-
rior too much because it has been unable to withstand the outside elements so that art-
work can be protected within it. Thus, the Wexner Center demonstrates how the
transformation of limit into possibility in turn creates new limits.

13. My intent is not to trivialize the serious pain that Deleuze was experiencing as
a result of his terminal cancer, nor to diminish the profound anguish that resulted from
what would today be identified as Septimus's "post-traumatic stress disorder"; rather I am
invoking their spectacular urban suicides (one enacted on the streets of London and one
on the streets of Paris) as especially visceral examples of how the seemingly stable order
provided by the city grid can be disrupted and rendered illusory in a moment's time.
The attack on the World Trade Center on 9/11/2001 provides yet another example of the
fragility of not only the city's fabric itself, but also the web of dreams, myths, and cultural desires that are woven through it.

14. Indeed, Sartre privileges these metastable experiences that result from the dynamic confrontation between limit and possibility, or what he terms, in *Being and Nothingness*, facticity and transcendence. In *Nausea* he offers an earlier, more extended
account of their embodied effects. In contrast to Sartre's almost exclusive focus on the
private reflections of *Nausea*'s main character, Roquentin, in whom these effects are
registered, I would like to emphasize the ways in which these effects are manifested in-
tercorporeally, inscribed not only in human bodies but in the city streets themselves.

8. Urban Flesh

I am especially grateful to members of the International Merleau-Ponty Circle for
their instructive comments when I presented an earlier version of *Urban Flesh*. A later
incarnation benefited enormously from the insights of members of the Society of Phenomenology and Existential Philosophy and was subsequently published in *Phenomenology Today* 49 (2005). Yet another version of "Urban Flesh" appeared in *Feminist
Interpretations of Maurice Merleau-Ponty*, edited by myself and Dorothea Olkowski, and
profited immensely from Dorothea's comments as well as those of the anonymous
reader commissioned by Nancy Tuana on behalf of Pennsylvania State University Press.
And finally, the excellent, detailed recommendations of wonderful philosophical colleagues, including most notably Ellen Feder and Eduardo Mendieta, have led to the
continued evolution of my thoughts on the possibilities and limitations of urban flesh.

1. See Judith Butler's essay, "Sexual Difference as a Question of Ethics: Alterities
of the Flesh in Irigaray and Merleau-Ponty" for a detailed working through of Irigaray's
critique of Merleau-Ponty on this issue. Butler provides a defense of Merleau-Ponty regarding his recognition of the differences between one experience and another whether
they are undergone by the same person or by two different people. She does not appeal
explicitly to his concept of style as I am doing to make this point, but focuses instead
upon his notion of the chiasm that separates the experience of being touched from that
of touching, guaranteeing that the one can never collapse into the other even if it is the
same hand that is both touched and touching.

2. Similarly, as Morrison has powerfully shown in *Playing in the Dark: Whiteness*

and the Literary Imagination, one cannot invoke whiteness without either implicitly or explicitly contrasting it with blackness. Moreover, as Fanon has also demonstrated in *Black Skin White Masks,* the more phantasmatically blackness is conceived, the more mythically entrenched the status of whiteness becomes.

3. Steven Vogel offers an extended critical discussion of this traditional binary approach in *Against Nature: The Concept of Nature in Critical Theory.* He advocates a social constructionist view of nature whereby nature is itself an ongoing product of cultural interpretation. See Mary Douglas's *Purity and Danger: An Analysis of Concepts of Pollution and Taboo* for one of the most influential accounts of the significance of the cultural distinction between purity and pollution.

4. There are many excellent resources to turn to for a discussion of the gendered dimensions of nature and culture, though less work has been done on how the city is gendered. Elizabeth Grosz's work is a notable exception in this regard. See "Bodies-Cities" in *Space, Time, and Perversion: Essays on the Politics of Bodies* and *Architecture from the Outside: Essays on Virtual and Real Space.* Sherry Ortner's classic essay, "Is Female to Male as Nature Is to Culture?" in *Making Gender: The Politics and Erotics of Culture* offers one of the best-known feminist accounts of the engendering of nature and culture respectively as feminine and masculine. Carol Bigwood's *Earth Muse: Feminism, Nature, and Art* offers a phenomenological analysis that supports Ortner's critique of the patriarchal identification of nature with an idealized feminine "earth mother" and culture with an idealized masculine master of *techné.*

Although urban analyses often concentrate on the racial and class implications of what Frankenberg calls a "racial social geography" in *White Women Race Matters: The Social Construction of Whiteness,* less work has been done on how nature is itself racialized. For excellent and disturbing accounts of the consequences of failing to acknowledge the racism inherent in human understandings of "urban flesh," see Gooding-Williams's edited collection, *Reading Rodney King/Reading Urban Uprising.*

5. I am indebted to Eduardo Mendieta for suggesting that I introduce Hannah Arendt's account of violence into this discussion.

6. Although Arendt's account of violence, and particularly racial violence, in *On Violence,* can certainly be mobilized for feminist and antiracist politics, it would be remiss not to call attention to her unfortunate linkage of emasculation and dehumanization to describe a human being who is incapable of experiencing or presumably expressing feelings of violence. Her account reinforces the fact that violence itself is a gendered phenomenon. This is not to deny that women as well as men may act violently, but suggests that the very expression of violence tends to be associated with masculinity. This has historically had deleterious consequences for women who have behaved violently, because their violation of gendered expectations has furthered their own dehumanization at the hands of others.

7. Of course, this is only temporary. Master plans for this exceptionally large piece of prime New York City real estate were solicited very soon after 9/11 from top international architecture firms, and Ground Zero will soon be a memory, albeit one that was materially incorporated in virtually all the designs for the site.

8. The willingness of the current U.S. government to endorse the displacement of others in order to maintain its own secure emplacement in the world helps to fuel charges of U.S. imperialism.

9. Notably, one of the reasons Kant's justification for political quiescence in the face of an unjust ruler in his political essay "On the Relationship of Theory to Practice

in Political Right" is so dissatisfying is because the universality of the law that demands obedience to the ruler does violence to a legitimate sense of outrage about the ruler's abuse of his power in determining the scope and application of the law. Kant unequivocally states his position as follows:

> It thus follows that all resistance against the supreme legislative power, all incitement of the subjects to violent expressions of discontent, all defiance which breaks out into rebellion, is the greatest and most punishable crime in a commonwealth, for it destroys its very foundations. This prohibition is *absolute*. And even if the power of the state or its agent, the head of state, has violated the original contract by authorizing the government to act tyrannically, and has thereby, in the eyes of the subject, forfeited the right to legislate, the subject is still not entitled to offer counter-resistance. The reason for this is that the people, under an existing civil constitution, has no longer any right to judge how the constitution should be administered. (Kant 1991: 81)

What Kant is advocating is precisely that citizens (and non-citizens?) tolerate injustices in order to preserve the authority of the ruler and the universality of the law, a position that is in direct contrast with later political thinkers such as Arendt, Beauvoir, and Merleau-Ponty.

10. Leaving aside the question of whether animals have a sense of futurity, it is clear that this curtailment of bodily agency when faced with the destruction of one's world applies to non-human as well as to human bodies.

11. In a conversation I had with Ed Casey after I presented an earlier version of this chapter, he told me that his more recent experience as a city dweller (in New York City) has led him to reject his earlier claim that the city could not be a home.

9. Death and the Other

1. Indeed, the extreme contrast between their respective views of what Heidegger might call "appropriate comportment" toward death is highlighted even more by his use of the impersonal, non-gendered term Dasein, which is most accurately referred to not as a "he" or a "she" but rather as an "it," and by Hainer's explicit references to her own idiosyncratic desires, interests, activities, and relationships.

2. The so-called problem of the Other has a long history within both phenomenology and existentialism, and it arises out of these latter's affirmation that each individual has his or her own subjective life that cannot be directly shared with others even when human beings share particular experiences. Regarding Heidegger's conception of authenticity, it is crucial to stress that neither meaningfulness nor ethicality is synonymous with authenticity for Heidegger. Authenticity is a very complex, rich notion in his work, and it cannot be done justice to through the notions of meaningfulness and ethicality. However, I do think that it is impossible to achieve any measure of authenticity in one's life if meaningfulness and ethicality are not present.

3. Heidegger never explicitly links his conception of the authentic individual (which remains a rather sketchy portrait for obvious reasons!) to the solitariness of Kierkegaard's knight of faith. Rather this is a connection I am making, and a similar echo is readily found in Sartre's equally strong assertion that being-for-others is not an ontological structure of the for-itself, in *Being and Nothingness* (Sartre 1956: 474). These radical distinctions between self and other are in large part responsible, I believe, for the

failure to banish the critiques of subjectivity so often leveled at both phenomenologists and existentialists. Both Merleau-Ponty and Beauvoir (and even the later Sartre) provide alternative views of subjectivity as constituted in and through intersubjective experience that I and many other continental philosophers (feminist and non-feminist alike) have found more compelling. Yet, despite this lack of unanimity in views concerning the complex relations between self and other among phenomenologists and existentialists, it is striking that the more extreme conception offered by Heidegger, Kierkegaard, and the early Sartre, which generates the problem of the Other in all its terrible glory, is the one that continues to serve as a straw man for many of phenomenology's as well as existentialism's critics.

4. There have been so many of these criticisms directed against so many major figures in the phenomenological tradition (including Heidegger, Sartre, Merleau-Ponty, Levinas, and Beauvoir) that they cannot all be mentioned here. Contemporary continental feminist theorists who have raised them include: Luce Irigaray, Julia Kristeva, Judith Butler, Elizabeth Grosz, Iris Young, Sonia Kruks, Kelly Oliver, Tina Chanter, Debra Bergoffen, Dorothea Olkowski, and Shannon Sullivan, and these are only the tip of the iceberg!!

5. Turning to God, an "otherworldly being," for comfort in dealing with the angst of one's own being-toward-death would seem to be, for Heidegger, yet another way in which the they seeks tranquillization about death. In his words, "The this-worldly, ontological interpretation of death comes before any ontic, other-worldly speculation" (Heidegger 1996: 230).

6. See www.nytimes.com/portraits for the complete group of biographical sketches that have been created to date, since more have been added since the revised edition of *Portraits: 9/11/01: The Collected "Portraits of Grief"* was published by Times Books in 2003.

7. I believe that this position is closer to Butler's than to Kristeva's or Irigaray's. For Butler rejects the possibility of preserving a separate domain of language such as Kristeva's semiotic or Irigaray's maternal-feminine from the symbolic order, and she is suspicious of claims that escape from the symbolic is necessary in order to subvert hegemonic interpretations of the subject and its others. What I am suggesting is that one does not need to escape conventional discourse in order to express truths about human existence that are unique and personal. See Butler's "The Body Politics of Julia Kristeva" for her detailed critique and response to the appeal to pre-symbolic experience as a way of getting beyond the limitations of the symbolic domain.

8. This is my term, not Oliver's.

9. See chapter 7 of my *Body Images: Embodiment as Intercorporeality* (Routledge 1999) for a description of bodily imperatives and their foundational role in motivating an embodied ethics.

10. Challenging Choices

I am grateful to Peg Simons and the copyeditor at Indiana University Press for their excellent suggestions that significantly improved a previous version of this chapter that was published in *The Philosophy of Simone de Beauvoir: Critical Essays* (Indiana University Press, 2006). I also profited immensely from the wonderful feedback I received when I first presented a much shorter, original version of "Challenging Choices" at the 9th International Simone de Beauvoir Society Conference, "Engaging with Simone de

Beauvoir," at St. John's College, Oxford University, in July 2001, and later as a Keynote Presentation for the "Women in Dialogue with Philosophy" conference at Boston College in April 2002.

1. See Paul Ricoeur, "The Human Experience of Time and Narrative" and "Life: A Story in Search of a Narrator," for discussions of the "configurational dimension" of human narratives, that is, of the stories people tell to make sense of their lives. According to Ricoeur, the process of configuration involves constructing "significant wholes out of scattered events," and he emphasizes throughout his work that it is always possible to reconfigure the meaning of human lives by generating a new configuration out of a particular succession of events (Ricoeur 1991: 106).

2. Not surprisingly, this almost always means the perspective of the one who does not share the oppressed person's experience!

3. As a guest on CBS's *The Early Show* shortly after the trial, Russell Yates stated that his wife should not have been taken off antipsychotic drugs in the period preceding the killings. "'She was never diagnosed, she was never treated and they didn't protect our family,' he said" (quoted in "Jurors: Yates' Drowning of Her Children Seemed Premeditated," *CourtTV.com*, March 18, 2002). In June 2002, a headline in the *Houston Chronicle* announced, "A Year Ago, Russell Yates Tragically Lost 5 Children; He's Still Fighting for his Wife." The article affirms Yates's love and concern for his wife: "Andrea is a woman who needs compassion, who needs to be held and comforted. But here she is, 23 hours a day in a cell, isolated for the rest of her life from everyone who loves her. It's hard to accept. That has caused me a lot of stress this last year" ("After the Horror," *Houston Chronicle*, June 6, 2002). In a later article appearing in *CourtTV.com* on July 23, 2004 sensationally entitled, "Lawyer: Yates Thinks Children Are Alive," Russell Yates's weekly visits to his wife in prison are mentioned, clearly implying that his support for his wife has continued throughout her incarceration. However, in a July 27, 2006, article that appeared in the *Washington Post* following the most recent July 26, 2006, verdict by a Houston jury that Andrea Yates was "not guilty by reason of insanity," her husband is not mentioned at all, and in the accompanying photograph, she is surrounded only by her two lawyers. It would seem that with the passage of time, the killing of the children at the hands of their own mother has remained of central interest, and Russell Yates's current views concerning his wife's actions are no longer deemed to be as newsworthy.

4. Frankenberg's expression "racial social geography" is particularly apt in distinguishing the radically different social, political, and physical landscapes that situated each woman's actions.

5. Although I am proffering interpretations of both women's behavior here, I do not mean to suggest that these are the only plausible explanations one could give of either woman's actions. Indeed, there are several possible theoretical frameworks that may be utilized to analyze their respective situations. The possible interpretations I am suggesting are therefore not intended to provide a comprehensive analysis of these two women's situations and their respective responses to them or to close off other interpretations.

6. Indeed, the July 26, 2006, reversal of this earlier verdict by a new Texas jury seems to support such an interpretation; this was, in fact, the central argument made by Yates's attorneys in her trials.

7. By horizons, I am referring to the temporal horizons of past memories and future anticipations that help to shape the meaning of the present, spatial horizons such as

the larger geographical region as well as the immediate locale in which the events unfolded, and the social and material horizons (such as horizons of race, class, and gender) that help to define the parameters within which everyday life attains its significance.

8. See chapter 1, "Context and Perspective," for a more comprehensive discussion of how individual perspectives are constructed on the basis of particular contexts of significance.

9. In his later work, most notably *Critique of Dialectical Reason*, as Young (1990b) and others have noted, Sartre affirms the Marxist recognition of the severe burdens that can be placed upon an individual by the material constraints of her existence, and in this latter text, he provides a much more satisfactory account of how these constraints can limit one's existential choices.

10. As with other notorious cases of violent bourgeois crime, especially the murder of children by their mother such as the 1995 South Carolina story of Susan Smith, who sent her car into a local lake, drowning her two sons who were securely strapped into their car seats, this case was tried publicly in the press in the days following the initial deaths. In Susan Smith's case, even her ex-husband, David Smith, testified that she deserved death for the drownings of their boys, Michael and Alex, a crime compounded, in his and the public's eyes, by her false claim that they had been kidnapped, triggering a nine-day national search for the boys and their abductor. (See *CNN.com*'s "U.S. News Year in Review," December 28, 1995, for an overview of the crime and the subsequent trial.) Indeed, just as in the case of Susan Smith, Andrea Yates's guilt was reassessed in great detail by the public as well as by the court several months later during her death-penalty trial. Both cases have also been explicitly compared in articles focusing on women who kill their children, such as *CNN.com*'s August 8, 2001, article by David Williams entitled "Postpartum Psychosis: A Difficult Defense."

11. Of course, it is not inappropriate to ask why Andrea Yates's husband did not notice how depressed she was even if she herself did not recognize the seriousness of her condition. Strangely (or depending on one's perspective, perhaps not so strangely), there was very little criticism, much less condemnation, of Russell Yates in the press. The criticism that did occur came primarily from Andrea Yates's immediate relatives in newspaper articles and media quotes, including the following statement by her brother, Brian Kennedy: "I think that any man and woman whose spouse was that severely down, confused, that sick, that I would do whatever it would take to make sure my other half would get the help that was necessary" ("Yates Family Members Decry Husband," *CourtTV.com*, March 18, 2002). With some minor exceptions, including feminist support by the National Organization for Women (NOW), which organized a candlelight vigil outside the courtroom where the original case was being tried (see "NOW Rallies to Mother's Defense," *Washington Post*, September 3, 2001), Andrea Yates was publicly vilified as a criminal who deserved if not the death penalty, then at least a life sentence for her actions. As one juror stated in the wake of the conviction: "I think she should be punished for what she did considering she did know right from wrong and I think prison's the way to go" ("Jurors: Yates' Drowning of Her Children Seemed Premeditated," *CourtTV.com*, March 18, 2002). The lack of blame for Russell Yates makes sense if one acknowledges the powerful role the (Kantian) notion that human beings are all autonomous moral agents plays in establishing the framework for societal moral judgments in post-Enlightenment Western civilization. Indeed, if anything, Mr. Yates has been presented as a double victim: first as a man who was married to a dangerous woman without realizing it, and second, as a man who has suffered, through no fault of his own, the loss

of his entire family in one fell swoop. Strikingly, Russell Yates has referred to both himself and his wife as victims of the crime, the criminal justice system, and the press: "They've really taken victims and victimized them further. They put our family through hell this past year and unnecessarily. She should have never gone to trial" ("After the Horror," *Houston Chronicle*, June 20, 2002).

12. Undoubtedly some people could claim that Yates's behavior is a response to the oppressive institutions of marriage and motherhood themselves, that she was reacting (whether or not she knew it), to the compulsory aspects of those institutions, including the rigid system that underlies both institutions that Adrienne Rich identifies as compulsory heterosexuality; however, there are important material, psychic, social, and cultural differences between the oppression of late twentieth century middle-class American women who have chosen (however constrained that choice might be) married life and the oppression of slaves in antebellum America, who were unable to enjoy even basic freedom of movement, much less the right to be educated, to marry, and to raise their children, without their master's approval.

13. I am using this expression "life-world" [*lebenswelt*] in the Husserlian sense taken up and elaborated upon by Alfred Schutz in *The Phenomenology of the Social World*. In this text, Schutz focuses his attention on the typifying structures that emerge out of, and in turn shape, human beings' social relations with others.

14. I am grateful to Peg Simons for pointing out that Beauvoir offers an example of the sincere individual, through the character of Françoise, that both preceded and influenced Sartre's own discussions of seriousness, sincerity, and bad faith in *Being and Nothingness*.

15. For a focused discussion of this very point, see the "Myth and Reality" chapter of Beauvoir's *The Second Sex*.

16. See chapter 5 of Sonia Kruks's *Situation and Human Existence* for a detailed account of how Sartre's understanding of freedom and the situation changed from *Being and Nothingness* to the *Critique of Dialectical Reason*. Kruks credits Beauvoir as being a major influence on Sartre in modifying his earlier view and in developing a more robust conception of praxis.

17. Indeed it is passages such as these that reveal how Beauvoir was already posing significant internal challenges to the ethics of the autonomous for-itself she propounds throughout most of *The Ethics of Ambiguity*.

18. Although it is beyond the scope of this discussion to develop in depth the connections between Beauvoir's existentialist ethics and Sartre's, Simons has provided a compelling analysis of the impact of Beauvoir's early work on Sartre's own concept of situation in the chapter "Beauvoir and Sartre: The Question of Influence" in her book *Beauvoir and* The Second Sex: *Feminism, Race, and the Origins of Existentialism*.

19. The original reads as follows: "Mon action n'est pour autrui que ce qu'il en fait lui-même: comment donc saurais-je d'avance ce que je fais?" (Beauvoir 1944: 51).

20. See my essay "Freedom, Oppression and the Possibilities of Ethics in Beauvoir's Work."

21. For a fuller description of these "bodily imperatives" and how they function to ground an ethical existence, see chapter 7 of my *Body Images: Embodiment as Intercorporeality*.

22. For instance, the language of choice is woefully insufficient to address the responsibilities a person may have to her family since these latter exceed one's choices even if it is in and through one's choices that a person assumes them or fails to uphold

them. As Young observes in her essay "Reflections on Families in the Age of Murphy Brown: On Justice, Gender, and Sexuality": "Family are the ones who care for you when you are sick, and for whom you care when they are sick. Family members are mutually obliged to remember one another's birthdays, the ones on whom we dump our troubles. Family entails commitment and obligation as well as comfort: family members make claims on one another that they do not make on others" (Young 1997: 106).

My point is that the commitments and obligations people have to their families are not solely, or even primarily, the product of choice. After all, human beings (or other animals for that matter) don't choose their families to begin with, even if people can consciously decide how they want to treat their families and live up to the responsibilities that they entail. As almost everyone knows from personal experience, moreover, deciding how one wants to treat one's family (and be treated in turn) is hardly a guarantee that things will work out as one has planned. Ultimately, I argue, the meaning and influence one's family has in one's life is never simply a matter of choice.

23. The National Civil Rights Museum in Memphis, Tennessee, provides an incredibly powerful illustration of the oppressive effects of segregated schools, buses, restaurants, pools, bathrooms, and even water fountains on the countless numbers of African Americans who suffered under the notorious Jim Crow laws that were so rigidly forced in the American South not only at the time of Beauvoir's 1947 visit but over two more decades. The museum accomplishes this not by fancy exhibits but by the sheer number of artifacts they have assembled (including an actual bus that one walks through as well as a re-creation of a diner counter that was the site of a sit-in) that document how these "laws" attempted to circumscribe the very movements and meaning of African Americans' lives from one moment to the next.

24. Louis Althusser, in his well-known essay "Ideology and Ideological State Apparatus," discusses the power of state institutions, which, in an ongoing way, shape the meaning of intercorporeal experience by interpellating subjects who are subjected to the dominant ideology that is promulgated through various ideological state apparatuses (ISAs) including: the religious ISA, the educational ISA, the family ISA, the legal ISA, the political ISA, the trade union ISA, the communications ISA, the cultural ISA (Althusser 2001: 96). If, as Althusser argues, it is the case "[t]hat an individual is always-already a subject, even before he is born," then it makes no sense to talk about "choosing" to be a subject in the first place (Althusser 2001: 119). Thus, for Althusser, the very term "subject" is ambiguous because of its two conflicting meanings, both of which come into play at once:

> In the ordinary use of the term, subject in fact means: (1) a free subjectivity, a center of initiatives, author of and responsible for its actions; (2) a subjected being, who submits to a higher authority, and is therefore stripped of all freedom except that of freely accepting his submission. This last note gives us the meaning of this ambiguity, which is merely a reflection of the effect which produces it: the individual *is interpellated as a (free) subject in order that he shall submit freely to the commandments of the Subject, i.e. in order that he shall (freely) accept his subjection, i.e.* in order that he shall make the gestures and actions of his subjection "all by himself." *There are no subjects except by and for their subjection. That is why they "work all by themselves."* (Althusser 2001: 123; emphasis in original)

In the passage above, Althusser radically problematizes the very notion of choice and even freedom for *any* human subject, not just those who are severely oppressed.

While a separate study would be needed to pursue his arguments at length, it is clear that Althusser offers an invaluable resource for elaborating how social and political institutions legitimize (and de-legitimize) a human being's existence as a subject whose life is always interwoven with those of other subjects, thereby revealing the essential limitations of the language of choice to characterize the significance human actions have in shaping the type of person one becomes.

25. For the reader is unclear by the end of the novel whether Beloved is merely a figment of Sethe's imagination or a real flesh and blood human being.

11. Mothers/Intellectuals

1. See Althusser, "Ideology and Ideological State Apparatuses (Notes toward an Investigation)," and Butler's chapter "Arguing with the Real" in *Bodies That Matter* as well as her subsequent book, *Excitable Speech: A Politics of the Performative*, for in-depth accounts of the power of interpellation.

2. Althusser emphasizes the role of the state even more than the role of other individuals in this process. Subjectivation, he argues, is ideological through and through. In his words, *"the category of the subject is only constitutive of all ideology insofar as all ideology has the function (which defines it) of 'constituting' concrete individuals as subjects"* (Althusser 2001: 116; emphasis in original). For Althusser (following Marx), the state ideology that "constitutes concrete individuals as subjects" is always the dominant ideology of the ruling class. In *Bodies That Matter*, Butler further develops Althusser's insight that the disabling aspects of subjectivation produce enabling effects by granting the subject recognition as a subject, albeit a subordinated subject. In her words, "This 'subjection,' or *assujettissement*, is not only a subordination but a securing and maintaining, a putting into place of a subject, a subjectivation" (Butler 1993a: 34). Butler traces this enabling/disabling view of subjectivation back to Hegel's famous discussion, in the lordship and bondsman chapter in *Phenomenology of Mind*, of the subordination of the master to the slave insofar as the master requires the slave's recognition of his status as master (and therefore a confirmation by the slave of the slave's own subordinated status) in order to secure his own subjectivation as master.

3. This goes against William James's strong claim in the "Habits" chapter of *The Principles of Psychology* that a person's character is "fixed like plaster by the time we are thirty," which I discuss in chapter 5, and is more in keeping with the existentialist emphasis upon the ongoing re-creation of the self espoused by both Sartre and Beauvoir.

4. I am using Lewis Gordon's expression "antiblack world" to capture the all-pervasive presence of antiblack racism in social life, that is, the ways in which antiblack racism operates as an "ontological limitation of human reality" for blacks (as well as for non-blacks) (Gordon 1995: 1).

5. Indeed, Bourdieu would simply say that individual, social, and cultural understandings of what it means to be a mother are co-constitutive, insofar as they collectively form part of the habitus within which individual mothers live their lives.

6. To say that men are by definition non-mothers does not mean that men are incapable of engaging in mothering practices. In *Maternal Thinking* Sara Ruddick points out that one doesn't need to be a biological female to engage in "maternal thinking," and I agree with her. However, even a father who engages in mothering as a primary daily practice, a "house-husband" for instance, is still viewed as a man (read non-

mother) who takes on a maternal role, and he is often lauded or blamed for doing so precisely because it is not seen as natural for his sex and gender.

7. Linda Alcoff provides an excellent historical survey of political as well as philosophical approaches to identity in *Visible Identities*, chapters 2 and 3. She concentrates at length upon the key role the self/other binary has played in discussions of identity, and her insights have been central to my thinking on these matters.

8. Eva Kittay offers one of the most moving accounts of just such a person in chapter 6 of *Love's Labor*, namely her oldest child, Sesha, who has had no trouble expressing her identity with caretakers, family, and friends, despite severe mental and physical disabilities that render her incapable of using language or of getting about in the world independently.

9. The same point holds for Sartre as well, and it is illustrated in depth in both the "Bad Faith" section of *Being and Nothingness* and in his play *No Exit*.

10. See chapter 9 for a discussion of how Kierkegaard's, Heidegger's, and Sartre's respective understandings of the authentic individual as someone who is at least conceptually able to separate herself from others has been integral to both the phenomenological and the existential traditions. It is a major reason for the ongoing critique of these traditions as being too "subjectivist." Alcoff provides an excellent explanation of this critique and a response to it in chapter 4 of *Visible Identities*. Sara Heinämaa also tackles this critique head-on in chapter 1 of *Toward a Phenomenology of Sexual Difference*, with reference to both Kierkegaard and Beauvoir, arguing that it is possible to affirm the "Kierkegaardian notion of the separation of the self" without this affirmation leading to "solipsism or subjectivism" (Heinämaa 2003: 10).

11. It is striking that Caws claims that identity, as reflexive, "can" be mediated rather than that it is mediated. This suggests that it might be possible for the self to relate to itself without mediation by others and/or by the world of her concern. In fact, Caws supports this interpretation when he maintains that one can and should transcend one's culture of origin, though he is quick to clarify that this "does not mean turning one's back on it" (Caws 1994: 385). To make one's identity one's own, he argues, involves stepping away from identifications that have been imposed on one by one's society. In his words, "the mature person is likely to leave his or her culture of origin behind as limiting to the development of personal identity" (Caws 1994: 372). While he acknowledges the positive role that an ethnic identification can play in an individual's life, he views it as exceedingly problematic for the individual merely to accept this identification as her identity. Instead, appealing to Sartre, Caws maintains that she needs to actively commit to this particular identity as a self-conscious choice in order to avoid the charge of bad faith. In contrast, I will argue that though this may seem like a very appealing view of identity, especially to individuals who were oppressed growing up within their native cultures, it presupposes that one can, indeed, transcend the influence of one's culture of origin through one's rational choices. Moreover, it is exceedingly problematic to imply, as Caws does, that the "mature" person leaves her native culture behind. This makes it seem as if one's native culture resembles the immature Freudian id that must be repudiated. However, even setting aside the problematic implications of such a comparison, implications that Fanon discusses at some length in *Black Skin White Masks* with reference to the colonial subject whose native culture is viewed as uncivilized when compared to the allegedly more sophisticated culture of the colonizer, Freud recognized that the desires of the id can never be transcended or vanquished altogether. Instead the individual must reckon with them on an ongoing basis, just as, I would argue, one must

continue to reckon with the influence of one's native culture, a culture that one may have a tendency to regard as immature when one is most in tension with it!

12. See the "Existential Psychoanalysis" chapter of *Being and Nothingness* for a good description of what it means to make an existential choice.

13. See part 3 of *Volatile Bodies* for an in-depth description of these types of theories. Grosz herself seems more sympathetic to "outside in" perspectives, despite her recognition of their shortcomings, than to the "inside out" perspectives she associates with the phenomenological and psychoanalytic traditions.

14. See my discussion of Bourdieu and the habitus in chapter 5 for a fuller development of this point.

15. Moreover, I would argue that this same point applies to any dual or even hybrid identity, from Gloria Anzaldua's discussion of the specific challenges faced by the *mestiza* in *Borderlands/La Frontera* to Alcoff's own discussion in *Visible Identities* of the obstacles and opportunities encountered by mixed-race people in a society that constantly seeks to reduce their identity to one race or the other.

16. This is not to suggest that the roles themselves are fixed from one culture to another or even one time period to another. While I am drawing primarily from the experience of contemporary women in the United States in this chapter, I believe that most of my claims regarding the difficulty of integrating one's life as a mother and one's life as an intellectual hold up in other cultures and other time periods as well. This is not only because the demands of an intellectual life and the demands of motherhood are different in kind but also because both require one's primary attention while one is attempting to fulfill them.

17. The intellectual life has traditionally been seen as self-justifying in at least two senses: (1) as worth pursuing for its own sake alone; (2) as justifying or legitimizing the one who pursues it.

18. This passage is striking for a number of reasons, one of which is that Heraclitus gives the credit for his own intellectual inspiration to the gods, not to himself. He suggests that divine inspiration can and does occur in the midst of mundane life, and does not require a special setting to take place. I believe that this view ties in well with Sara Ruddick's (1989) work on maternal thinking, a complex epistemological activity that occurs in an ongoing way while one is most (rather than least) encumbered with one's parenting responsibilities.

19. See "The Mother" chapter of Simone de Beauvoir's *The Second Sex*.

20. However, it should be noted that the unconventional topic of my talk and of our larger panel (which contained the expression "mothers/intellectuals" in its title) could itself lead more traditional scholars to view our panel as non-intellectual from the outset. Perhaps this is why we had such a small audience for the papers at this session (as I recall, it was attended only by women and most of them were mothers)! This goes to show that the subject matter one addresses also influences whether or not one's thought, speech, and/or writing are viewed as intellectual. Historically speaking, topics that address what have typically been viewed as "women's issues," such as motherhood, tend not to be regarded as intellectual, though this is thankfully starting to change.

21. And given how meager most academics' annual conference travel budgets are, even those with the interest and inclination may be unable to participate in this professional venue for the formal exchange of ideas!

22. Of course, for those who live the both/and it must be noted that it rarely feels

like "having one's cake and eating it too." Indeed, as most mother/intellectuals soon discover, one may have made or bought the cake, but the kids or one's colleagues could wind up eating it before one even gets a bite!

23. Though it should be added that an individual may be called upon to make the "infinite movement of resignation" by resigning one ethical duty in order to satisfy a higher one. Kierkegaard's discussion of the tragic hero and the particular example of Agamemnon, who chose to sacrifice his daughter Iphigenia to save his country, is a case in point.

24. For an important discussion of the wartime rape of female civilians by soldiers whose goal is to produce unwanted children who will not be accepted in their communities, and the significance of the landmark designation of these acts as crimes against humanity by the International Tribunal operating in The Hague, see Debra Bergoffen's 2005 essay, "How Rape Became a Crime against Humanity: History of an Error, Modernity and the Problem of Evil."

25. The anti-intellectualism championed by U.S. president George W. Bush may make the intellectual life seem less appealing than it has in the past; however, it is politicians, not mothers, who seem to be benefiting from Bush's and other Republicans' attacks on the intellectual.

26. Even the call to come together as Americans is problematic because the generic term "American" applies to Canadians as well as Central and South Americans; despite this fact, over time, it has come to designate the identity exclusively of people who reside in the United States.

27. I am thinking here about the numerous unprovoked physical and psychological attacks that have been experienced by Muslims, Sikhs, and Middle Eastern peoples who reside in the U.S., which are part of the "collateral damage" caused by the terrorist attacks of September 11, 2001.

28. In Alcoff's words, "Identities themselves—meaning not the mere representation but the lived bodies—are fluid, complex, open-ended, and dynamic, which is why reductive and overly homogeneous characterizations of identity are inaccurate." For this reason she maintains that "there is no ultimate coherence between anyone's multiple identities; there will always be tensions between various aspects" (Alcoff 2006: 112). Alcoff's notion of identity as an interpretive horizon, articulated in chapter 4 of *Visible Identities*, reinforces the point that identities can never be understood or assessed apart from the horizons within and through which they are constituted.

Bibliography

"After the Horror." *Houston Chronicle*, June 6, 2002. http://www.chron.com/cs/CDA/ ssistory.mpl/special/drownings/1462406 (URL no longer active); accessed February 9, 2005.

Agamben, Giorgio. 2002. *Remnants of Auschwitz: The Witness and the Archive*. Trans. Daniel Heller-Roazen. New York: Zone Books.

Alcoff, Linda Martin. 1991. "The Problem of Speaking for Others." *Cultural Critique* (Winter 1991–1992): 5–32.

———. 2001. "Toward a Phenomenology of Racial Embodiment." In *Race*, ed. Robert Bernasconi, 267–283. Malden, Mass.: Blackwell.

———. 2006. *Visible Identities: Race, Gender, and the Self*. Oxford: Oxford University Press.

Al-Saji, Alia. 2007. "A Phenomenology of Critical-Ethical Vision." Unpublished paper presented at the "Embodiment and Sexual Difference" Workshop at the University of Alberta, Edmonton, Canada, October 2007.

Althusser, Louis. 2001. "Ideology and Ideological State Apparatus (Notes towards an Investigation)." In *Lenin and Philosophy and Other Essays*, 85–126. Trans. Ben Brewster. New York: Monthly Review Press.

Anderson, Benedict. 1991. *Imagined Communities: Reflections on the Origin and Spread of Nationalism*. Rev. ed. London: Verso.

Andrews, Jorella. 2006. "Vision, Violence, and the Other: A Merleau-Pontian Ethics." In *Feminist Interpretations of Maurice Merleau-Ponty*, ed. Dorothea Olkowski and Gail Weiss, 167–182. University Park: Pennsylvania State University Press.

Anzaldua, Gloria. 1987. *Borderlands/La Frontera: The New Mestiza*. San Francisco: Aunt Lute Books.

Arendt, Hannah. 1970. *On Violence*. San Diego: Harcourt, Brace.

Barthes, Roland. 1975. *The Pleasure of the Text*. Trans. Richard Miller. New York: Noonday Press.

———. 1989. "The Death of the Author." In *The Rustle of Language*, 49–55. Trans. Richard Howard. Berkeley: University of California Press.

Bataille, Georges. 1985. *Visions of Excess: Selected Writings, 1927–1939*. Ed. and trans. Allan Stoekl with Carl R. Lovitt and Donald M. Leslie Jr. Minneapolis: University of Minnesota Press.

Baudrillard, Jean. 1984. "The Precession of Simulacra." In *Art after Modernism: Rethinking Representation*, ed. Brian Wallis, 253–281. New York: New Museum of Contemporary Art.

Beauvoir, Simone de. 1944. *Pyrrhus et Cinéas*. Paris: Editions Gallimard.

———. 1976. *The Ethics of Ambiguity*. Trans. Bernard Frechtman. New York: Citadel Books.

———. 1989. *The Second Sex*. Trans. H. M. Parshley. New York: Vintage Books.

———. 1990. *She Came to Stay*. New York: W. W. Norton.

———. 1999. *America Day by Day*. Trans. Carol Cosman. Berkeley: University of California Press.

Benhabib, Seyla. 1992. *Situating the Self: Gender, Community and Postmodernism in Contemporary Ethics*. New York: Routledge.

Bergoffen, Debra. 1997. *The Philosophy of Simone de Beauvoir: Gendered Phenomenologies, Erotic Generosities*. Albany: SUNY Press.

———. 2005. "How Rape Became a Crime against Humanity: History of an Error, Modernity and the Problem of Evil." In *Modernity and the Problem of Evil*, ed. Alan D. Schrift, 66–89. Bloomington: Indiana University Press.

Bergson, Henri. 1955. *An Introduction to Metaphysics*. Trans. T. E. Hulme. New York: Macmillan.

Bigwood, Carol. 1993. *Earth Muse: Feminism, Nature, and Art*. Philadelphia: Temple University Press.

Bourdieu, Pierre. 1977. *Outline of a Theory of Practice*. Trans. Richard Nice. Cambridge: Cambridge University Press.

———. 1984. *Distinction: A Social Critique of the Judgment of Taste*. Trans. Richard Nice. Cambridge, Mass.: Harvard University Press.

———. 1990. *The Logic of Practice*. Trans. Richard Nice. Stanford, Calif.: Stanford University Press.

Buber, Martin. 1970. *I and Thou*. Trans. Walter Kaufmann. New York: Charles Scribner's Sons.

Burns-Ardolino, Wendy. 2003. "Woman Interrupted? A Response to Weiss." *Cultural Matters 2: Changing Our Ways*. http://culturalstudies.gmu.edu/cultural_matters/issue2/index.html; accessed June 12, 2007.

Busch, Thomas. 1999. "Sartre on Language and Politics (with Reference to Particularity)." In *Circulating Being: From Embodiment to Incorporation, Essays on Late Existentialism*, 62–79. New York: Fordham University Press.

Butler, Judith. 1989a. "Sexual Ideology and Phenomenological Description: A Feminist Critique of Merleau-Ponty's *Phenomenology of Perception.*" In *The Thinking Muse: Feminism and Modern French Philosophy,* ed. Jeffner Allen and Iris Marion Young, 85–100. Bloomington: Indiana University Press.

——. 1989b. "The Body Politics of Julia Kristeva." *Hypatia: A Journal of Feminist Philosophy* 3, no. 3: 104–117.

——. 1990. *Gender Trouble: Feminism and the Subversion of Identity.* New York: Routledge.

——. 1993a. *Bodies That Matter: On the Discursive Limits of "Sex."* New York: Routledge.

——. 1993b. "Endangered/Endangering: Schematic Racism and White Paranoia." In *Reading Rodney King/Reading Urban Uprising,* ed. Robert Gooding-Williams, 15–22. London: Routledge.

——. 1997. *Excitable Speech: A Politics of the Performative.* New York: Routledge.

——. 1998. Foreword to *The Erotic Bird: Phenomenology in Literature,* by Maurice Natanson. Princeton, N.J.: Princeton University Press, ix–xvi.

——. 2004. *Undoing Gender.* New York: Routledge Press.

——. 2006. "Sexual Difference as a Question of Ethics: Alterities of the Flesh in Irigaray and Merleau-Ponty." In *Feminist Interpretations of Maurice Merleau-Ponty,* ed. Dorothea Olkowski and Gail Weiss, 107–125. University Park: Pennsylvania University Press.

Camus, Albert. 1954. *The Stranger.* Trans. Stuart Gilbert. New York: Vintage Books.

——. 1983. *The Myth of Sisyphus and Other Essays.* Trans. Justin O'Brien. New York: Random House.

Casey, Edward S. 1993. *Getting Back into Place: Toward a Renewed Understanding of the Place-World.* Bloomington: Indiana University Press.

Caws, Peter. 1994. "Identity: Cultural, Transcultural, and Multicultural." In *Multiculturalism: A Critical Reader,* ed. David Theo Goldberg, 371–387. Oxford: Blackwell.

Chanter, Tina. 1995. *Ethics of Eros: Irigaray's Rewriting of the Philosophers.* New York: Routledge.

——. 2001. *Time, Death, and the Feminine: Levinas with Heidegger.* Stanford, Calif.: Stanford University Press.

Collins, Patricia Hill. 2000. *Black Feminist Thought: Knowledge, Consciousness, and the Politics of Empowerment.* 2nd ed. New York: Routledge.

Crenshaw, Kimberlé, and Gary Peller. 1993. "Reel Time/Real Justice." In *Reading Rodney King/Reading Urban Uprising,* ed. Robert Gooding-Williams, 56–70. London: Routledge Press.

Deleuze, Gilles. 1994. *Difference and Repetition.* Trans. Paul Patton. New York: Columbia University Press.

Derrida, Jacques. 1976. *Of Grammatology.* Trans. Gayatri Chakravorty Spivak. Baltimore: Johns Hopkins University Press.

——. 1982a. "Signature Event Context." In *Margins of Philosophy,* 307–330. Trans. Alan Bass. Chicago: University of Chicago Press.

——. 1982b. "Différance." In *Margins of Philosophy,* 1–27. Trans. Alan Bass. Chicago: University of Chicago Press.

——. 1995. *The Gift of Death.* Trans. David Wills. Chicago: University of Chicago Press.

Descartes, René. 1980. *Discourse on Method and Meditations on First Philosophy.* Trans. Donald A. Cress. Indianapolis: Hackett.

Dewey, John. 1980. *Art as Experience.* New York: Perigee Books.

Didion, Joan. 2005. *The Year of Magical Thinking*. New York: Alfred A. Knopf.

Dilthey, Wilhelm. 1976. *Dilthey: Selected Writings*. Ed. and trans. H. P. Rickman. Cambridge: Cambridge University Press.

Diprose, Rosalyn. 2002. *Corporeal Generosity: On Giving with Nietzsche, Merleau-Ponty, and Levinas*. Albany: SUNY Press.

Di Quinzio, Patrice. 1999. *The Impossibility of Motherhood: Feminism, Individualism, and the Problem of Mothering*. New York: Routledge.

Douglas, Mary. 1966. *Purity and Danger: An Analysis of Concepts of Pollution and Taboo*. New York: Routledge and Kegan Paul.

Dreyfus, Hubert L., and Stuart E. Dreyfus. 1999. "The Challenge of Merleau-Ponty's Phenomenology of Embodiment for Cognitive Science." In *Perspectives on Embodiment: The Intersections of Nature and Culture*, ed. Gail Weiss and Honi Fern Haber, 103–120. New York: Routledge Press.

Fanon, Frantz. 1967. *Black Skin White Masks*. Trans. Charles Lam Markmann. New York: Grove Press.

Feder, Ellen. 2007. *Family Bonds: Genealogies of Race and Gender*. Oxford: Oxford University Press.

Fielding, Helen. 2006. "White Logic and the Constancy of Color." In *Feminist Interpretations of Maurice Merleau-Ponty*, ed. Dorothea Olkowski and Gail Weiss, 71–89. University Park: Pennsylvania State University Press.

Foucault, Michel. 1970. *The Order of Things: An Archaeology of the Human Sciences*. New York: Random House.

———. 1977. *Discipline and Punish: The Birth of the Prison*. Trans. Alan Sheridan. New York: Vintage Books

———. 1984. "What Is an Author?" In *The Foucault Reader*, 101–120. Ed. Paul Rabinow. New York: Pantheon Books.

———. 1988. *The Care of the Self*. Vol. 3 of *The History of Sexuality*. Trans. Robert Hurley. New York: Vintage Books.

Frankenberg, Ruth. 1993. *White Women, Race Matters: The Social Construction of Whiteness*. Minneapolis: University of Minnesota Press.

Gadamer, Hans-Georg. 1982. *Truth and Method*. New York: Crossroad Publishing.

———. 1992. "The Political Incompetence of Philosophy." In *The Heidegger Case: On Philosophy and Politics*, ed. Tom Rockmore and Joseph Margolis, 364–369. Philadelphia: Temple University Press.

Garreau, Joel. 1991. *Edge City: Life on the New Frontier*. New York: Doubleday.

Gilligan, Carol. 1982. *In a Different Voice: Psychological Theory and Women's Development*. Cambridge, Mass.: Harvard University Press.

Goldberg, David Theo. 1990. "The Social Formation of Racist Discourse." In *Anatomy of Racism*, ed. David Theo Goldberg, 295–318. Minneapolis: University of Minneapolis Press.

Gordon, Lewis R. 1995. *Bad Faith and Antiblack Racism*. Atlantic Highlands, N.J.: Humanities Press.

———. 2000. *Existentia Africana: Understanding Africana Existential Thought*. New York: Routledge.

Grosz, Elizabeth. 1993. "Merleau-Ponty and Irigaray in the Flesh." In "Sense and Sensuousness in Merleau-Ponty." Special issue, *Thesis Eleven*, no. 36: 37–59.

———. 1994. *Volatile Bodies: Toward a Corporeal Feminism*. Bloomington: Indiana University Press.

———. 1995. "Bodies-Cities." In *Space, Time, and Perversion: Essays on the Politics of Bodies*, 103–124. New York: Routledge Press.

———. 2001. *Architecture from the Outside: Essays on Virtual and Real Space*. Cambridge, Mass.: MIT Press.

———. 2004. *The Nick of Time: Politics, Evolution, and the Untimely*. Durham, N.C.: Duke University Press.

Guillaumin, Colette. 1995. *Racism, Sexism, Power and Ideology*. Trans. Andrew Rothwell et al. London: Routledge.

Hainer, Cathy. 1998–1999. *The Cathy Hainer Journals. USA Today*. (The original articles appeared between March 10, 1998, and December 6, 1999, in the "Life" section of *USA Today*). These articles are available through the USA Today electronic archives at http://www.usatoday.com.

Hastings, Howard. 2003. "Also an Ambivalence of Individuality: A Response to Weiss." *Cultural Matters 2: Changing Our Ways*, http://culturalstudies.gmu.edu/cultural_matters/issue2/index.html; accessed June 12, 2007.

Hegel, G. W. F. 1967. *The Phenomenology of Mind*. Intro. George Lichtheim. Trans. J. B. Baillie. New York: Harper and Row.

Heidegger, Martin. 1971a. "Building Dwelling Thinking." In *Poetry, Language, Thought*, 143–161. Trans. Albert Hofstadter. New York: Harper and Row.

———. 1971b. "The Origin of the Work of Art." In *Poetry, Language, Thought*, 17–81. Trans. Albert Hofstadter. New York: Harper and Row.

———. 1993a. "What Is Metaphysics?" In *Martin Heidegger Basic Writings*, 89–110. Trans. David Farrell Krell. New York: HarperCollins.

———. 1993b. "Letter on Humanism." In *Martin Heidegger: Basic Writings*, 217–265. Ed. David Farrell Krell. Trans. Frank A. Capuzzi and J. Glenn Gray. San Francisco: Harper Collins.

———. 1996. *Being and Time*. Trans. Joan Stambaugh. Albany: SUNY Press.

Heinämaa, Sara. 2003. *Toward a Phenomenology of Sexual Difference: Husserl, Merleau-Ponty, Beauvoir*. Lanham: Rowman and Littlefield.

Homer. 2000. *The Odyssey*. Trans. Stanley Lombardo. Indianapolis: Hackett Publishing.

Hooks, Bell. 1984. *Feminist Theory: From Margin to Center*. Boston: South End Press.

———. 1990. "Marginality as Site of Resistance." In *Out There: Marginalization and Contemporary Cultures*, 341–343. Ed. Russell Ferguson, Martha Gever, Trinh T. Minh-ha, Cornel West. Cambridge, Mass.: MIT Press.

Hoy, David Couzens. 1999. "Critical Resistance: Foucault and Bourdieu." In *Perspectives on Embodiment: The Intersections of Nature and Culture*, 3–21. Ed. Gail Weiss and Honi Fern Haber. New York: Routledge Press.

Husserl, Edmund. 1965. *Phenomenology and the Crisis of Philosophy*. Trans. Quentin Lauer. New York: Harper and Row.

———. 1970. *The Crisis of European Sciences and Transcendental Phenomenology*. Trans. David Carr. Evanston, Ill.: Northwestern University Press.

———. 1982. *Ideas Pertaining to a Pure Phenomenology and to a Phenomenological Philosophy*. First Book. Trans. F. Kersten. Dordrecht: Kluwer Academic Publishers.

———. 1989. *Ideas Pertaining to a Pure Phenomenology and to a Phenomenological Philosophy*. Second Book. Trans. F. Kersten. Dordrecht: Kluwer Academic Publishers.

Irigaray, Luce. 1985a. *Speculum of the Other Woman*. Trans. Gillian C. Gill. Ithaca, N.Y.: Cornell University Press.

——. 1985b. *This Sex Which Is Not One.* Trans. Catherine Porter. Ithaca, N.Y.: Cornell University Press.

——. 1993. *An Ethics of Sexual Difference.* Trans. Carolyn Burke and Gillian C. Gill. Ithaca, N.Y.: Cornell University Press.

James, William. 1950. *The Principles of Psychology.* Vol. 1. New York: Dover.

Jay, Martin. 1993. *Downcast Eyes: The Denigration of Vision in Twentieth-Century French Thought.* Berkeley: University of California Press.

Johnson, Mark. 1987. *The Body in the Mind: The Bodily Basis of Meaning, Imagination, and Reason.* Chicago: University of Chicago Press.

——. 1993. *Moral Imagination: Implications of Cognitive Science for Ethics.* Chicago: University of Chicago Press.

"Jurors: Yates' Drowning of Her Children Seemed Premeditated," *CourtTV.com,* March 18, 2002. http://www.courttv.com/trials/yates/031802-b_ap.html; accessed February 9, 2005.

Kafka, Franz. 1996. *The Metamorphosis and Other Stories.* Trans. Stanley Appelbaum. New York: Dover.

Kant, Immanuel. 1964. *Groundwork of the Metaphysic of Morals.* Trans. H. J. Paton. New York: Harper and Row.

——. 1991. *Kant: Political Writings.* Ed. Hans Reiss and trans. H. B. Nisbet. Cambridge: Cambridge University Press.

Keenan, Thomas. 1997. *Fables of Responsibility: Aberrations and Predicaments in Ethics and Politics.* Stanford, Calif.: Stanford University Press.

Kierkegaard, Søren. 1983. *Fear and Trembling/Repetition.* Ed. and trans. Howard and Edna Hong. Princeton, N.J.: Princeton University Press.

——. 1987. *Either/Or.* Part 2. Ed. and trans. Howard V. Hong and Edna H. Hong. Princeton, N.J.: Princeton University Press.

——. 1992. *Concluding Unscientific Postscript to Philosophical Fragments.* Vol. 1. Ed. and trans. Howard and Edna Hong. Princeton, N.J.: Princeton University Press.

Kittay, Eva. 1999. *Love's Labor: Essays on Women, Equality, and Dependency.* New York: Routledge.

Kristeva, Julia. 1980. *Desire in Language: A Semiotic Approach to Literature and Art.* Ed. Leon S. Roudiez. Trans. Thomas Gora, Alice Jardine, and Leon S. Roudiez. New York: Columbia University Press.

——. 1982. *Powers of Horror: An Essay on Abjection.* Trans. Leon S. Roudiez. New York: Columbia University Press.

Kruks, Sonia. 1990. *Situation and Human Existence: Freedom, Subjectivity, and Society.* London: Unwin Hyman.

——. 2001. *Retrieving Experience: Subjectivity and Recognition in Feminist Politics.* Ithaca, N.Y.: Cornell University Press.

Lacan, Jacques. 1977. *Écrits.* Trans. Alan Sheridan. New York: W. W. Norton.

"Lawyer: Yates Thinks Children Are Alive," *CourtTV.com,* July 23, 2004. http://www.courttv.com/trials/yates/072204 _alive_ap.html; accessed February 9, 2005.

Levinas, Emmanuel. 1969. *Totality and Infinity.* Trans. Alphonso Lingis. Pittsburgh: Duquesne University Press.

Long, J. Z. 2003. "On Becoming-Habitual: A Response to Weiss." *Cultural Matters 2: Changing Our Ways.* http://culturalstudies.gmu.edu/cultural_matters/issue2/index .html; accessed June 12, 2007.

Lorde, Audre. 1990. "Age, Race, Class, and Sex: Women Redefining Difference." In *Out There: Marginalization and Contemporary Cultures*, ed. Russell Ferguson, Martha Gever, Trinh T. Minh-ha, and Cornel West, 281–287. Cambridge, Mass.: MIT Press.

Lugones, María. 1990. "Playfulness, 'World'-Travelling, and Loving Perception." In *Lesbian Philosophies and Cultures*, ed. Jeffner Allen, 159–180. New York: SUNY Press.

MacIntyre, Alasdair. 1981. *After Virtue: A Study in Moral Theory.* Notre Dame, Ind.: University of Notre Dame Press.

McCourt, Frank. 1996. *Angela's Ashes: A Memoir.* New York: Scribner Press.

McRuer, Robert. 2006. *Crip Theory: Cultural Signs of Queerness and Disability.* New York: New York University Press.

McWhorter, Ladelle. 1999. *Bodies and Pleasures: Foucault and the Politics of Sexual Normalization.* Bloomington: Indiana University Press.

Mead, George Herbert. 1938. *Philosophy of the Act.* Ed. Charles W. Morris. Chicago: University of Chicago Press.

——. 1962. *Mind, Self, and Society from the Standpoint of a Social Behaviorist.* Ed. Charles W. Morris. Chicago: University of Chicago Press.

Merleau-Ponty. 1962. *Phenomenology of Perception.* Trans. Colin Smith. London: Routledge and Kegan Paul.

——. 1964a. *Signs.* Trans. Richard C. McCleary. Evanston, Ill.: Northwestern University Press.

——. 1964b. *The Primacy of Perception.* Ed. James M. Edie. Evanston, Ill.: Northwestern University Press.

——. 1968. *The Visible and the Invisible.* Ed. Claude Lefort. Trans. Alphonso Lingis. Evanston, Ill.: Northwestern University Press.

——. 1969. *Humanism and Terror.* Trans. John O'Neill. Boston: Beacon Press.

——. 1993. "Eye and Mind." In *The Merleau-Ponty Aesthetics Reader*, 121–149. Ed. Galen A. Johnson. Translation editor Michael Smith. Evanston, Ill.: Northwestern University Press.

——. 2003. *Nature: Course Notes from the Collège de France.* Compiled and with notes by Dominique Séglard and trans. Robert Vallier. Evanston, Ill.: Northwestern University Press.

Morrison, Toni. 1987. *Beloved: A Novel.* New York: Knopf.

——. 1992. *Playing in the Dark: Whiteness and the Literary Imagination.* Cambridge, Mass.: Harvard University Press.

——. 1993. *The Bluest Eye.* New York: Knopf.

Natanson, Maurice. 1998. *The Erotic Bird: Phenomenology in Literature.* Princeton, N.J.: Princeton University Press.

Naylor, Gloria. 1982. *The Women of Brewster Place.* New York: Viking.

New York Times. 2001. "A Nation Challenged: Portraits of Grief" series. September–December 2001. www.nytimes.com/portraits.

Nietzsche, Friedrich. 1956. *The Genealogy of Morals.* Trans. Francis Golffing. New York: Anchor Books.

"NOW Rallies to Mother's Defense." *Washington Post*, September 3, 2001, A3.

Oliver, Kelly. 2000. "Beyond Recognition: Witnessing Ethics." *Philosophy Today*, Spring 2000, 44, 31–42.

——. 2001. *Witnessing: Beyond Recognition*. Minneapolis: University of Minnesota Press.

Olkowski, Dorothea E. 1999a. *Gilles Deleuze and the Ruin of Representation*. Berkeley: University of California Press.

——. 1999b. "Phenomenology and Feminism." In *Edinburgh Encyclopedia of Continental Philosophy*, 323–332. Edinburgh: Edinburgh University Press.

——. 2000. "The End of Phenomenology: Bergson's Interval in Irigaray." *Hypatia: A Journal of Feminist Philosophy* 15, no. 3: 73–91.

Ortner, Sherry. 1996. "Is Female to Male as Nature Is to Culture?" In *Making Gender: The Politics and Erotics of Culture*, 21–42. Boston: Beacon Press.

Paris, Jeffrey. 2001. "Overcoming Our Empathy-Deficit: Phenomenological Reflections on the WTC-Event." http://pages.prodigy.net/gmoses/nvusa/paris1.htm; accessed October 29, 2007.

Plato. 1951. *The Symposium*. Trans. Walter Hamilton. London: Penguin Books.

——. 1991. *The Republic*. Trans. Allan Bloom. New York: Basic Books.

Portraits: 9/11/01: The Collected "Portraits of Grief." 2003. New York: Times Books.

Proust, Marcel. 1981. *Remembrance of Things Past*. Vols. 1–3. Trans. C. K. Scott-Moncrieff and Terence Kilmartin. New York: Random House.

Rich, Adrienne. 1976. *Of Woman Born: Motherhood as Experience and Institution*. New York: Bantam Books.

——. 1983. "Compulsory Heterosexuality and Lesbian Existence." In *Powers of Desire: The Politics of Sexuality*, ed. Ann Snitow, Christine Stansell, and Sharon Thompson, 177–205. New York: Monthly Review.

Ricoeur, Paul. 1991. *A Ricoeur Reader: Reflection and Imagination*. Ed. Mario J. Valdés. Toronto: University of Toronto Press.

Ruddick, Lisa. 1990. *Reading Gertrude Stein: Body, Text, Gnosis*. Ithaca, N.Y.: Cornell University Press.

Ruddick, Sara. 1989. *Maternal Thinking: Toward a Politics of Peace*. New York: Ballantine Books.

Sartre, Jean-Paul. 1956. *Being and Nothingness*. Trans. Hazel E. Barnes. New York: Washington Square Press.

——. 1964. *Nausea*. Trans. Lloyd Alexander. New York: New Directions.

——. 1975. "Existentialism Is a Humanism." In *Existentialism from Dostoevsky to Sartre*, 345–369. Ed. and trans. Walter Kaufmann. New York: New American Library.

——. 1976. *Critique of Dialectical Reason*. Trans. Alan Sheridan-Smith. London: Verso. *Critique de la Raison Dialectique*. Paris: Editions Gallimard, 1960.

——. 1988. *"What Is Literature?" and Other Essays*. Cambridge, Mass.: Harvard University Press.

Scarry, Elaine. 1985. *The Body in Pain: The Making and Unmaking of the World*. Oxford: Oxford University Press.

Schutz, Alfred. 1967. *The Phenomenology of the Social World*. Trans. George Walsh and Frederick Lehnert. Evanston, Ill.: Northwestern University Press.

Sen, Amartya. 2006. *Identity and Violence: The Illusion of Destiny*. New York: W. W. Norton.

Silverman, Kaja. 1992. *Male Subjectivity at the Margins*. New York: Routledge Press.

Simons, Margaret A. 1999. *Beauvoir and* The Second Sex: *Feminism, Race, and the Origins of Existentialism*. Lanham, Md.: Rowman and Littlefield.

Spivak, Gayatri. 1995. "Can the Subaltern Speak?" In *The Post-Colonial Studies Reader*, 24–28. Ed. Bill Ashcroft, Gareth Griffiths, Helen Tiffin. London: Routledge.

Stein, Gertrude. 1914. *Tender Buttons*. Los Angeles: Sun and Moon Press.

Sullivan, Nikki. 2001. *Tattooed Bodies: Subjectivity, Textuality, Ethics, and Pleasure*. Westport, Conn.: Praeger.

Sullivan, Shannon. 2001. *Living Across and Through Skins: Transactional Bodies, Pragmatism, and Feminism*. Bloomington: Indiana University Press.

Susser, Daniel. 2007. "Challenging the Binary: Toward an Ecological Theory of Intentionality." Enosinian Honors Thesis in Philosophy, The George Washington University.

Thomson, Rosemarie Garland. 1997. *Extraordinary Bodies: Figuring Physical Disability in American Culture and Literature*. New York: Columbia University Press.

Tolstoy, Leo. 1981. *The Death of Ivan Ilych*. Trans. Lynn Solotaroff. New York: Bantam Books.

"U.S. News Year in Review." *CNN.Com*, December 28, 1995. http://edition.cnn.com/EVENTS/year_in_review/us/smith.html; accessed February 9, 2005.

Vogel, Steven. 1996. *Against Nature: The Concept of Nature in Critical Theory*. Albany: State University of New York Press.

Weiss, Gail. 1999. *Body Images: Embodiment as Intercorporeality*. New York: Routledge Press.

———. 2002. "Freedom, Oppression, and the Possibilities of Ethics in Beauvoir's Work." *Simone de Beauvoir Studies* 18 (2001–2002): 9–21.

———. 2004. Introduction to "Introduction to an Ethics of Ambiguity (1946)." In *Simone de Beauvoir Philosophical Writings*, ed. Margaret A. Simons with Marybeth Timmerman and Mary Beth Mader, 281–288. Urbana: University of Illinois Press.

Wigley, Mark. 1992. "Untitled: The Housing of Gender." In *Sexuality and Space*, ed. Beatriz Colomina, 327–389. New York: Princeton Architectural Press.

Williams, David. "Postpartum Psychosis: A Difficult Defense." *CNN.Com*, August 8, 2001. http://archives.cnn.com/2001/LAW/06/28/postpartum.defense/; accessed August 22, 2007.

Williams, Patricia. 1991. *The Alchemy of Race and Rights*. Cambridge, Mass.: Harvard University Press.

Wittgenstein, Ludwig. 1968. *Philosophical Investigations*. Trans. G. E. M. Anscombe. New York: MacMillan.

Wittig, Monique. 1992. *The Straight Mind and Other Essays*. Boston: Beacon Press.

Woolf, Virginia. 1957. *A Room of One's Own*. San Diego: Harcourt Brace Jovanovich, Publishers.

———. 1981. *Mrs. Dalloway*. San Diego: Harcourt, Brace, Jovanovich.

"Yates Family Members Decry Husband." *CourtTV.com*, March 18, 2002. http://www.courttv.com/trials/yates/031802_ap.html; accessed February 9, 2005.

"Yates Is Not Guilty by Reason of Insanity." *Washington Post*, July 27, 2006, A3.

Young, Iris. 1990a. *Throwing Like a Girl and Other Essays in Feminist Philosophy and Social Theory*. Bloomington: Indiana University Press.

———. 1990b. *Justice and the Politics of Difference*. Princeton, N.J.: Princeton University Press.

———. 1997. *Intersecting Voices: Dilemmas of Gender, Political Philosophy, and Policy*. Princeton, N.J.: Princeton University Press.

Index

perception *(continued)*
  ground, 18; perceptual field, 15, 18, 21–22, 27–29, 100–101, 103–104; perceptual system, 15
perspective, 6, 11–25, 99, 101, 110, 132, 149, 157, 169, 175, 184–186, 193–194
Phenomenology of Mind, 226n2
Phenomenology of Perception, 16, 22, 68, 118, 131, 143, 162–163, 169, 206n13
Plato, 45
Portraits: 9/11/01: The Collected "Portraits of Grief," 159
The Principles of Psychology, 77, 226n3
Proust, Marcel, 76–77
Pyrrhus et Cinéas, 167, 172

quantum mechanics, 28

Racism, Sexism, Power and Ideology, 106
reader, 41–61, 104, 192
Reading Rodney King/Reading Urban Uprising, 116
Remembrance of Things Past, 76
Repetition, 47
The Republic, 81
reversibility, 6, 31, 35–36, 66, 128, 150
rhetoric, 55, 66
Rich, Adrienne, 197, 224n12
Ricoeur, Paul, 65–67, 69, 164
Ruddick, Lisa, 210n3
Ruddick, Sara, 197, 199, 226n6

Sartre, Jean-Paul, 13, 124, 133, 162–163, 166, 173, 176, 185–186, 206n13, 208n8, 209nn7,8,10, 218n14, 220–221n3, 223n9; bad faith, 169–170; individual freedom, 4, 50, 56, 171 174, 178; intentionality, 57, 60, 150; writing, 46–48, 50–52, 55–57, 59–60
Scarry, Elaine, 168
Schneider, 79, 169
The Second Sex, 163, 167, 170–171, 174, 177
September 11 (also referred to as 9/11), 7, 84–85, 87, 91, 128, 131, 135, 138, 159, 201, 212n6, 218n13, 229n27
sexual difference, 116, 128
Silverman, Kaja, 14
Smith, Susan, 223n10
"The Social Formation of Racist Discourse," 216n4

Spivak, Gayatri, 198
St. Augustine, 161
Stein, Gertrude, 210n3
The Stranger, 154
subjectivity, 55–57, 59–61, 92, 95, 101, 119, 159, 168–170, 173, 185, 187, 196, 198
suffering, 5, 121, 132, 135, 152–154, 163, 167
suicide, 30, 124
Sullivan, Nikki, 51, 209n12
Swann's Way, 76
Symposium, 49

temporality, 21, 29, 35, 76, 119–120
Tender Buttons, 210n3
terrorism, 131–133, 138; war on, 84, 135
text, body as, 62–63
Time Regained, 76
Tolstoy, Leo, 151–153
The Trial, 70
Truth and Method, 3

Undoing Gender, 71, 142
USA Today, 148, 149, 151
utopia, 137

Velasquez, Diego, 14
The Visible and the Invisible, 35, 127
visibility, field of, 102–103
Visible Identities, 103, 109, 143, 205n8, 227n7, 228n15, 229n28
vision, 14–15, 30, 99–100, 137, 143, 154–155, 159, 172
Vogel, Steven, 130–131
Volatile Bodies, 187

What Is Literature, 59, 209n10
White Women Race Matters: The Social Construction of Whiteness, 217n7, 219n4
Wigley, Mark, 123–124
Wittgenstein, Ludwig, 3
Wittig, Monique, 203n2
Woolf, Virginia, 120–124, 140, 201
writer, 41–42, 46–48, 50–60.
  See also author

Yates, Andrea Pia, 165–168, 172–173, 176, 179, 222n3, 223n11
Yates, Russell, 222n3, 223–224n11
The Year of Magical Thinking, 1
Young, Iris, 140